THE SUCCESSFUL LAW FIRM

New Approaches to Structure and Management

THE SUCCESSFUL LAW FIRM

New Approaches to Structure and Management

by Bradford W. Hildebrandt and Jack Kaufman

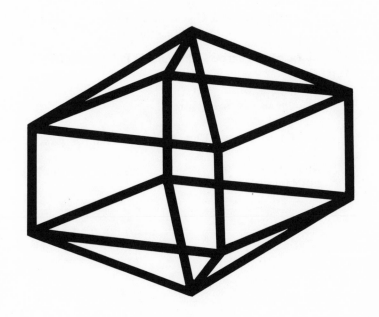

LAW & BUSINESS, INC./HARCOURT BRACE JOVANOVICH, PUBLISHERS

Printed in the United States of America
Second Printing, April 1985

Library of Congress Cataloging in Publication Data:

Hildebrandt, Bradford W.
    The successful law firm.

    1. Law offices — United States. I. Kaufman, Jack.
II. Title.
KF318.H54   1983   340'.068   83-22857
ISBN 0-15-004289-2

Acknowledgments

We are indebted to everyone at Hildebrandt, Inc. for their help in providing us material and insights, particularly to our partner, Donald S. Akins, for all his good counsel and for his work on the Marketing and Business Development Chapter; to Ken Lowe for his assistance on long range planning. Gerry Malone helped us edit and proofread. Betty Shipley deserves special mention for working with impossible handwriting, and for retyping the manuscript more times than she, or we, would like to remember.

Larry Gordon of Washington, D.C. provided material for the chapter on Investments and we appreciate that help. We also acknowledge all of the writers and speakers on law office management, who have added to our knowledge and continue to do so, and to our clients who provided us with material and with real examples of good and bad governance, management, and administration.

Perhaps the most important contribution was made by our wives, Barbara Hildebrandt and Judy Kaufman who pushed us "to get on with it," and who sacrificed (we hope not happily) some of the free time we might have had available to spend with them had we not added this book to our other work.

Preface

As consultants to the legal profession, and from prior work in administrative/management capacities in law firms, we believe there is a need for a book that covers the major management issues facing the profession now and in the years ahead.

We are often asked to consult on such matters as technology, including word processing, data processing, communications systems, associate training and partner compensation. However, on at least two-thirds of these assignments, we find that management problems must be addressed and solved before we can deal with the specific project.

In the course of our work, we meet lawyers who are financial experts, lawyers who understand the computer and what it can and should do for the firm, lawyers who work well in the personnel area, or have other specialties or skills. Unfortunately, few understand good management; and even if they understand it, they are unable, unwilling, or not permitted to apply it to their own organizations.

Our book covers what we consider some of the major management challenges of the years ahead. We hope it gives the readers a basis from which to work, rather than the answer to a specific problem. Consulting work in the legal field appears to some to be easy, because we face the same problems over and over. True, the problems are often the same, but law firms like snowflakes are unique, and solutions must be geared to the particular entity, its stage of evolution and its cast of characters. We hope the reader keeps this in mind when trying to apply to his or her law firm many of the things we suggest.

Examples we cite in the book are real. However farfetched they may seem, when you work with lawyers everyday, you do not have to make up anything. They provide us with more material than we could ever use.

We hope our readers learn something they did not know before, find an answer to a problem, or merely think about the material we cover and how it might apply to them. Few doubt that the years ahead will be challenging ones for the legal profession. We hope we have helped to identify both the challenges and possible solutions to them.

Bradford W. Hildebrandt
Jack Kaufman

November, 1983

Contents

CHAPTER I

Management Styles

This book contains a great deal of advice on a number of topics, including partners' compensation, mergers and acquisitions, and business development. Very little can be accomplished, however, unless the basic management structure of the firm is understood and is able to provide a leadership capable of addressing the important issues of the unusually complex organization we call the law firm.

This chapter is intended to provide the basis on which a firm can understand its structure and design its management systems. It traces the evolution of law firms and their progression from small entrepreneurial firms to more organized establishments. It enables you to find your firm in the evolutionary process and to recognize management structures suitable for your needs.

THE EVOLUTION OF A LAW FIRM

Most law firms take a rather predictable course in their development. A typical firm usually starts with a dominant senior partner who, by-and-large, runs the firm and dictates its management policies. A common term for such an individual is the "benevolent dictator." While in some firms the dominant force may be more than one partner, the effect is the same. This style of management usually provides strong, consistent leadership and leaves little doubt about the leadership of the firm or the decision-making process. Such leadership is essential to the development of firms but is not without its deficiencies, which include:

- Lack of communication with other partners;
- Failure of the dominant leaders to adopt policies to meet the realities of the developing firm;

1

- Failure of the dominant leaders to teach other partners how to lead the firm; and
- Waiting too long to replace a leading partner as he ages, thereby setting in motion all of the political infighting that usually results in a power struggle.

As a firm moves through its development stages, there comes a time when the senior partner steps aside. If the senior partner has not helped shape the leadership under him (which is generally the case) or if he refuses to step aside at an appropriate time, it is almost certain that a partner revolt and power play will follow. Simply stated, the departure of the strong leader, without careful planning for future management, opens the door in which every partner wants to place a foot. Very often this set of circumstances results in a desire for a "democratic" firm run by numerous committees. In the partners' minds such a structure affords the opportunity for every partner to be on a committee and be involved in some aspect of management. Unfortunately, the committee form of management, while almost inevitable in the evolutionary process, is the worst of all forms of management, because it leads to indecision and lack of direction. Partners become more involved in the administration of the firm than in the more substantive management issues. This is costly because it diverts attention from the practice to areas of administration where most lawyers are least trained to function.

The most unfortunate aspect of the committee system is that while it may appear to work initially, it almost always degenerates to management by indecision. Rather than achieving the goal of meaningful partner involvement, the committee structure becomes an excuse for indecision and a "pass the buck" attitude.

In their thirst for power, partners in the evolving firm jump at every opportunity for involvement without realizing that involvement in meaningless areas is none at all and causes costly management mistakes. One example of this might be service on a paralegal committee which neither hires, supervises, or evaluates paralegals. Another would be serving on a staff personnel committee, or a word processing committee.

You would think that understanding the dangers of the evolutionary process just explained—and given the fact that countless firms have been through this process—intelligent lawyers by planning carefully would avoid this step in the management of the firm. Unfortunately, such is not generally the case. More often than not, the democratic committee step must be endured if for no other reason than to prove how ineffective and destructive it can be.

GOVERNANCE, MANAGEMENT, AND ADMINISTRATION

Firms going through the evolutionary process must keep several things in mind.

1. First and foremost, do not think that the basic problem of structure can be solved by hiring a high-powered, high-priced, professional manager. Such an individual is an important part of the overall management structure of the firm but should be hired only after or as a part of the basic reorganization of the firm. The professional manager who must report to numerous committees in a firm where strong leadership is lacking will soon become frustrated with the inability to reach decisions. In such cases it does not take long before the manager looks for other opportunities.

2. In order for an effective structure to evolve in an orderly fashion, the re-education of partners on the need and desirability for strong leadership and centralized management is required.

3. In order to arrive at strong centralized management, while still preserving the desirability for partners to feel involved in their firm, a firm must understand the structure of an effective management system. The basic parts of such a system include:

Governance: This refers to the overall policy-making of the firm and covers such areas of decision-making as partners' compensation, selection of leaders, development of specialization, long-range planning, budgeting, branch offices, and practice structure.

Management: Management on the lawyer level involves executive decision-making both as it relates to overall firm management and to practice management. Depending on the size of the firm, lawyer management might mean working on the higher levels of policy-making in the large firm—leaving the implementation of decisions to a business executive—while in small firms, the role might encompass more mundane areas of management such as staff employment policies, staff salaries, equipment selection, and other areas more related to administration. (See page 16 for a further discussion of areas of responsibility.)

Administration: This refers to the day-to-day running of the law firm and covers such topics as staff personnel, systems and procedures, finance, and the like. In more and more firms, even smaller ones, this function is being turned over to a professional.

It should be evident that the lines between these three areas of management are not black and white, and a great deal of gray exists.

Policy management concerns the overall decision-making of the partners in terms of the nature and philosophy of the firm. Regardless of how talented a professional manager might be, a law firm is unlike other corporate management structures in that it has resident ownership, and it is foolhardy to think that someone else can establish policies that drastically affect the overall desires of these resident owners.

Typical policy level decisions include:

- partners' compensation
- lawyer and paralegal recruiting
- legal staff compensation
- type of practice
- size of firm
- location of offices
- budget approval
- philosophy relating to expense accounts
- capital improvements
- specialization
- practice management
- billing practices.

Administration is the execution of management policies established by the partners. This is not to say, however, that a well-trained business manager cannot advise the partners in setting policy, but that ultimately, final policy decisions should be made by the appropriate partners. Once established, the everyday supervision of the firm and carrying out of the management decisions should be left to an administrator.

In the very small firm almost all of these functions may be handled by the partners, with some minor delegation of responsibilities to a good secretary, paralegal, or combination bookkeeper/office manager. As the firm evolves, however, the functions will have to be more clearly defined and the level and expertise of the administrative support staff will change dramatically.

As mentioned earlier, in law firms where partners are calling for greater "democracy," few partners truly understand what they are asking for. In fact in their own ignorance they establish procedures that slow down decision-making, resulting in a stagnant law firm unable to cope with its own management.

Here again, firm size can make an enormous difference. It is not difficult for a small firm to convene the partners and discuss most management issues. Interestingly enough though, even here one tends to hear comments such as, "we discuss everything to death" or "we never seem to make a decision." As a firm gets larger, this problem compounds itself, and some form of central management with a substantial delegation of authority to a partner or partners is not only essential, but inevitable.

How important is democracy in decision-making as a factor in the health of the partnership? The answer to this question is not simple, and the degree of democracy will depend somewhat on the individual character of the law firm. In reality, though, partners of most law firms—given an opportunity to think about democracy—are much more satisfied with a sense of involvement than with true democracy in all issues. The need for the decision-making participation is probably important in a number of instances, which can be easily defined. For example, a firm might determine that specific partnership approval, by some voting method, is needed in the following areas:

- Admission of new partners
- Determination relating to questions of expulsion, dis-

ability, retirement, withdrawal, and death
- Name change
- Approval of acquisition or merger
- Capital expense in excess of "X" amount
- Overall approval of hiring philosophies
- Selection of management/executive committee.

Other decisions, such as approval of partnership percentages or admission of laterally hired associates, will vary from firm to firm, so no general statement can be made on what items should or should not require partnership approval in a particular firm.

The key to centralized management is effective communication between the management group and the other partners. Communication allows partners to feel they have a voice in the destiny of the firm. The following are some guidelines that should be kept in mind for establishing communication channels and keeping them open.

A pre-printed agenda of items to be considered and a written report of decisions made are very effective. Each communication should encourage partners to give their inputs, either formally or informally, on agenda items and to ask questions about the committee decisions.

Secrecy is the worst enemy of effective management, and it creates rumors and suspicions that usually are unfounded. This is not to say, however, that a managing partner or a management committee has to divulge the nature of internal discussions. Indeed, partners who are given management responsibilities must feel they can have open and free interchanges without worrying about being directly quoted.

The lack of dissemination of financial information to the partners establishes the aura of a dual class of partnership and results in a "we and they" attitude. This does not mean that every piece of financial information should be distributed to all partners. Dissemination of such information as a profit and loss statement, accounts receivable, and unbilled time generates a better sense of responsibility among the partners. The "employee mentality" that exists among many of the partners, a very serious problem in an expanding law firm, is often brought about by the management style of older or senior partners in the firm, rather than the other way around. It is interesting to note how many "seniors" criticize younger partners for their attitudes toward the management of the firm and client development efforts, while failing to recognize that *they* created the atmosphere for such attitudes.

"Self-perpetuating" management of the firm is ultimately doomed to fail and is often responsible for the departure of many partners. There is something to be said for ensuring continuity of management in a firm; no system will function without the reasonable participation by the natural leaders or those who constitute a power base. Therefore, as firm management evolves to meet current needs, careful consideration must be given to the selection of those who will govern.

It is far better to give away some power when the delegation of the power can be controlled than to have it taken away by a group of partners because the managing partner has lost credibility. That is to say, controlled management evolution is far better than "palace revolts."

A firm must have a structure that permits leadership and direction. There is nothing worse than a law firm that has lost its leadership.

More attention should be paid to practice management and development than to everyday overall administration. Yet, in most firms the reverse is often true. Indeed, a partner's desire for involvement can be much better served in establishing a role in an area in which the partner may have some expertise, such as heading a department, working with associates in his practice area, or studying ways in which existing clients within his department can be better served. Many partners can serve in these areas, rather than in the firm management which requires abilities for which most partners are untrained and are in reality, uninterested.

Partners must recognize that time spent in firm governance and management, if properly controlled, is as valuable as, if not more so, than the same time recorded as a billable hour. Too many firms penalize, either directly or indirectly, partners who devote time to firm management. Compensation arrangements, covered in Chapter V, often either do not recognize the management time at all or put too much emphasis on billable hours, financially penalizing the managers. A few firms make sure management is compensated by designating a percentage of the net profits of the partnership to be used for this purpose before paying the partners.

Recognize that the complexities of managing the modern firm, regardless of size, may outgrow the abilities of the partners. The solution to such a situation, which exists in many firms, is to admit that it may be true. Once it is admitted, the firm can take concrete steps to obtain the assistance necessary to begin to correct the situation. (Note the discussion on the executive director in Chapter II.)

Be prepared to deal with major management problems. Do not think that the firm is well managed because you have allowed the partners to study all the major word processing systems on the market and to prepare a position paper on each one, while problems of inequitable partners' compensation, partner performance, no specialization, lack of a marketing plan, no long range planning, and others continue to fester.

Remember that the practice of law is a business (a rather trite but true statement) and that two basic decisions have to be made on a regular basis:

(1) What type of law should be practiced from a professional standpoint?

(2) Can the firm have such a practice from a business standpoint?

In formulating policy, the firm must ensure that overall management recognizes this duality.

Do not play lawyer with business problems. Business problems require decision-making ability (a quality lacking in a large number of lawyers) on a reasonable and timely basis. Giving advice to a business client on the legal aspects of business decisions and actually making practical decisions are very different.

As a firm grows larger, it must necessarily delegate some management functions to other partners and/or the administrator. A large firm's Management Committee simply cannot handle all the decision-making necessary for effective management.

Now that we have an overview of the main concepts of firm management, let us examine in detail specific situations along with their good and bad points.

MANAGING PARTNER

The most popular form of management until approximately the mid 1960's was the managing partner. This was a natural step in the evolutionary process, since law firms had grown relatively slowly until that time and were either not really managed at all, or continued to be governed by the founding partner. The manager partner concept can best be explained by looking at different approaches to this role.

Benevolent Dictator

The managing partner in the 1950's and 1960's normally filled his position as part of the evolutionary process rather than through any elective process. He may have been the founder of the firm who had generated most of the clients, had picked the lawyers necessary to do the work as the firm grew, determined the compensation, decided the direction in which the firm was to go, and even took care of the day-to-day administration, handling much of it himself and delegating the balance to his secretary. There were no questions relating to authority. The firm *belonged* to the founder, carried his name, and existed because of him.

There is little question in the minds of students of government, of experts in law firm management, or, for that matter, in the minds of lawyers who grew and succeeded under the benevolent dictator, that this was an extremely effective and efficient manner in which to run an organization. The lawyers spent 100 percent of their time practicing law. They did not have to worry about where the business was coming from, how the work would be billed, or when a document would be typed. The firm was a protected environment, similar to law school. You had an assignment given to you, did the work, and went on to the next project.

Obviously, the benevolent dictator, or more kindly, the senior partner, had attained his status and continued in his role not necessarily through any inherent ability to manage (though there were and are excellent managers within this group) but rather from an unquestioned position of authority. Power had not been granted to him by others and, therefore, could not be taken away. Inroads might be made by another lawyer who started coming into his own and generating substantial clientele or by the scholar who directed the work or was available to counsel on the legal problems. These partners were granted some role in the inner circle—but not enough to challenge the leader.

When lawyers who grew up in firms led by benevolent dictators are asked, "What made the firm prosper and grow?" an initial response is, "He was a phenomenal business getter." But as they expand on this, usually they bring into their reasoning the facts that, right or wrong, decisions were made on a timely basis, action was taken when action was necessary, and more that was done was right rather than wrong.

There are few successful law firms of almost any size, however, in which a dictator was able to bring about and sustain success. Along the way, minus the benevolence, there were split-offs or enough turnover to keep the firm in a static or declining growth pattern.

While the benevolent dictatorship is an excellent system for law firm management and governance and for that matter, administration, there will not be as much of it in the 1980's and 1990's as in the 1930's through the 1960's. Society has changed. People want to be involved. "Quality of life," "doing one's own thing" and questioning—even fighting—the system are accepted and even expected. The benevolent dictator arose and prospered in the depression years and while the economic future of the country cannot be predicted, it is doubtful that the society and economic environment that fostered the growth of benevolent dictators in the first place will return.

Managing Partner

The managing partner was often the title given to the previously described benevolent dictator. When a change became necessary due to a retirement, death, or disability, rather than through a revolt, usually a hand-picked successor took over with the advice and consent of the predecessor. Since this individual normally did not control the clients, the role did not assume the same proportion as that of the predecessor. Either gradually or at the outset, some "power was given to the people."

DUTIES

Managing partners are less authoritarian than benevolent dictators, and the position normally evolves to one of supervision as opposed to control. Few operate under a written position description, but most recognize there is a line they do not cross. Though few managing partners operate under a written position description, and most firms do not spell this out in their partnership or shareholders agreement, the role often is tailored to include the following duties:

1. Execution of firm policies
2. Direction and control of the training, work, and evaluation of the legal staff
3. Supervision of financial and other firm records
4. Cost control supervision
5. Supervision of furnishing and maintenance of the office
6. Supervision of firm expenditures and collections
7. Arranging partner (shareholders) and office meetings and chairing these
8. Preparation and dissemination of minutes of meetings
9. Preliminary work relating to any merger, acquisition, or branch office
10. Preliminary preparation of annual budget
11. Supervision of administrator or office manager, and in the absence of such positions, of all staff personnel
12. Such other duties as the partners (shareholders) shall delegate

The definition of duties obviously varies based on whether the firm also has an executive or management committee and by how much power the partners are willing to delegate.

Unfortunately, today there is a good deal of confusion as to what a managing partner is, or should be. In no more than perhaps 50 percent of those law firms with the position is the managing partner filling the role previously described. In another 25 percent the position relates solely to administration, and though some of these firms designate this person "Administrative Partner," most do not. In the 25 percent of firms remaining, the title is used either to honor a senior partner, to designate the partner who takes the calls and mail no one knows what to do with, or some other basically undefined role. It is not unusual to meet a young managing partner and to learn the practice in the firm is to have this position filled by someone having more time available and serving until the next young partner comes along.

SELECTION

The concept of a true managing partner is probably a good one, however, even though there are fewer lawyers in this role today than in years past, and the trend seems to be away from this form of management. When the benevolent dictator filled this role, law firms were smaller and less complicated environments. As law firms grow in size, the role becomes more difficult to fill. Often the partner who might be acceptable to a large majority does not want to devote the time, or there is not one partner with enough support, respect, and management ability to assume this mantle. Also, unless the lawyer in the firm of 75 or more lawyers is willing to give up a substantial portion of his practice, he is not going to have enough time available to do an adequate job.

The true managing partner is usually a mature lawyer with an active practice, often the lead partner in a practice area. Are his skills put to better use in managing the firm, or in both practicing law and managing his area of practice? In the legal field, it is easier to find and/or train good lawyers than it is to find or train good managers.

The managing partner question is often solved by the desire for involvement of other partners, or by the necessity of delegating responsibility to others. The concept of assistant managing partner has never taken hold, since the delineation of responsibilities between two individuals is often difficult. (Such an arrangement is not unlike the role of most United States vice presidents.) The natural inclination is to some other form of committee structure. Many of today's managing partners have evolved into chairmen of the management or executive committees, though they may still carry the managing partner title.

While there is no general rule and a great deal depends on the firm's stage of evolution, it is normally advisable to make the managing partner position an elected one. Unlike the dictator, the managing partner needs a mandate. He must be invested with power by his peers if he is to succeed. The election process alleviates the natural fear other partners have of control resting in one person. A normal term should be three to five years, since an opportunity to consider both the individual and the position should be reviewed at regular intervals. We believe it is advisable to insist on the election, even when there is no contest, or no doubt in anyone's mind that the person holding the office can or will continue as long as he wants. The mere existence of the election process provides the sense of "involvement" most of today's partners feel is necessary.

Many firms force rotation of the managing partner. This is done to avoid placing too much power into one partner's hands. While this may be necessary following a dictatorship, if one partner has the proper management skills and can lead the firm, other partners should recognize this and change their agreement to allow for reelection. Otherwise, the firm will be hurting itself in order to preserve more democracy.

Not inconsequential in the selection of the managing partner is the impact such a role will have on the partner's practice and relationship with clients. One of the criteria for the selection of an individual to fill such a role is that individual's ability to delegate not only work but also client relationships. The fact that a lawyer is busy, is a business getter, or is responsible for numerous clients is not a reason to eliminate such a person from consideration if that individual can delegate effectively and see that the time required will be given to the position.

One of the problems with having litigators in management roles is that they are often unavailable for long periods of time and cannot give the leadership and direction when it is required. This is not to say that litigators cannot be managing partners, but they must understand the time commitments that will be necessary to do an effective job.

CO-MANAGING PARTNERS

One last comment on this subject. In some firms, there are co-managing partners or up to five or six lawyers carrying this title. The plural of managing partner should not exist in the law firm. Bifurcation seldom works, and the concept of co-managing partners eventually evolves to this: One takes over, for example, the financial area, either from desire or expertise and the other worries about the myriad of other areas. Neither one, however, feels able to make decisions without consultation, thus delaying and complicating the decision-making process.

Having many managing partners creates a problem that is more psychological than anything else, but the end result is no different from its being an actual problem. It is, in effect, a problem in semantics. Four or five managing partners are really a management committee, and though being a member of the management committee may give a certain prestige within the firm, it does not particularly impress those outside the legal community. Managing partner, on the other hand, delivers a message about the lawyer's place in the firm. Partners have little difficulty accepting a title carried by one lawyer, but a problem when the term is used for a number of others.

MANAGEMENT COMMITTEE

While a strong, capable, elected managing partner can do an effective job in managing a medium size law firm, larger firms, firms without a natural leader, and those at the evolutionary stage in which no democrary (or the appearance of it) is necessary, would do better under a management or executive committee system.

The most common form of management in firms with fifteen or more partners is the management or executive committee. How this committee is formed, what it does, its areas of authority and responsibility, whether it is elected, rotated, self-perpetuating, and similar considerations, usually depends on what stage the firm has reached in its evolution.

Law firm A retained an outside consultant to help it determine whether it needed a change in structure, or if not, what it could do to make the management of the firm operate in a considerably more efficient fashion than it had in the past year or two. The feeling of inefficient management, incidentally, is a good warning sign that the partners charged with the management function are a) not making decisions, b) functioning at too low a level, and c) are being second guessed by the other partners. The 16 partners had designated one of their members as managing partner. This was done to provide a chairman for meetings, a name to the outside world, and a representative to a group of local managing partners who met three or four times a year. There was little or no authority granted, and the partners continued to manage the firm through regularly scheduled partners' meetings at which decisions, if made, were based on a wide concensus after hours of discussion.

The firm had grown through merger, lateral hiring of partners, and a good local economy. No partner or group of partners dominated, and the business base was spread fairly evenly. The partners were all under fifty, hard-working and aggressive. They were bright enough to know that concensus was not working, but stubborn and individualistic enough not to want a smaller governing body—unless they were on it.

Individual interviews were held with every partner, and short discussions were held with a cross-section of the more senior associates. These sessions were used to accomplish several purposes:

- To educate the interviewees on successful management;
- To convince them that a change in structure did not have to result in an elimination of their role or participation as partners; and
- To elicit names of partners, who, if the firm ever went to a management committee, had the best skills and acceptance to help assure the success of at least the initial committee.

This process provided the basis for a report to the partners that outlined alternative management structures, and the benefits and detriments to each one of those presented.

Based on the above set of circumstances, particularly the small age spread and the fact that the business base was not centered in a few people, the favored recommendation was for a five partner management committee, elected by the partners on a staggered term basis, with a limitation on the number of consecutive terms a partner was eligible to serve. The role of the management committee was defined and put in writing, with areas of responsibility and authority outlined. Decisions that were to remain under the control of the partnership as a whole were set forth in a position paper.

In a subsequent meeting the consultants were asked for their opinion on who might make up the best first slate, and the names presented were subsequently elected. The committee consisted of five partners elected to serve staggered terms. The number of consecutive terms to be served was limited.

Through this exercise, done in an orderly fashion with open communication and written job descriptions, the partners became convinced they would still have a say and a vote on major issues, yet the firm would run more efficiently with less lawyer involvement.

Duties

Though the job description of a management committee may vary from firm to firm and would be different if the firm also had a true managing partner, the description that follows is typical for many law firms, regardless of size.

MANAGEMENT COMMITTEE

JOB DESCRIPTION
This committee shall direct the day-to day business affairs of the firm. The duties of this committee are as follows:

(a) Executing firm policies.

(b) Hiring first-year associates and hiring and firing professional employees, including paralegals and the Administrator, but excluding attorneys.

(c) Directing and controlling associates' training and work.

(d) Supervising and controlling firm records and control of office supplies.

(e) Supervising and controlling the library, including book purchases.

(f) Supervising and controlling firm expenditures and collections.

(g) Assigning personnel, telephone and mail requests for services, not specifically directed to any partner or associate.

(h) Arranging partnership and office meetings.

(i) Supervising the firm's finances, including all bank accounts and investments.

(j) Distributing the firm's profits.

(k) Determining compensation for the office staff and establishing annual compensation reviews.

(l) Compiling and disseminating a record of decisions made at meetings of the partners.

(m) Reviewing billings, collections, and profitability of all firm business.

(n) Meeting present and future space needs.

(o) Reviewing and placing insurance; reviewing and managing retirement plans and other fringe benefits.

(p) No later than thirty (30) days after the end of each fiscal year, reporting to the partnership on the profitability and growth of the firm.

(q) Reviewing attorneys' workloads and reassigning cases and/or clients where appropriate.

(r) Reviewing all present business and prospective new firm clients and determining whether, in each instance, representation should be continued or undertaken and under what fee arrangements.

(s) Making all determinations on matters arising under the Code of Professional Responsibility.

(t) Appointing such ad-hoc committees as it deems appropriate to carry out its duties.

(u) Appointing such partners as it may deem appropriate to be responsible for designated areas of the firm's practice and business.

(v) Such other duties as the partners shall delegate or as may be necessary to fully carry out the duties hereinabove delegated.

It is understood that the management committee may delegate any of the above items to the firm's Administrator as it deems appropriate and may cause any records or reports to be established that assist it in fulfilling its responsibilities.

Areas Reserved to the Partnership

Earlier in the chapter some of the areas normally reserved to the partners were mentioned (see page 5). A more complete list, based on the aforementioned committee description, would be along the lines of the following:

Among those areas normally reserved to the partnership are the following:

1. Admitting new partners.
2. Hiring lateral-entry associates.
3. Expelling a partner or terminating an associate.
4. Dissolving the partnership.
5. Amending the partnership agreement.
6. Dealing with matters relating to death, disability, retirement, and withdrawal of partners.
7. Approving expenditures exceeding $25,000.00 for equipment or capital improvements.
8. Considering new areas of practice.
9. Merger.
10. Changing firm name.
11. Other matters partners may feel should be reserved to the partnership as a whole.

To the firm trying to set up an effective management committee, the discussion, creation, and approval of these descriptions is often enough to dissipate the partners' fear of a form of management that is something less than purely democratic. It is also a way of involving the partners in making the transition from a strong managing partner and dictator to another management system.

Common Questions

Questions frequently arise over size, election procedures, and limitation of terms of the management committee.

SIZE

Interestingly enough, few management committees number more than seven partners and few less than five. Odd numbers are more common than even, probably under the theory that tie votes are less likely. The size, five or seven, appears to be based on the perception that fewer than five is not a representative enough number, and that more than seven becomes unwieldy. It is not unusual to encounter a 150-lawyer firm with a five-partner management committee, nor the twenty-five lawyer firm with the same size committee. Seven is normally a compromise in order to accommodate diversity in age groups or areas of practice, rather than because a larger number is necessary to manage properly.

ELECTION PROCEDURES

Length of term for management committee members varies, with three year terms the most common. Shorter terms are usually indicative of a law firm that has not yet passed into the stage of its evolution where it is fully comfortable with the management committee.

It is wise to stagger the terms so that there is experience and continuity on the committee. This is often done by electing two partners to a three-year term, two to a two-year term, and one to a one-year term at the first election. Subsequent elections fill three-year terms.

Should the number of consecutive terms a partner is allowed to serve be limited? In a more established firm, a rule of this nature is probably a mistake. The purpose of the committee is to manage the firm, and if one or two (or more) partners have the respect of the other partners, as well as recognized management skills, the firm is not served by such a restriction. Those advocating limitations normally fear a return to a dictatorship or oligarchy, not realizing that the election procedure offers enough protection.

Many people have suggested that management committee representation should be based on age ranges or areas of practice, under the theory that this will be a more representative committee. While this should not be totally discounted, those serving on the committee should be the partners best able to manage. A practice management committee can provide input to the management committee so that representation by area of practice is not necessary.

Often there is a strong push to have a "junior" seat on the committee so younger partners in the firm will have a voice. Occasionally this position does not have a vote, which is pointless if the reason for the seat is representation. If the firm is offering a placebo, it would do better to forget it. If a younger partner is nominated and elected, fine, but a place should not be created for this partner, since those best able to manage should do so.

MEETING PROCEDURES

The management committee should meet regularly, probably at a minimum twice a month. A specific time should be determined, and a meeting held if there is a quorum. Agendas should be prepared in advance, and partners should always be invited to submit agenda items they feel should be considered.

In order to maintain the communication necessary to assure the success of the committee, many firms open the meeting to partners wanting to attend. Others schedule partners for specific dates, though attendance is voluntary.

Also to foster communication, minutes should be kept, and most decisions reported to the partners.

Removing any aura of mystery, coupled with frequent and meaningful communication, will do more to alleviate the fear of uninvolvement than anything else.

PERMANENT MANAGEMENT COMMITTEE

Many larger firms have a permanent management committee. There are no elections; the committee determines who will and will not sit on it. Committee members are usually the senior partners in the firm, or partners selected by a retiring dictator.

Though a permanent, standing committee often does an excellent job in managing the law firm, partners in most firms with this system have an employee mentality, and "we–they" is an everyday expression. This is not, however, a management problem, but rather a communication problem. By seeking input from partners and allowing a free flow of information in both directions this system is often the most effective.

COMMITTEE STRUCTURE

Another common form of management is through a series of partners' committees, set up to deal with various management responsibilities. In some cases a committee structure (operating under a management committee or managing partner) may be appropriate or even desirable. The danger, however, is in having committees proliferate from a desire for involving the partners in supposedly meaningful management areas.

Someone once said that a committee would be defined as the unwilling, picked from the unqualified to do the unnecessary. Unfortunately, this is the case in many law firms. A far better approach to the delegation of responsibility is to select individual partners to have overall responsibility for a specific area and to permit each to select others to assist him. This method establishes an accountability relationship between the individual partner, the management committee and/or the partnership as a whole. Such an arrangement works much more effectively and gives the partner chosen to handle a responsibility more involvement and control over the task.

Responsibilities

In order for partners in the firm to perform effectively, they must recognize one timeless rule of management. It is essential that the appropriate amount of authority accompany the responsibility in order to get the task done. If a partner is asked to handle the firm's professional liability insurance (a task, incidentally, that could easily be delegated to an administrator), then he should be allowed to do the necessary work and establish the insurance coverage. His decision, however, should be made within the framework of broad policy set by the management committee on levels of coverage, amount to be deductible and form of coverage. To give such an assignment to a partner and then quiz him on what companies he talked to, or the cost as compared to others, will only lead to disenchantment. Such second guessing and/or need to be involved in every minor detail makes a mockery out of the assignment. It is meaningless to involve other partners, only to allow them no meaningful authority.

Let us examine a number of responsibilities for which either a committee or one partner might be assigned.

RECRUITING

Partners responsible for the recruitment of young lawyers are almost universally criticized. This criticism stems from the very nature of the responsibility and usually includes

a. The partner spends too much time;
b. The process is too costly;
c. We cannot seem to attract the quality of student we want;
d. We do not get individuals from "my" law school; and
e. We pay too much attention to law schools' placement rules.

Yet there is almost no better way of involving younger partners and even senior associates in management than in the selection of young lawyers. Indeed, it can be argued that it is the very lawyers joining the firm who will eventually become the partners of the young partner, so the latter should have more to say about the selection. There is, of course, nothing wrong with having senior partners involved in the process, but it is the younger partners who generally have more interest in and are better at identifying with the law school students.

A proper way to delegate recruiting responsibilities is for the partners, in a smaller firm, and the management committee, in a larger firm, to determine the number of young lawyers to be hired, and then to turn the operation over to the recruiting committee/partner, including the absolute authority to make offers to qualified candidates. (Some firms are beginning to use personnel and recruiting professionals to do initial recruiting work, including campus interviewing. There are also a few administrators doing this work.)

ASSOCIATE EVALUATION

As a firm begins to add associates, it soon realizes that effective supervision and training require time and effort. At some point in the firm's development, a partner should be placed in charge of the associates program to ensure proper evaluation and training. This function, however informal or unstructured, should be established when a firm hires its second associate, and then developed and formalized as more associates are added. Incidentally, if you think the lack of communication is a problem even among a few partners, listen to what associates have to say about it.

BILLING COMMITTEE

One of the most neglected functions in firms is monitoring billing procedures. As a firm grows and hires an administrator, this function can, with the exception of peer review of bills, be delegated to that individual.

Peer review, based on the theory that a partner not billing properly is affecting everyone's profit, not just his own, can have excellent results. One way to obtain these results is to establish responsibility for billing review and control. This can be accomplished by having all bills over a certain amount reviewed by someone else; or by having only bills with write offs of time or costs reviewed. This function also envisions a review of unbilled time to avoid extensive build-ups and to encourage regular billing habits.

There are, of course, various ways of looking into administrative details. This may be handled by the management committee in a small firm or delegated to a billing committee or quite possibly a department chairman in large firms. But the function is important and can have a direct impact on profitability.

FINANCE

In too many firms financial management is limited to very few partners. As a firm grows this function should be totally delegated to a professional having accountability to the management committee or partner. In small firms, one partner, who should be on the management committee, should be responsible for financial management.

PRACTICE MANAGEMENT

Firms are beginning to give more and more attention to professional practice management, as opposed to business management. Practice management is the management of the substantive practice of law. It includes such areas as allocation of work, quality control, supervision of associates, evaluation and training of associates, development of specialization, and other areas impacting directly on the sub-stantive production of the legal product. This is an area that, indeed, needs much more attention than most firms tend to give this function (see comment later in this chapter).

BUSINESS DEVELOPMENT

Business development is the organized effort to obtain busi-ness from both existing and potential clients. It requires care-ful attention and planning by every firm regardless of size. This should be delegated to a partner or partners who have the drive and ability to draw a plan and to set it in motion (see chapter VI).

LONG RANGE PLANNING

More and more firms are slowly realizing that it is not enough simply to try to get through the coming week, but that like any other business, some forecasting, not just based on economics, is essential. A look ahead at the firm for sever-al years can be revealing and alarming (See chapter VIII for more on long-range planning).

This, of course, is not an all inclusive list of areas that should be delegated to individuals and partners. The number of individuals involved and the degree of overlap of assign-ments still varies from firm to firm.

It is important, however, to emphasize the basic assump-tions underlying the need for the above breakdown of respon-sibilities:

- There are functions in the modern law firm that must be addressed.
- A managing partner, management committee, or even a professional administrator cannot do every-thing effectively.
- Some plan must exist for the evolution of manage-ment and the training of partners as part of the management structure.
- Involvement creates a sense of controlling one's own destiny and generally results in partners who have a

better understanding and sympathy for the problems of managing a firm.

A firm should avoid an overproliferation of meaningless committees. Such delegation does nothing for the effective management of the firm and only leads to a sense of stagnation and ineffective leadership. One law firm had the ultimate in committee structure with the appointment of the "Committee on Committees." This makes a mockery of intelligent management and probably results more in an effort to see to it that every partner is *involved* in something than to determine what is in the best interest of the firm.

THE FUTURE

One of the most perplexing problems lies in trying to predict what is going to happen to law firm management in the future. There are forces at work in society and within the profession that are going to have drastic effects on governance, management, and administration. Among them:

Competitiveness For a law firm management book to have a chapter on "marketing" would have been considered absurd only a few years ago. Yet, today there is a general recognition by firms of all sizes and types that time, effort, and money are going to have to be directed at the marketing effort.

This new emphasis is going to have some effects on management structure. Many philosophies, such as the lack of willingness to pursue clients aggressively, the reluctance to spend money, and the lack of recognition or encouragement of the entrepreneurial partner, will have little place in most successful firms in the future. The law firm that has hired only the law review editors of certain elitist law schools may find themselves with excellent lawyers and very little marketing skill.

Ultimately, those partners in management positions who fail to recognize this changing climate should plan, or will be forced, to step aside.

Profit squeeze Everyone reads about the lawyers who in certain law firms are earning exorbitantly high incomes from the practice of law. The simple truth, however, is that few

law firms are "money machines," and overhead costs are ris-
ing faster than net profits in a majority of firms. Firms that
do not have partners who can manage effectively, that do not
rely on the expertise of progressive, well-trained administrators, and that are unwilling to handle the age-old problem of
progress will find themselves unable to deliver legal services
at costs acceptable to clients. Again, management must address policies that affect the "we always did it this way" or "I
am a partner and deserve my own secretary" or "I can do it
faster myself" mentality.

Life style An enormous number of partners still talk about
the fact that the associates do not work as hard as they did
when they were associates, or "if you walk around here at
night or on Saturday, you find only a few associates." Both of
these statements are true and yet, partners who exhibit
depression mentality are unfortunately still setting the tone
for many firms. The concerns these individuals express are
real, but their desires do not reflect reality. This is not to say
that the practice of law is a 9-5 occupation—far from it. But
the attitude of work for work's sake is simply no longer acceptable in our society. Those partners who lived it and demand it from others usually also cannot understand why
their firm is a revolving door for both partners and associates.

Enlightened management should understand the changing
nature of those who pursue the practice of law and, while
establishing reasonable and even demanding work and performance standards, must not fail to recognize the human element of management.

A severe problem in law firms today is that most of the
pressure of the practice is self generated and much of the resistance to high legal fees has its roots in poor management
and direction.

Merger and acquisition The national, even international,
tendency toward mergers and acquisitions in the legal profession is going to have profound effects on the ability of
smaller firms to compete effectively.

Several years ago most experts on legal economics scoffed
at the idea of huge law firms of national and international
scope. Few would scoff today, and there is every reason to believe we are fast moving to such entities. The one underlying
problem, however, is whether lawyers can accept overall cen-

tralized management, which is required for the success of such entities. Accountants at the large firms learned this lesson years ago and as a result have developed very successful organizations. Lawyers have yet to learn the lesson of delegation. They confuse the need to be involved in practice management with the desire to tamper with overall policy management.

Specialization There are still many older lawyers who hold on to the belief that the practice of law is the "greatest of all professions" and should never be considered a business. They claim that clients want to deal with lawyers who are generalists and who have a grasp of many aspects of the law. They further argue that a lawyer should be capable of handling almost any transaction regardless of its nature. This is an outdated, unrealistic view of the practice of law today. The delivering of legal services is a business and one that is becoming more competitive by the minute.

Specialization in the practice is essential if the demands of clients are going to be met and if law firms are going to be able to deliver services with reasonable cost. Even the single practitioner is a specialist in the area of his service, not unlike the old family doctor who has been replaced by the "family medicine specialist."

The development of specialization in a growing firm is inevitable for the following reasons:

    a. the complexity of the law
    b. the desire of clients to get the best possible advice in a given area
    c. the need to control the quality of the work product
    d. in the larger firm the task of controlling large numbers of lawyers.

Specialization does not mean, however, that a firm has to become overdepartmentalized. Lawyers can work in one or more related areas and in broader departments with subspecialties, where teams of lawyers can work with clients. This is an effective approach.

To be avoided at all costs is the development of departments in the firm to satisfy the ego needs of a partner rather than creating a structure designed for the purpose of delivering legal services in accordance with the nature of the practice and the needs of the clients.

The development of specialization, the training of lawyers, and the delivery of the legal product is the definition of practice management and will become the byword of the well managed law firm.

Practice management Practice management in the small firm may mean nothing more than keeping some reasonable records of each lawyer, work-load, the types and volume of cases worked, and a review of quality of the ultimate product. For example, not allowing opinion letters to go to clients without a review by another partner is a form of quality control.

As a firm grows, however, practice management can become even more significant and, properly structured, can help spread the management role among more partners. What happened at one forty lawyer law firm might help to illustrate this point.

The firm of Able, Baker & Charlie had grown very rapidly in the last few years following many years of slow but steady growth. The lawyers had prided themselves on being generalists and being able to do everything for a client. However, they turned to outside help after discovering:

- While the firm was growing, the net income was not keeping pace with inflation.
- The firm was experiencing a high turnover in associates.
- The firm was having some difficulty in competing for the type of client it felt it deserved.
- The partner who was doing tax work was complaining that everybody was "writing simple wills." The firm had just been sued for mishandling an estate. The managing partners felt there were no grounds for the suit. (What else is new?)
- The firm had a five person executive committee that was spending more and more time on "management."
- Many of the partners had more than one area of expertise and did not want to be "confined" in their practice.

In order to advise this firm, consultants interviewed all of the partners and associates. The interviews revealed some interesting information:

- There existed almost no communication among the partners.
- All of the partners felt some structure was necessary and blamed the "other partners" for the current problems.
- The associates said that though during their employment interviews the concept of a non-structured firm seemed attractive, having experienced it they were convinced that something had to be done to develop some training and evaluation procedures.
- To get a different perspective on the firm the consultants interviewed several clients. These meetings revealed a nervousness by the clients that they were too reliant on a partner who was often unavailable and that the firm had not developed sufficient expertise to serve them.

Many recommendations were made to this firm but several were directed at the practice area.

The firm established four broad areas of practice: business; litigation; real estate; and tax. Each partner, except the firm's three senior partners who were also the chief business getters, was assigned to a department for a primary area of specialization but was also listed with a secondary area of expertise.

Each associate was assigned to an area.

Each area of practice selected a chairman who had overall management responsibilities including:

- Establishing section goals and objectives for each year and for the reasonably foreseeable future, including desired staffing, organization and business development efforts, and coordination with other sections and the appropriate committees to accomplish the firm's objectives.
- Insuring that the work of clients is promptly, responsibly, and competently completed and that services are economically performed, with work being delegated downward to the lowest competent level.
- Insuring that work undertaken is likely to be profitable and that fees are billed and collected in a timely manner.

- Insuring that all members of the section are meeting budget and other requirements and allocating workload with a view to efficiency, development of expertise in various substantive areas, and providing opportunity for professional fulfillment.
- Monitoring supervision of professional, paralegal, and secretarial staff, coordinating evaluation of and communication concerning individual performance, and otherwise being attentive to staff morale.
- Devising and implementing means of keeping professional staff regularly informed of developments in the law and making known and encouraging specialized learning opportunities.
- Developing and maintaining forms, systems, and procedures peculiar to the section, and orienting new personnel in the same, including file maintenance and client communication.
- Insuring that satisfactory supporting staff is available and properly supervised.
- Insuring that all section members support and perform within firm policies, including adjustment of personal lifestyles, preferences, etc.
- Insuring that policies of the firm and section (including prompt submission of time reports and client billing) are enforced and policed in coordination with the executive committee.

The four department chairmen formed a practice management committee and the following duties, formerly handled by the executive committee, were delegated to this new committee:

- Supervise the intake of new work.
- Set procedures for properly assigning work.
- Create an ongoing dialogue such that cooperation exists between lawyers in each department.
- Set up billing review procedures.
- Determine manpower needs for partners, associates, and paralegals and make recommendations to the management committee.
- Set standards for quality control including procedures for issuing opinion letters.

- Work with the associates committee to establish evaluation and review procedures.
- Establish both in-house and outside programs for "CLE."
- Act as a committee to evaluate potential mergers, possibly augmented by other individuals appointed by the management committee.
- Such other duties as the management committee might delegate.

Each department began a regular schedule of meetings, which any lawyer working on a project within the jurisdiction of that department was expected to attend.

Each department chairman was introduced to clients through a structured client education program.

A department organizational chart was developed and given to clients.

A review of the firm one year after these recommendations had been instituted revealed the following results:

- Reduction in associate turnover
- More work from existing clients and more referrals of clients
- The development of a long range plan and a partners' retreat to discuss future growth
- A substantial increase of income

While the recommendations contained in this case study may not totally apply to every firm's situation, the analysis of the problems and the suggested solutions should be carefully studied because they clearly illustrate what can be accomplished when the energies of the partners are directed toward the control of the practice. Earlier in this chapter we discussed at length the problem of partners wanting to be involved in management, and we urged that overall management be delegated and centralized. If the desire of partners to be involved in overall firm management could be redirected so that each and every partner had a role in practice management, law firms would be generally better managed and clearly more profitable.

In this chapter we have attempted to "set the stage" for other material in the book which will cover many of the items discussed in this chapter in greater detail.

Understandably, the overall impact of a carefully thought out management plan and further understanding the evolutionary nature of management will allow firms to avoid the pitfalls of poor management and, we hope, build a structure that will allow them to deliver a quality legal product and to accomplish many of the things that will keep them competitive in today's legal practice.

CHAPTER II
Administration

The preceding chapter concentrated on the the policymaking role of the benevolent dictator, the managing partner, and the management committee. Lawyer participation in these areas, though vital, is also time consuming. If once policy is made by the benevolent dictator or management committee, it is necessary for this same individual or group to carry out the policy, the firm will find itself losing hundreds of billable hours, normally those billed at the highest rates. This is not only a waste of assets, but a poor use of manpower. Carrying out policy often requires skills for which lawyers are neither trained nor capable of handling. The disciplines required, at least in carrying out administrative policy, are better handled by trained personnel who are able to take the necessary time and, not the least important, at substantially less cost to the firm.

In this chapter we will discuss administrative personnel, following what is the normal evolution from office manager to executive director. We will cover what these employees do or should do, and why some succeed and others fail. We have discussed the importance of strong governance and management, but do not feel that is enough to run the legal organization successfully. Strong administration is also required.

The use of staff personnel to perform administrative duties is not a new concept in the law firm, though acknowledging that this exists, and putting names to it, is a trend of the last 10 to 12 years. The person handling administrative duties in a newly established firm was initially either the senior partner's secretary or the bookkeeper. As a law firm grew, this person was designated office manager, or a new employee was hired, either because he or she was more skilled in the work required or because the lawyer or the firm felt the employee was more valuable in the original role. Initially, larger firms either created a position above the office manager, or designated the employee administrator, legal administrator, director of administration, or a similar title deemed to be more dignified or important than office manager. As small firms grow, they follow a similar evolution. Though there are no real definitions for the titles, for the sake of clarity in understanding the material that follows, we will briefly try to differentiate between the positions, or rather what we believe the positions to be.

OFFICE MANAGER

Most firms graduate from the senior secretary to an office manager. The office manager has more responsibility than a secretary, but less authority than an administrator. The hiring of an office manager marks the beginning of an adjustment period for the law firm that realizes non-lawyer personnel should be used for support but, at this stage, is unwilling to give up both the day-to-day consultation on all administrative matters and also the authority to make such decisions.

The office manager position may be an effective one in the firm not yet ready to delegate authority, since having the employee will take some of the pressure off the lawyers and free some of their time. An efficient office manager can change lawyer attitudes about "non-professionals" running the firm and, therefore, is an orderly step in the evolution toward a higher level position. Incidentally, the larger firm may have an administrator, with an office manager to back up this person on the more clerical portions of the job.

The position description that follows lists the areas in which an office manager might work. Though the responsibilities of the administrator are similar, many of the areas would be delegated to others. The important difference is in authority. Thus, the office manager will recommend salary increases for employees, but these will be approved by lawyer management. The administrator has a budget for salaried personnel and within that budget handles salary administration without lawyer involvement. Similarly, operating under a furniture and fixtures budget, the administrator will make purchases (such as new desks or chairs). The office manager will recommend the purchase, but normally has to have management approval for each specific purchase (other, perhaps, than office supplies).

Office Manager
Job Description

1. Financial records (Supervision of bookkeeping)
2. Periodic financial reports to partners
3. Financial systems (Check drawing, petty cash, bookkeeping methods, control of disbursements for clients, control of accounts receivable)
4. Cost control
5. Liaison with firm's public accountants
6. Overseeing firm's accounts with suppliers
7. Time records (Collection, submission, and retrieval of data)
8. Firm insurance (Accident, non-owned automobile, improvements, liability, etc.)
9. Firm memberships (Memberships in professional business organizations maintained at firm expense)
10. Filing systems (Current, transfer, general, and "office")
11. Periodic inter-office informational bulletin
12. Library (General housekeeping, updating of reference material, purchase of new books, binding, and repair of books)
13. General supervision of non-exempt staff (Promulgation and enforcement of office rules, establishment of holiday schedules, general supervision of court, and messenger runs)
14. Procurement of non-exempt staff
15. Supplies (Inventory maintenance and purchase)
16. Safety and security
17. Housekeeping of premises (General housekeeping of all but lawyers' offices)
18. Maintenance of premises (Inspection, liaison with building and outside contractors)
19. Cleaning of premises (Inspection, liaison with cleaning contractors)
20. Maintenance and renewal of office equipment and furniture (Inspection, dealing with complaints and repairs)
21. Data processing systems, reports, and analysis

22. Partners' and employees' benefits (Hospitalization insurance, retirement benefits)
23. Communication systems (Telephone, postal, telex, internal, telecopier—overseeing use; consideration of adequacy, etc.)
24. Liaison with other tenants
25. Maintenance of vacation schedules

Initial Hire or Promotion From Within

Though it is difficult to make a general statement, and there are a number of exceptions to the rule, it is advisable to hire a new employee to serve in this role, as opposed to promoting from within. There are a number of reasons for this, the primary one being the difficulty both lawyers and staff have in adjusting to someone in a new role. This is often compounded by the promoted employee's having an equally difficult transition period, one day being one of the employees and the next day being part of firm management. The adjustment period is often so difficult that the problems, rather than gradually disappearing are compounded, almost insuring failure or at least making success considerably more difficult.

Though the office manager seldom has a great deal of authority in dealing with the legal staff, it is necessary that the person command a good deal of respect, almost more so for what the lawyers convey to their secretaries or other support people than what they feel themselves. It is an equally difficult adjustment for staff members who have considered the employee on their own level suddenly to think in terms of "reporting" to their former co-worker. "How can she tell us what to do? She broke plenty of rules herself" are often-heard refrains. These problems can be overcome if the firm is patient and willing to offer a great deal of support during a settling in period. Employee turnover during this period is common, and often increases the office manager's chances for success.

The major benefits to promotion from within are that it indicates to the staff that the firm is interested in their advancement and career, and also cuts down the introduction and integration period for the office manager to office systems, procedures, and personnel. Though these are desirable goals, our experience indicates the likelihood of success is greater with the new hire. We are not sure of the reasons for this, but suspect that management attitude has a good deal of weight. Once the decision to have an office manager is made, the management wants to move at full speed and feels it will accomplish its purpose and can also be more demanding with a new employee than with the employee promoted from within.

Sources

The background of successful office managers varies. While specific personality characteristics, educational and work background cannot really be pinpointed, having worked in a professional environment does seem to cut down on the training time necessary to adjust to the legal environment. Office managers or supervisory personnel from the medical, accounting, educational, or architectural environment make a quicker and more successful transition than those whose background is in other disciplines, such as manufacturing, wholesale, or retail.

In looking for an office manager, personnel skills are probably more important than any other. While expertise in finance may be helpful, it is not nearly so important as interpersonal relationships. (Law firm finance is a more easily learned skill.)

An excellent source of candidates is other law firms. The employee who is in charge of personnel, purchasing, and other administrative duties, yet is unable to make a transition in his present position, may be the perfect candidate for another law firm.

Time for a Change

There is seldom a "failure" of office managers. Either they end their careers with the firm, outgrow the job and leave, or the job outgrows them. In the law firm that has experienced a certain amount of growth, it is common to find lawyers complaining about the day-to-day operations of the firm, that the office manager is in over his or her head, and that the firm needs someone with more capability, certainly someone who can stand up to them. This is a sign that the firm is, perhaps, ready to graduate to a new system of administration. When the lawyers and staff start losing patience with the office manager for not taking care of matters over which the person has no control and for not taking more authoritative positions in areas in which, for years, the manager was told he or she had no authority, there is a reasonable likelihood that an administrator may succeed.

The point at which the consideration of an administrator begins is probably the same point at which serious thought in helping relocate the office manager should take place. As a general rule, the law firm is a humane environment, and letting people go above the lowest level employee is difficult. The customary solution in the case of the office manager is to keep the person on, but bring someone in over him. This is generally a mistake and makes the initial months more difficult than they otherwise would be for the new employee. A law firm usually solves the problem by telling the new administrator that the continuation of the office manager as an employee is up to him. Three to six months later, presuming the office manager is terminated, the office manager becomes a martyr or saint and the administrator a tyrant, or an uncaring individual. Though some resentment may be focused on the administrator if the law firm releases the office manager before the former starts work, this is shorter lived, makes the firm the culprit, and generally assures a smoother transition. The theory that having the office manager around to show the administrator the ropes and help train him, sounds reasonable, but the positions have basic differences so that "training" is difficult, and the top level administrator would normally rather find his or her own way.

ADMINISTRATOR

Delegation

It is understood that the administrator is expected to establish administrative procedures to implement the provisions of this position description and to delegate such functions as he deems appropriate.

As mentioned earlier, there are a few very basic differences between the administrator and office manager. Among the major ones are:

1. The administrator attends all partnership meetings, and often operates as secretary to the partnership.
2. The administrator should attend all management committee meetings, though this in an ex officio capacity.
3. An administrator must have the authority to hire and discharge all staff personnel and to administer salaries within approved guidelines.
4. The administrator will normally have authority to make purchases of furniture, fixtures, supplies, and equipment within approved guidelines.

In principle, and on paper, this sounds easy for the law firm to accept. There are, however, initial steps that should be taken before the search and interview procedure begin.

The position description should be reviewed by the partners. Unless the firm's governing body operates as a dictatorship, hiring an administrator without the advice and consent of the partners will almost surely result in an unsatisfactory experience for all concerned.

The word "review" is probably too mild. The firm's partners must probe their intentions and positively determine that they are not only psychologically ready to give up certain areas of management and responsibility, but also ready to accept the concept of an "outsider" telling them what to do. To accept quickly the lawyer's comments that "All I want to do is practice law" would be a mistake.

Although few lawyers want to be involved in the day-to-day management of the law firm, they want to reserve their right as partners to get involved any time they might feel the urge. Unless the vast majority are willing to accept both the concept of the administrator and the fact that he will report to the lawyer management (be it a managing partner or executive committee) rather than directly to them, there is little likelihood of success.

There are no specific statistics, but most experts in the field would account for the failure of a firm's first administrator by pointing to both the lack of a clearly defined job description, along with a lack of real acceptance of the concept by the firm's partners. Should you talk to a group of experienced legal administrators, you might find several willing to make a job change, but few would consider being a firm's first administrator (at least without intensive investigation and/or an employment contract).

A position description for a law firm administrator follows. Note that this encompasses many, or all, of what was contained in the office manager description. The major difference is in authority as opposed to the areas of responsibility. In addition, the administrator has a closer working relationship with management and firm committees.

Job Description

I.   Summary

The administrator, an experienced, executive level manager, has the day-to-day and general responsibility for all support functions and staff personnel of the firm, as detailed later in this description. In recognition of the importance of the position, the administrator is expected to creatively and continuously define and redefine the scope of the position by searching for new areas to be improved upon (rather than simply reacting to problems as they arise).

II. Reporting

The administrator shall report directly to and be responsible to the executive committee and the managing partner, although in appropriate instances he may perform assignments for special committees of the firm.

III. General Requirements

A. Financial background.

B. Ability to understand, evaluate, and supervise operation of technologically and operationally complex equipment (e.g., data processing, word processing, and document reproduction).

C. Analytical ability.
D. Ability to communicate and deal with people:
    1. Sensitivity to human needs
    2. Ability to command respect and inspire confidence
    3. Strong powers of persuasion
    4. Ability to channel effectively activities of numerous strong-willed partners and associate attorneys.
E. Creativity.
IV. Membership
    The administrator will serve as recording secretary of the executive committee and will prepare agendas for its meetings. He shall attend meetings of the executive committee and any other committee meetings required by his position, except when his own remuneration and compensation shall be under consideration. He shall gather information and prepare reports requested by members of the executive committee. He will attend partnership meetings, serve as a resource person, and participate in decision-making as requested.

He shall be encouraged to join appropriate organizations; and his membership dues and expenses will be borne by the partnership within an approved budget. In this regard, he shall guard the confidentiality of all firm information.
V.   General Responsibility
    The administrator shall have overall responsibility for the performance of all of the functions described in VI below (and others as they arise). Fulfillment of these responsibilities, however, may occur directly, or in conjunction with and supervision of subordinates (e.g., personnel manager, data processing manager, word processing supervisor, librarian, or file manager).

In this connection, it shall be the administrator's ongoing responsibility to make recommendations to the executive committee with respect to continuous refinements and staffing of the support hierarchy so that it functions smoothly and efficiently with the least number of people.

VI. Authority

    A. Personnel

He has the authority to engage the services of any staff employee at such compensation as may be available within his budget. He has authority to discipline or discharge any staff employee.

    B. Purchasing

The administrator has the authority to contract for purchases within the limitations of an approved budget.

VII. Specific Responsibilities

    A. Personnel (staff)

1. Determine staff personnel needs.
2. Locate, recruit, screen, test, and engage the services of staff employees.
3. Conduct employee evaluation and recommend levels of and changes in compensation for staff employees.
4. Maintain confidential personnel files for all employees and partners.
5. Develop systems of personnel utilization for staff employees, and provide general supervision and discipline for the staff.
6. Maintain methods of communications with partners and employees, study and recommend benefit programs and administer such programs.
7. Indoctrinate all new employees with regard to office procedures, security, and other matters of firm policy.
8. Schedule vacations for all staff employees.
9. Consult with employees to assist in resolving personal or job-related problems, and, where appropriate, act as spokesman in dealing with attorneys.
10. Develop programs for maintenance and improvement of employee morale.
11. Counsel staff employees who are not meeting the firm's standards and direct their improvement program.
12. Arrange for termination of employment of personnel who must leave for personal reasons or because of the inability to perform tasks assigned them.

13. Maintain and develop compliance programs for equal employment opportunity.
14. Assist the lawyer recruiting committee in contacting law schools for interviews, responding to requests for and scheduling interviews, screening resumes, arranging visits to the office for candidates for summer clerkship or associate employment, greeting law students or graduates who come to the office for interviews, assuring the candidate's visit is meaningful to the candidate and the office, and making all necessary transportation, lodging, and entertainment arrangements.
15. Regulate work flow within the firm and the work load, including overtime, of individual staff employees.
16. Develop individual job descriptions for all staff positions within the firm.
17. Assist in outplacement of terminating associates, attorneys, and paralegals.
18. Supervise administrative aspects of departmental rotation of new associate attorneys.
19. Assist the associate evaluation committee by coordinating the schedule of semi-annual evaluations, developing and circulating the evaluation reporting forms, digesting the results of the individual evaluations for consideration by the committee, and compiling all necessary materials for presentation to the committee for consideration of compensation changes.
20. Prepare and transmit to new partners copies of all pertinent firm documents, and conduct financial briefings on firm operations for all new partners.
21. Assist the points committee by gathering data and compiling all necessary materials for presentation to the committee for consideration of partner compensation.
B. Finance and Accounting
1. Develop financial plans and budgets for the executive committee.

2. Provide periodic reports regarding performance against budgets.
3. Provide other financial reports, including summaries of time recorded, accounts receivable, and cash flow, as requested by the executive committee and the managing partner.
4. Supervise the timekeeping, billing, and general accounting functions.
5. Maintain controls on delinquent accounts and disbursements to encourage the collection of both.
6. Study and recommend improved systems for accounting, timekeeping, billing, and collections.
7. Act as the firm's liaison with its public accountants.
8. Insure the timely preparation and filing of tax returns, forwarding of withholding and other reporting requirements of all levels of government.
9. Administer the firm's pension plan, including computation and payment of contributions and filing of appropriate reports.
10. Approve payment of accounts payable.
11. Take responsibility for maintaining bank relationships.
12. Take responsibility for investment of the firm's liquid assets.
13. Assist in tax planning for the firm.
C. Long Range Planning
1. Project growth and needs for the future of the firm
2. Develop and analyze costs for proposed new areas of practice and potential mergers with other firms.
3. Keep the executive committee advised on the firm's financial needs, and prepare for consideration proposed billing rates necessary to meet those requirements.
4. Prepare and update long-range budget projections.

D. Office Equipment and Supplies
1. Contract for and insure timely delivery of furniture, office machines, and equipment, supplies, printed material, and other purchases.
2. Insure that the firm obtains proper value for funds expended, considering both cost of purchase and client and community relationships.
3. Establish and maintain a complete inventory of all firm property.
4. Supervise storage and distribution of office supplies.
5. Assume responsibility for purchasing, indexing, and distribution of preprinted forms.
6. Become familiar with new developments and equipment through regular contact with technical representatives, attending and participating in business shows, subscribing to professional and trade publications, attending and participating in seminars.
7. Set up and supervise maintenance schedules on all equipment.
8. Prepare cost studies and recommendations to the executive committee, comparing various equipment alternatives and methods of acquisition.
9. Negotiate as required with vendors to secure purchase agreements and/or lease or rental contracts.
E. Physical Facilities
1. Make appropriate recommendations for adding or divesting space, for use of space, and for location and relocation of attorney offices when required.
2. Work with outside architects or consultants in planning the space requirements of the firm.
3. When construction is underway, maintain files and records of construction contracts, progress reports, change orders and payment schedules, and arrange all physical move-

ments of people, furniture, and functions necessary to expedite construction.

4. Maintain ongoing relationship with landlord.
5. Insure proper maintenance, appearance, cleanliness, and security of facilities.

F. Systems, Procedures, and Services

1. Generally study and recommend changes in office procedures and systems, or recommend procurement of outside assistance as required.
2. Supervise the operation of, and continuously refine and improve, the firm's systems and procedures, including:
   a. data processing
   b. automated word processing
   c. document production (including dictation and typing procedures)
   d. document reproduction
   e. document retrieval (including filing, indexing, storage, microfilming, file purging)
   f. docket control systems
   g. conflict of interest systems
   h. litigation support
   i. mail and document flow (including incoming and outgoing mail, mailing equipment, special messenger services, telecopies, in-house messengers)
   j. dining and food services
3. Be alert to opportunities for computerization and other cost-saving or service-expanding concepts and ideas, and make recommendations to the executive committee.
4. Develop, publish, and constantly update staff, attorney, and other office policy and procedure manuals concerning the operation of the firm.

G. Library and Continuing Legal Education

1. Assume general administrative responsibility for the library and its staff understanding, however, that a librarian may report directly to a lawyer for the purpose of direction and

decision making concerning actual operation of the library.

2. In cooperation with department heads, coordinate continuing legal education programs and arrange for attendance at seminars by attorneys.

H. Community and Client Relations

1. Supervise personnel and procedures employed in telephone answering and client reception, including reception areas and other public/client areas.

2. Oversee operation of, and seek ways to improve, the firm's telephone system.

3. Develop and refine, and supervise maintenance and constant updating of, the firm's general and specialized mailing lists.

4. Develop, and thereafter update, a firm resume, and provide input for published lists (e.g. Martindale-Hubbell).

5. Supervise the preparation and distribution of announcements.

6. Provide for in-house dissemination of information important to the partners and employees.

7. Arrange for client seminars.

8. Assist in implementing public relations (press, government, bar associations, and relations with other firms).

I. Uniformity and Quality Control

1. Consult with, assist, and guide department heads and individual attorneys, as well as the practices and standards committee, in achieving the firm's goal of uniformity of format and work product whenever feasible.

2. In cooperation with the word processing operation, maintain, index, expand, and oversee continuous updating of standardized forms prepared by attorneys.

J. Insurance

1. Administer the existing insurance programs for the firm, make recommendations for changes to modify coverages as appropriate

and to reduce costs, and analyze new programs as needed:
a. accident and health
b. casualty
c. professional liability
d. bonding
e. disability

Selection of the Employee

The employee selected for an administrator position should
have good educational background and work experience, but
equally important, must fit the needs of the firm and administer in a manner consistent with the firm's philosophy.

Salary

One guideline to keep in mind is that you will probably not
be able to hire a qualified legal administrator for less than
you would hire a senior associate. An administrator with several years experience will normally command a higher salary. Should you be unwilling to accept the concept of a non-
lawyer employee earning an income in the same range as a
partner, you are not mentally prepared to accept the professional legal administrator and would be advised to postpone
creating this position.[1]

In addition to salary and fringe benefits on a par with the
lawyers, the administrator must be treated in all ways as part
of the professional staff. If the firm encourages membership
in professional associations, continuing legal education, and
the like for the lawyers, it should be similarly encouraged
and financed for the administrator. The lawyer has daily contact with clients, other lawyers, the courts and can keep

---

[1] We have not included specific salary information since this varies by size of
firm, geographic location, the position description, and numerous other factors. We have recently placed administrators with their salaries ranging
from $38,000 to over $75,000. The Association of Legal Administrators
publishes an annual salary survey, available to non-members of the Association at $75.00. (Association of Legal Administrators, 1800 Pickwick, Glenview,
Illinois 60025 312/724-7700)

abreast of his profession. The administrator's job keeps him in the office; without the opportunity for social, educational, and intellectual stimulation, he will soon grow stale and perform much less effectively.

Hiring

When you are ready to proceed, a few suggestions for your actual interviewing process might be in order.

An interviewee who has had experience as a legal administrator and does not have as many questions to ask you as you have to ask him is probably looking for a job and not for a career with your firm.

Do not be turned off by the forceful individual. The vast majority of successful, respected administrators are not "yes" men or women. It is flattering for an interviewer to have an applicant agree with everything he says, but law firms are not managed on flattery. Lawyers are combative by nature, and will walk all over the weak administrator. Look for someone willing to stand up for his practices, theories, and principles but whose mind is open.

Do not rule out the candidate who has been released by another firm without thorough investigation. You will often find firms willing to admit that the administrator's failure was the firm's fault, normally by giving the administrator a good deal of responsibility, but no authority. This is often also the reason for a currently employed administrator to seek a change of employment.

Be alert to the floater. The good legal administrators are career oriented and do not go from firm to firm or city to city. Make sure your applicant is looking for more of a challenge along with a possible salary increase, rather than just a new place to hang his hat. You should be able to determine this both by the answers to the questions you pose, "What did you like most about your last position?" "What did you like least?" as well as by a thorough checking of references.

Interview the prospective administrator with as much depth as you would an attorney being considered by the firm. His or her role will be equally significant, will affect the lawyers, staff and clients, and will, in many cases, have as much or more effect on the future of your firm. A qualified legal administrator will allow you to devote more time to the practice of law in an environment you enjoy. Proper legal administration will allow the lawyer a good income, while providing quality legal services for clients at a price they can afford to pay.

With the accent on law office management and economics increasing every year, the day may come soon when law firms hire an administrator after proper analysis of the position and the firm—an intensive soul searching coupled with educated screening, interviewing and hiring. Too many law firms today are willing to function in a fashion they would not, in good conscience, permit to exist in their clients' businesses. A willingness to place your own business on a level with your clients' businesses will help you hire the right administrator, work with him, and make the experience a beneficial and rewarding one for both the administrator and the firm.

In most cases the firm is better off with a generalist than a specialist. The skills required to be effective are so diverse, that unless the firm is hiring an administrator to fill a specific need at a specific time (such as the investigation of and implementation of an in-house computer), a well-rounded background augurs better for success.

Surveys conducted by the Association of Legal Administrators indicate that those serving in the position came from a wide variety of backgrounds and disciplines. While there are many exceptions, here is how we feel some of these backgrounds measure up:

- *C.P.A.'s*: This background is attractive to law firms that feel an in-house CPA will be of great benefit in the financial area. While this has some merit, accounting in most firms is relatively simple and will not really utilize the CPA's skills. More important, accountants are generally not effective in the personnel area, which is a vital skill in dealing with lawyers and staff.
- *Retired military*: Initially, a number of firms hired retired army personnel, feeling they had good administrative skills and, usually unstated, could be hired at a relatively low salary due to their generous pensions. Though a great deal depends on the command area in which these people were engaged, it was often not

a successful transition. The structure of most law firms is quite different from the military. There is seldom a recognizable chain of command, and there are large numbers of commanders in chief. People used to issuing orders and having them followed with little or no question have difficulty with the average legal secretary.

- *Lawyers*: The major advantage to hiring someone with a law degree is that the individual comes in with a good deal more immediate acceptance and respect than most other administrators. There is little doubt that this is an excellent way in which to begin, but often success stops short at this point. Though legal education is excellent, it does not provide the training necessary to administer a law firm. The lawyer-administrator also has a tendency to consider himself one of the lawyers, and does not relate well to the staff.

Among the fields which seem to be excellent training grounds for legal administrators are:

- *Education*: The educational administrative area, on both the secondary and college level, has been an excellent source of successful administrators. This environment attracts a high level person, interested in service, who through dealing with faculty, staff, parents, and the Boards of Education and school board, understands the politics necessary to do the job. These skills all seem to transfer well to the legal environment.
- *Hospital, medical, clinic administration*: Administrators transfer skills quite well from the medical to the legal environment. They are used to high overhead, operating within budgets, dealing with professionals in pressured situations, and are attuned to the public image presented by the group they represent.
- *Managers of brokerage firms, accounting, architectural, and business firms*: Most of the managers or administrators of other professional firms understand the importance of providing service to professionals. Most of them have dealt closely with law firms and seem to understand the legal profession and its needs.

The structure of these organizations is similar to a law firm, as are the areas of responsibility and authority.

Two of the other considerations concerning candidates are age and sex. No general rules apply, but most administrators would admit that the male administrator has an easier start, although he is not necessarily any more successful in the long run. There seems to be a desire for some gray hair by the law firms, under the theory that the younger individual will have neither the experience nor the maturity to cope with the lawyers and staff. The applicant in his or her forties or fifties will normally be given the edge over the younger applicant. These are changing concepts; however, since the average age of lawyers in medium to large firms is younger than it was twenty years ago and the number of women lawyers is increasing dramatically, we would expect this to have a definite bearing on those selected by law firms in the future.

Insure the Success of the Administrator

Though it would seem to be an obvious management principle that a manager or administrator get to know the organization before trying to run it, it is surprising to find law firm after law firm, and administrator after administrator expecting to manage effectively on the first day on the job. This is usually a terrible mistake and can damage the administrator so that he is not salvageable.

There is no set period, but three to six months is a reasonable amount of time to get to know the lawyers in the firm, the management style, the staff, and the tone in the office. The time spent doing this is very definitely not wasted; in fact it unquestionably saves time in the long run. In addition, both lawyers and staff are nervous about the new employee, wonder how or if this person will make their lives more difficult, and how much to give in to new ideas, policies, and systems. The best advice to give the new administrator is to tell him the firm expects him to get to know it before doing anything else.

Another way in which to insure the success of the administrator is to hold lawyer involvement in administrative matters to a minimum, but not eliminate it. Some firms in their desire to let the lawyers practice law totally withdraw from administration, giving the administrator no forum, no one to test ideas on, no one to bounce things off. When or if he makes an error, the blame is all his. There is a happy medium.

For example, administrator C was asked to investigate in-house computerization for the firm. A data processing committee was appointed to work with him. A meeting was held every other week, with four lawyer committee members, the bookkeeper, and the administrator. Visits were made to three law firms and two vendor offices, and two other vendors made presentations to the committee. Approximately 350 hours of lawyer time was spent, at an average hourly rate of $100. Three of the lawyers involved knew nothing about data processing before hand, so a good deal of time was spent in educating them rather than in meaningful work. The experience was frustrating for the administrator who had to coordinate meeting dates, visits, and topics.

Administrator D had a similar project for another firm. Two lawyers with some background in finance or data processing were appointed to work with him. An initial meeting was held, and the needs of the firm were determined. The administrator then proceeded to investigate the market. A short report was written to spell out what he had eliminated and what his first and second choices were. The committee reviewed the report, had the two vendors make a presentation, and also visited two installations. Not only did the firm save a great deal of lawyer time, but it provided a reasonable amount of good meaningful backup to the administrator.

Another important aid in helping the administrator succeed is a frequent evaluation of the job he is doing. Lawyers have a tendency to give negative feedback, or none at all, and the administrator who thinks he is doing a good job often finds he has failed only when he is terminated. This serves neither the firm nor the administrator.

Turnover and Failure

Presuming the selection process was handled intelligently and that there are no basic philosophic differences in the manner in which the administrator operates and the manner in which the firm generally wants him to operate, and elimi-

nating the administrator who leaves because he has out-
grown the job and for whom there are no longer challenges,
you are still left with a good number of administrator turn-
overs that must be explained. These failures normally fit into
one of two major categories:

- The law firm that forces the administrator to fail;
  and
- The administrator who causes his own failure.

There are no measurable or really reliable statistics available on this, but our experience with law firms and administrators would indicate a fairly even ratio.

Let's examine these two areas, discussing the major causes
for failure within these two categories.

FAILURE CAUSED BY THE LAW FIRM

Probably the major cause of administrator failure is the un-
willingness or inability of the law firm to accept the basic
concept of a "non-lawyer" involved in areas the lawyers consider their own. The legal staff will almost always give lip
service to the concept of professional administrator, and it is
not unusual to hear, "All we want to do is practice law. We'll
be thrilled to have someone else do the other things around
the office." Unfortunately, though the words are right, the actions often are not. A great deal also depends on the point at
which the firm is in its evolution.

For example, firm B hired an experienced administrator
who reported to a strong managing partner. The administrator worked independently, within the guidelines of his position description, and the lawyers in the firm appeared to be
happy with the arrangement. After two years, the firm started having problems with partners who wanted more involvement, and as a first step to satisfy them, ten committees were
formed. Among these were committees on data processing,
personnel, word processing, and office decor. The administrator spent a good deal of his time attending committee meetings, listening to lawyers who knew little or nothing about a
subject discuss and analyze it, and generally delay action and
decision–making. He gradually became a resource person for
a committee, performing only those functions the lawyers did
not want to do themselves. Six months later he left the firm,

leaving the lawyers puzzled as to the reasons. They had hired a professional administrator, and due to a change in management philosophy, turned him into an office manager.

This points out a major reason for administrator failure—hiring the wrong person for the position, or hiring the right person but then changing the rules in the middle of the game. Many administrators have the patience to live through the attempt to manage and/or administer by committee, recognizing that it is doomed to fail, and anticipating a return to their original role. But the majority have neither the patience nor the desire to do so, and move on to another firm that will better utilize their talents.

In another case, Alex Jay was the administrator for the X, Y, Z law firm. During his first year with the firm he had problems with a secretary who was assigned to work with partner Jones. Jay felt he should not pursue this until he had been with the firm for awhile and the partners were comfortable with him. After a reasonable period of time he called the secretary in and told her that she must start abiding by the rules on office hours, and that he would also expect her to help out when she had time available. He later met with Jones and advised him of the meeting. A few months later he met with Jones again, told him there had been no improvement, and that he was going to put the secretary on probation. In the middle of the probationary period he suggested that Jones talk to the secretary, since there had been no improvement in her attitude. A month later the secretary was given a final warning and Jones was notified of this. Two weeks later Jay advised Jones that he was going to terminate the employment, and this was eventually done. The chain of events that followed is basically immaterial, but the administrator was told that the secretary must be retained on the staff, "to keep partner Jones happy." The administrator resigned two days later, and was told that he was behaving in a juvenile manner, since this was a rather trivial matter.

The merits of this case are basically immaterial, and whether the discharge could, or should have been handled in another way does not really matter. The point is that the management of the firm did not back the administrator's decision, telling him something about his authority, and clearly communicating to the staff that though he was to be considered their "boss," with the right mix of politics, he was not the final word.

Another major cause of turnover is boredom, and this is often caused by the law firm that does not let the administrator become truly involved in everything that is going on, or that considers the administrator a maintenance man, rather than someone who can be extremely helpful not only in administration, but also in management. While they do not make the policy, their involvement in almost everything other than the direct practice of law will keep them challenged and stimulated.

Lawyers respect educational accomplishment, and in hiring an administrator, look for candidates with an M.B.A. degree, or comparable. Many firms consider a law degree a decided plus. Experience in another law firm or a responsible administrative position are considered pluses. If this is the caliber candidate interviewed and hired, the skills for which he was hired must be utilized or he will leave. The administrator is in a "limbo" position which is, in itself, difficult enough. He is not staff, and, though he is a professional, is not on the legal staff. There is no promotional ladder to climb, and advancement is only through salary increases or more challenge and stimulation. Administrators leaving a position seldom complain that they were expected to do more than they were able to, that they were overworked, or challenged beyond their capabilities. Unless the law firm recognizes this, the credentials for which it hired the administrator in the first place are what will cause the administrator to leave.

It is not unusual to walk into an administrator's office and to see him studying the firm's income and expense statement. On the side of the desk sits a can of three-in-one oil to take care of the squeaking desk chair for the complaining lawyer. It is when the oil can becomes more important to the firm than the financial statement that the whole concept of effective professional legal administration will fail.

FAILURE CAUSED BY THE ADMINISTRATOR

A great deal has been written about the turnover of administrators, particularly a firm's first on the job. Conferences have covered the failure of law firms to give the administrator sufficient authority to do the job. Informal bull sessions have dealt with the sufferings of administrators at the hands of difficult partners and obnoxious or aggressive associates.

However, little time and attention have been devoted to discussion of administrators who caused their own failure or who were "turned over" by the law firm for completely justifiable reasons. Perhaps a review of some of the reasons for this turnover will cause the administrator to recognize himself and to deal with the problem, or will call to the firm's attention some reasons the administrator is not performing to its "expectations," prompting the firm to discuss it before dismissal is the only solution. Some of the most common failures follow.

The administrator who tries to build the great law firm in the sky. This administrator goes to all the conferences, reads all the articles, knows all the theories, and tries to apply them to his law firm, regardless of whether they fit the particular makeup and personality of his firm. He does not take time to think about the fact that whether something is great theory or management practice is not really as important as whether it will work *in his firm.* By the time he has learned to deal with the firm he works for rather than trying to turn it into the great law firm in the sky, he has failed so often that his credibility is gone. True he may succeed once in awhile, but lawyers seem to keep better scorecards on administrators' failures than on the successes.

The monkey-see, monkey-do administrator. This is one who does little work on his own but picks up on everything the biggest firm in town, or a particular administrator he admires, is doing in the way of carrying out policy or purchasing equipment. This administrator is successful as long as his example is, and as long as the example applies to his firm. This administrator doesn't learn from his friends; he copies them. And while imitation may be a sincere form of flattery, it normally doesn't keep the monkey-see, monkey-do administrator on the job very long. While the law firm may be curious as to what other firms are doing, it should be suspicious of the administrator who justifies most decisions or proposals on the basis that the prestigious firm down the street is doing this.

The administrator who can't find the middle ground. The staff feels the administrator represents management to them but does not represent them to management. A variation of this is the administrator who is so busy representing the staff's position to management that he becomes an employee rather than a manager in the eyes of the attorneys. This is not fatal for someone content to be classified with the staff rather than as part of the attorney group, but it will prevent the administrator from gaining the acceptance necessary to insure his future as an integral part of the firm. Successful administrators find the middle ground and relate on all levels.

The administrator who plays the management committee or letterhead game. Perhaps more sad stories have been told about this administrator than all others. He has a strong position and a good salary, and he curries favor with the "important people" in the office. He often ignores the associates and treats certain of the partners as second-class citizens. You usually hear about his being a little nervous when it appears there may be a change in firm management, and you usually learn of his availability to fill another position when that management change takes place and some of the former "second-class citizens" now run the firm. If the management recognizes that it is getting special treatment, it would be well advised to discuss this with the administrator.

The administrator who doesn't understand politics. This is not a contradiction of the previous example in which the administrator played politics to some extent. This one can't play them, since he doesn't understand them. In his effort to be "fair" he feels the first year associate and the senior partner must be treated the same way. He makes sure the managing partner knows his position doesn't entitle him to anything extra and that the partner bringing in $350,000 a year in fees can't have any extras or special support services. When he loses his job he just doesn't understand why.

The administrator who forgets who is paying his salary. This administrator has all sorts of problems, such as lawyers who "unreasonably" request overtime secretarial help, messenger service or a file cabinet, or use of a conference room. He really would enjoy his job if it weren't for the lawyers. The addition of summer clerks and associates and the work connected with this infringes on his more important duties. If everyone would leave him alone, he'd have time to get his job done. Unfortunately, he really doesn't know that his job is to serve the people paying his salary, and he usually learns this too late.

The law firm is to blame for a great many administrator failures—perhaps the majority of them—but these are some of the ways in which an administrator fails through no fault of the law firm. If you see your administrator in one or more of these six examples, discuss the matter with him before it's too late. A little timely communication on both sides can do wonderful things for the management, the administrator and, most important, the law firm.

Executive Director

Several large firms, with more than a hundred lawyers, are carrying the concept of strong administration to an even higher degree than might be encompassed by an administrator. This often is done because the firm feels it needs the equivalent of a full time managing partner, but does not have a lawyer in the firm with the skills, time, or inclination; and it is difficult to recruit a lawyer to assume this role. Though the executive director makes policy only occasionally, because he is close in age or older than the average of the partners, has an extremely professional manner, and excellent experience, he is given more latitude than most administrators. He often fills the role a managing partner would, and if the person in the job has a law degree would be given the title managing partner, though the role is the same as an executive director. Another common reason for hiring an executive director is that the administrator is so busy running the day-to-day affairs of the firm, even with a staff handling most of the details, that he does not have time to do the financial planning, marketing, and long range planning the firm feels is necessary.

The firms with executive directors, and those trying to fill this position, say that the role is suited for "a top level corporate executive type." Often a requirement will be an MBA, PhD, or a law degree. Seldom will a true executive director be under 45 years of age. The salary will normally exceed $85,000, with benefits equal to those given to lawyers. Though the firm's administrator may have the necessary qualifications, the Executive Director is seldom promoted from within. Most Executive Directors operate on a partner level, are part of the Management Committee, and are expected to fill a role similar to that of a chief operating and financial officer in a corporation.

Today there are probably not more than thirty true executive directors in law firms. Though it is too soon to judge the success and acceptance of these people, early indications are that the firms are happy with this concept, and we would expect to see the trend to higher and higher levels of administration continue.

Official Recognition of the Administrator

A recent change in material issued by the American Bar Association allows the law firm to compensate the administrator or executive director on a basis that makes the position more attractive to top level candidates. Though the firm always could have paid a high salary, salaries higher than what partners might earn met with a great deal of resistance, and the Canons of Ethics prevented any profit sharing arrangement. Gradually there was recognition of the fact that good management requires delegation to competent professionals.

The American Bar Association recognized the contribution of administrators in their Informal Opinion 1440 of August 12, 1979:

> You have requested the Committee's advice on the matters set forth below. We understand the facts to be as follows:
> You indicate that you are of a firm of about forty lawyers, with a total staff of about one hundred people, lawyers and nonlawyers, and that you have instituted a sophisticated management organization. The firm employs a lay office administrator who is generally in charge of all nonprofessional business matters within the firm. Further, the administrator has no professional responsibility and does not participate in any decisions involving professional judgment, including the determination of fees which remain under the control of the lawyers. The administrator does not participate in the acceptance of legal fees or the decision concerning collection of fees. You indicate that you would like to pay your office administrator primarily on the basis of a fixed, predetermined annual salary, but in addition, a percentage of net profits which might

represent one-fourth to one-third of the administrator's total compensation. You indicate that it is the firm's belief that such a compensation structure for the administrator would provide an incentive and reward for unique talents and dedicated services in achieving greater efficiency and productivity in the operation of the law firm.

You have requested our advice as to the ethical propriety of your law firm compensating the lay office administrator in the foregoing manner.

It is our opinion that the compensation structure you describe for your lay office administrator would not be inconsistent with the Model Code of Professional Responsibility. In our view, the foregoing proposal does not constitute dividing legal fees with a nonlawyer under DR 3.102, because the compensation relates to the net profits and business performance of the firm and not to the receipt of particular fees. An organization practicing law may employ many nonlawyers. The source of funds to pay them for their services will be fees for legal services rendered. See Formal Opinion 303. We have previously found that a lawyer or law firm may include nonlawyer employees in a retirement plan even though the plan is based in whole or in part on a profit sharing arrangement. See Formal Opinion 325. With the development of professional business management within law firms, and given the fact that a fixed salary plus incentive compensation is not an uncommon form of compensation, we do not believe that such compensation structure is proscribed by the Model Code.

Though no more than 10 percent of those in administrative positions in the law firm now have a share in the profits or other incentive compensation, profit sharing is becoming more common. While it is difficult to sell to partners a salary of $125,000 for a top administrative person, they will often buy a salary of $75,000 with the opportunity to earn a much larger amount, if the firm has a good year or if net profit exceeds a particular figure.

We believe the results accomplished by good administration are no longer an issue. Today, good management in a law firm takes advantage of the contribution made by professional administration. The firms which recognize this are, and will be, far ahead of those that believe it is the lawyer's role not only to make policy, but to administer it.

CHAPTER III

New Era May Call for New Structures

As the nature of the practice of law continues to undergo vast changes, the relationships that exist between the partners of a law firm are under new strain. Gone are the days when partners simply did not move from one firm to another or where firms only hired graduates immediately out of law school. Also gone are the days when partners could ignore moral obligations to other partners with regard to such unforeseen circumstances as death or disability.

Yet as the practice of law has developed into a big business, it is astonishing how many firms operate without so much as an understanding of the basic relationship between partners and, even worse, have neglected to commit necessary understandings to writing. In fact, were the test of quality of legal work of many firms judged on the basis of their internal agreements, they would surely have problems attracting and keeping clients.

There are a number of issues that tend to create problems for a law firm and which go to the very heart of the relationship among partners, including:

- Admission of a new partner
- Death of a partner
- Disability of a partner
- Withdrawal of a partner
- Expulsion of a partner
- Definition of fees
- Management Structure
- Capital Structure
- Compensation methods
- Voting provisions

To ensure its success, the firm must not only address the above issues but also prepare a written agreement setting forth the basic understandings of the partners. For those

firms that already have such an agreement, the issues must
be re-evaluated and the agreement reviewed periodically to
see if it, indeed, sets forth a proper understanding or is relevant to the current thinking of the partners.

Each firm should consider one underlying question before
it plans to write or re-write its agreements, "What type of
firm do we want to be? Are we striving for an institutional[1]
situation, or are we actually a group of lawyers merely sharing office space?" It is interesting that a vast majority of
firms of all sizes will respond that they are, of course, true
law firms rather than simply lawyers sharing office space
and splitting fees. But it is remarkable to find how many
firms, based on their agreements and compensation arrangements, fit into the latter category.

This assessment should not be interpreted as a slanted
statement in favor of any particular mode of practice. Rather
it is offered as advice for a firm to be honest with itself and
to match its arrangements among partners with the true nature of the law firm.

ADMISSION OF NEW PARTNERS

This subject continues to undergo much change, as the
needs and economics of law firms continue to demand new
approaches.

---

[1] The term "institution" is used throughout this and other chapters, and there
should be a clear understanding of its meaning as it is used here. An institutional firm does not necessarily mean a firm who services banking, corporate, or other institutional clients. Rather, it is directed at the basic
underlying relationship that exists between partners and sets the tone for the
structure of the firm. A firm having partners with an institutional mentality
is one in which all recognize that the entity is more important than the individual and where certain reasonable agreements exist that stress the continuity of the entity over the interest of any one member. Accountants have
developed more stable, larger and, in many cases, more profitable organizations because they have learned the value of such an organization. Lawyers,
on the other hand, are trained from law school forward, as single practitioners and generally have little understanding of the value of a well organized
firm. Furthermore, they tend to look at clients as personal property and foster such relationship rather than educating the client in the benefits of firm
practice.

Traditional Approach

Historically, there was generally one class of partners who were admitted after careful scrutiny and after meeting a high and very demanding set of criteria. Much of the criteria were unwritten, mostly unspoken, and rested in the hands of a small group of senior partners. The truth is, however, that many of the most successful partnerships were initially put together on such terms. In the 1960's and 1970's, the admission to partnership became much easier; and the "good old boy syndrome," under which all associates were given partnership almost solely on the test of having endured four to six years as an associate, became the norm in many firms. This change was well received by young lawyers, but its effects have not been very good. Today there are many firms that are trying to deal with weak, employee-type partners, that is, partners who do not understand the risk-taking nature of a partnership and who, because of high income needs, expect compensation to come automatically with little awareness of client development and the profitability of the firm. As a result, many firms are aggressively moving to change their old policies. Small firms are hit even harder by this situation, since they cannot easily compete with the large firms in either recruiting or compensation and so tend to "sell" easy partnership as their one attractive feature over larger firms. There may be some benefit in this situation, however, since the larger firms, in tightening the qualifications for partnership and lengthening the time to admission, are forcing a number of well-trained associates, who will be even more easily attracted to the opportunities of the smaller firm, into the job market.

New Approaches

As the profit squeeze hits, more and more firms of all sizes are seeking new approaches to deal with partnership admission. Here are a few suggestions to consider:

INCOME PARTNERS

This arrangement is sometimes referred to by other names, including "non-equity partner," "participating associate" and "special partner." We recommend the term "income partner" since it more clearly defines the concept. Basically, it creates an intermediate step between associate and partner that is designed to give a lawyer the sense of partnership without all of the participation and trappings of a partner. One way to accomplish this is to give the individual in this position a base salary and a bonus based on a percentage of income.

Example One:		
Associate Salary		Bonus
A	45,000	.02%
Example two:		
Associate Salary		Bonus
A	45,000	.01% of a profit
		pool based on .03% of
		firm income

Example One is quite straightforward in that it provides for a bonus in the traditional sense by giving the associate/partner a percentage of the net income. The advantage of this method is that it is simple to calculate and treats the individual more like a conventional partner. This advantage may also be its biggest disadvantage, since one of the goals is to create a different class of partners, and this method makes that aspect of the arrangement more difficult.

Example Two provides for a bonus as part of a bonus pool of the net income, this pool being shared 100 percent among all non-equity partners. The advantage of this system is that it does in fact create a clear distinction between partners and more clearly defines the non-equity partners. It is, on the other hand, more complex to administer, and decisions of what percentage of profit should be reserved for the bonus pool each year can be difficult.

Generally speaking, an associate who is put into this classification has no equity or liability and limited or no voting rights.

The non-equity arrangement has advantages and disadvantages. Among the advantages:

• Gives associates an earlier opportunity to participate in profits.
• Educates associates about partnership responsibilities.

- Encourages a team approach to the practice.
- Allows a longer time to full partnership status.

Disadvantages include:

- Creates a second class status for partners, which can cause turnover and recruiting problems.
- May permit a firm to carry marginal associates by putting them in this intermediate class thereby creating an even tougher situation for weeding out nonperformers.
- Can create problems in the years of no net income growth, since the "capital" partners might resent the money going to the non-equity partners.

By and large, however, this arrangement can work in firms of all types and can allow limited admission to partnership at an early date. Such an arrangement does require careful selection and evaluation techniques of associates and an aggressive weeding out philosophy to ensure that only qualified individuals are put into this category.

The most significant development in the role of the income partner is the thinking by numerous larger firms that a permanent, second tier of partnership will, in the long run, make sense of the structure problems covered by having too many partners. Some firms have been comparing this change to the large accounting firms who have "partners" and "principals." The underlying theory at work in this arrangement is that there are many associates who are good lawyers and who can be profitable to the firm but who should not become full partners. We feel that the concept has merit and recommend its consideration.

NORMAL ADMISSION—GUARANTEES

If the non-equity arrangement does not seem attractive, a firm might want to consider a totally different approach. In this situation, a firm admits an associate to partnership but for somewhere from one to three years sets compensation on an absolute basis and guarantees the new partners no downside risk. Some firms also provide for non-equity sharing above the guaranteed amounts, while others permit participation either on some budgeted net income or when the net income exceeds a specific amount.

Generally speaking, guaranteed partners are given equity, make capital contributions, and vote on partnership interests.

The advantages of this arrangement are that it:

- Helps alleviate the problem of insufficient monetary increase for new partners based on percentage arrangements.
- Gives the new partner a greater sense of belonging to the partnership.
- Encourages senior partners to share income with juniors especially in years of limited net income growth.

Among the disadvantages are that it:

- May create a situation that overrewards a new partner, thereby creating unreasonable expectations in subsequent years.
- Creates the possibility that in a poor net income year a young partner under guarantee might earn more than a second or third year partner.

NORMAL ADMISSION—EXTENDED TIME

A large number of firms of all types are extending the time to partnership admission, causing complaints from associates that the "rules of the game are being changed."

The reason for this change is most often voiced by young partners (who incidentally were admitted under the more lax standards) and is based on the rationalization that the profit squeeze almost always created by high associate salaries has not left enough money to be distributed to the partners. Therefore, the argument continues, a reduction in new partners will help remedy this situation.

This is a case of "lawyers' solutions to management problems," coupled with a real lack of understanding of law firm economics. Consider the following:

- The move from associate to partner does not constitute a dollar for dollar reduction in net income—the firm has all along incurred costs both in salary and fringes that will be returned to the partners' bottom line.

- A lack of growth in the partnership is almost always caused by problems that have little to do with the qualifications of associates; but when a firm is experiencing economic problems, it's an easy way out for the partners to point their fingers at the associates, blaming them for all of the firm's ills. When a firm is having either economic or management problems the cause and, indeed, the solution is with the partners and not generally with the presently employed associates. It is interesting to note that it is often the partners who scream the loudest about the associates who are the cause of the economic problems. Such partners often do not utilize associates effectively but at the same time complain that associates are under-utilized and unprofitable.
- If partners placed more emphasis on both new client development and more efficient and realistic methods of operation, there would be plenty of room for new partners, because the economic base of the firm—that profit made from the associates—would permit reasonable growth.
- The moment a firm takes a no-growth attitude, it opens the door for valuable people to be lost.

It would be far better to have a shorter time period with a high set of standards than to keep a lower standard and to extend the time period for partnership.

This does not mean that we are contradicting earlier statements about extending partnerships or creating a two tier partnership, but rather to imply that many firms turn to such methods as a way of solving a basic economic problem. Adopting longer tracks to partnership and/or two-tier partnerships must be accompanied by long range plans to solve the overall economic problems that may be causing the partners to focus on the associate admission policy in the first place.

Partnership Criteria

The subject of admission brings up the question of criteria for partnership. Many firms have tried (most unsuccessfully) to define in writing the criteria for partnership admission. This is a very difficult task since the decision to admit a partner always comes down to some subjective decisions. Furthermore, a single set of criteria does not fit every associate. Nevertheless the following items (without regard to order) should be important in selecting partners.

1. Work habits—
   Billable and non-billable hours
   Organization of work
   Efficiency
2. Quality of work
3. Attitude toward firm management and structure
4. Ability to relate to clients
5. Ability to relate to other partners
6. Ability to supervise other associates
7. Client development *potential*

More recently many firms have also been applying a "need" criteria-Does the firm need another partner? This is a difficult decision to face, but in a time when many law firms have too many partners it is time that the question of need be be raised. Furthermore, the firm should ask itself whether it can afford another partner. That is to say are the economics of the firm growing enough to allow for compensation of a new partner without penalizing other partners.

It is our opinion that written criteria for partnership are unnecessary and unwise but that some standards as set forth in this paragraph should be anticipated and understood by all concerned.

VOTING

Admission of a Partner

Many firms have difficulty deciding on what basis a new partner is approved for partnership. In a vast majority of firms actual votes are not taken on every issue, but rather, the firm operates on a "consensus" basis. Indeed, the firm that has to count votes on issues may have much deeper problems. This is particularly true of smaller firms where partners should be able to reach a consensus on most matters without an actual vote being taken.

Nevertheless, all firms should have in their agreements the stipulated vote that it takes to admit a partner. This vote should be substantially high enough to assure that most partners are in agreement, but should never permit a "blackball" situation to occur. We recommend that a vote of 85 to 90 percent of the partners be required in firms of up to 15 partners and that the percentage drift downward in larger firms but should probably never fall below about 75 percent.

Also, in some firms the senior partners feel that they should have more weight in voting on some or all issues. While a case can be made for such a position, it should be kept in mind that when voting on admission of new partners takes place, the individuals who are most affected on a long term basis are the young partners.

Voting Rights of New Partners

Some firms give a young partner a lesser vote than partners who have been with the firm for an extended period of time. This practice is objectionable since it flies in the face of the whole basis for a partnership. If the seniors in the firm cannot obtain the support of the young partners by leadership example, then arbitrarily attempting to control their voice is treating a symptom rather than the problem.

General Voting Provisions

The voting arrangements in a law firm reflect to a large degree the heart of the relationship of the partners and often tell a good deal about the management philosophy in the firm. Some of the more common voting arrangements follow.

ONE–MAN ONE–VOTE

There are many firms, usually small, where each partner has one vote on partnership issues. This method of voting usually results from a feeling of need for democracy in the firm or when the young partners are attempting to have more to say in the decision-making process. It is interesting to note that stagnant firms and those experiencing partnership problems generally have this type of voting arrangement.

One–man one–vote arrangements generally give the partners a better sense of democracy, since all partners technically have an equal vote on partnership matters. Partners, especially younger partners, should recognize, however, that those partners who are in leadership roles or who are responsible for major clients generally have more leverage with their one vote than does a partner who recently joined the partnership. This type of voting system is recommended in firms that have strong leaders and sound management structures.

Where a firm utilizes the one–man one–vote rule, the number of votes required to oppose a particular issue should be set relatively low to eliminate the problem of a few partners stopping the progress of the firm.

A sample clause for a one–man one–vote arrangement might be as follows:

> All partnership decisions will require a 60 percent vote of all partners with each partner having one equal vote. Notwithstanding the above, a vote for the admission of a new partner, the dissolution of the partnership, or the expulsion of a partner will require an 80 percent partner vote.

WEIGHTED VOTING

Each partner in this arrangement has a vote corresponding to his or her percentage in profits. For example, a partner with a 10 percent interest in profits would have a weighted vote of 10 percent compared to a five percent partner, who would have half as much.

The weighted voting system gives those individuals receiving more of the compensation a higher degree of control of the firm. In order to insure some protection for the younger partners, the number of votes needed for approval should be set high enough to avoid a small number of partners from having too much leverage. This voting structure works better in firms where democracy tends to play too dominant a role or where the position of the leadership has to be well defined.

A sample clause for weighted voting might be as follows:

> All partnership decisions will require a 65 percent vote of the partners voting according to their current interest in profits. Notwithstanding the above a vote for the admission of a new partner, the dissolution of the partnership, or the expulsion of a partner will require an 85 percent vote.

COMBINATION SYSTEMS

Some firms use a combined system of voting in which it takes an "X" amount of interest in profits voting on a weighted basis and a majority of the partners measured on a one–man one–vote concept. Where a firm feels it has to have a complex voting system and both has to give leverage "officially" to the "seniors" and to have a feeling of democracy for all the partners, a combined system may be appropriate.

A typical clause for such a voting structure might be as follows:

> The admission of a new partner will require a 75 percent vote of partners' profit interests as well as a 51 percent vote of partners on a per capita basis.

GENERAL OBSERVATIONS

Those firms in which partners have to worry extensively about the voting criteria are usually ones in which problems exist. A need for carefully defined voting generally reflects a lack of trust among the partners and in the leaders of the firm. Those firms which seem to have the best relations among partners are ones where consensus decision making takes place and where the partners have delegated most of the management of the firm to one or more partners.

This is not to say that the voting system for partners should not be carefully documented in the firm's agreement. Each firm has different historical management and is at a different place in its management evolution, thereby requiring the reader to be certain to take the recommendations on management and tailor them for his specific firm.

For example, a firm that has been through a period of leadership by a dictator, especially if the dictator was not very benevolent or if decisions on major items were made with little consultation with other partners, would probably be better off with a more democratic voting arrangement provided, however, that some strong central management is put in place to follow the dictator.

Conversely, a firm that needs leadership, or where democracy has brought decision–making to a standstill, might be well advised to put the leadership and power in the hands of a few partners.

Lateral Entry Partners

In the last few years many firms have increased their acquisition of partners who have some level of experience, as
opposed to hiring strictly from law school and "promoting
from within." Indeed, the number of "headhunters" who are
attempting to serve the legal profession has increased dramatically.

The old concept that all lawyers should be taken out of law
school and work through the ranks still has some merit in
that it tends to bring about a more planned growth of the
firm and to allow an orderly development of the economic
pyramid. Since, however, lawyers may have the worst "people
judgment" of any group known to man, the recruitment effort
of many firms has been less than outstanding. Furthermore,
the "depression mentality" that still exists with many partners has caused firms, especially smaller ones, to fail to recruit on some planned basis and has therefore created gaps
in the experience level of associates. Also, the high cost of
law school graduates, coupled with the lag time in generating
profits from them, has caused many firms to resume their
lateral recruiting efforts.

There are several situations when the lateral entry of a
lawyer would be desirable.

- Where a firm's recruiting has been spotty, lateral
  entries can bring an immediate level of expertise and
  maturity to a firm.
- Where a firm is developing a new level of expertise
  and there would be a time lag in getting people to the
  necessary experience level.
- Where a firm has a highly specialized litigation practice and obtaining lawyers with a few years trial experience is more efficient than direct law school
  hiring.
- Where a firm that has become so "in-bred" that it has
  not balanced the personalities and abilities of its people, lateral hiring may be the cure. This is especially
  true where firms have developed good working lawyers but have paid little attention to the entrepreneurial skills needed to develop future clients.

Law firms can no longer ignore the growing trend of
lawyers who move from one firm to another. Industry today

looks favorably at the executive who has made a few well-planned moves, and it may well be that law firms will also come to understand this method of thinking.

Capital Structure

While the question of firm capital may seem rather clear and straightforward, it is amazing how many partners do not understand this subject. Worse yet, many firms have not come to grips with their capital needs. Many cash flow problems are the result not only of poor billing and collection habits but of a lack of understanding of the need for working capital to fund the operations of the firm.

Comments such as "We do not need capital," "Our capital is in furniture and fixtures," "We need enormous amounts of money in the bank" reveal a lack of understanding of this subject. Furthermore, many firms tell new partners that they do not have to make capital contributions when they become partners. Such a position is not in the best interest of either the new partner or the firm. It tends to create employee-minded partners—a partner who does not make a capital contribution has little sense of the risk-taking role of a partner—while at the same time not addressing the working capital needs of the firm.

Here are two examples of capital arrangements:

- A non-institutionalized firm may see it as the value of the depreciated hard assets plus the value of work-in process and accounts receivable and in fact give a withdrawing partner an interest in these assets.
- A firm that is trying to institutionalize, however, will consider the value of hard assets as costs of doing business with no interest allocated to partners except on dissolution. Certainly work-in-process and accounts receivable should not be counted when looking at assets for the purpose of defining working capital, despite what some accountants say on the subject.

The question then is "What is capital?" For the purpose of understanding the concept of working capital, consider capital as an amount of money either contributed by or held back from net income for the purpose of funding the firm's operations. While many readers may feel that this is a large-firm concept, the fact is that it applies to small firms as well, since firms of all sizes require working capital to provide cash for operations.

Working capital should be determined in a rational way, rather than by the arbitrary whim of a partner or two. Some of the reasons for working capital are:

- A fund to finance poor billing and client disbursement practices.
- A fund to provide a cushion for expenses and draws and to even out cash flow cycles.
- A reserve for major capital improvements (more and more handled by bank borrowing).
- A fund to allow for expansion, especially the hiring of new lawyers.

There are a couple of methods for calculating paid-in capital that are worth considering.

The first method looks at the various factors listed below to arrive at a goal for capital.

Factors
2 months of partners' draws
plus 3 months of expenses.

Total of the factors results in the establishment of capital based on a cash reserve philosophy.

The second method considers different factors.

Factors
1. Cost of accounts receivable lag time
2. Outstanding client advance at year end
3. Cost of billing write-offs
4. Loss on first year associates

These factors evaluate the use of cash as it affects current economic performance. This method is, we feel, a more scientific method of estimating capital needs.

An example is as follows:

1. Accounts Receivable lag	$250,000
2. Difference between client costs advanced and those received at year end	200,000
3. Cost of billing write-offs net of overbillings	150,000

4. Investment in new associates
   = Total cost of new associates
   less collection on their time   100,000
            Paid in capital requirement $700,000

Some firms having arrived at such a number then calculate that number as a percentage of gross income and adjust it annually at that percentage. For example:

	Year 1	Year 2
Gross	10,000,000	11,000,000
Capital	700,000	770,000
%	07%	07%

Regardless of the method, it is important to be certain that all partners understand the issue and how it will affect them since it is the individual partners who will be contributing the working capital. Here secrecy or lack of communication is devastating.

Once the amount of capital is determined, the issue of how it is raised must be considered. Too many firms simply dismiss this question without giving it any real thought or without an understanding of the ramifications it might have on the partners personally. Some of the typical ways to raise capital are as follows:

- At the end of the year withhold any undistributed profits and credit such amounts to capital. The disadvantage of this method is that it is usually totally unplanned and cyclical. It often creates confusion because it is an after-tax contribution, and it may prove totally unacceptable in its application when considering income levels of various partners.

One way to improve this situation is to establish a capital account as already explained and simply credit undistributed profits each year only to the extent of the requirement for each partner. Thereafter, undistributed profits are paid out as soon as cash is available in the subsequent year.

- Determine the amount of capital required from each partner and take a "note" allowing the partner to pay it at his convenience. Many small firms as well as larger ones that do not require a great deal of working capital tend to use this method.

There is, however, a serious disadvantage that is often overlooked by firms following this method. It lies in the inequities of actually paying off the note. Some partners almost always pay off their capital notes on or before the due date, while others will look for every excuse to delay payment. Since most firms do not like to be enforcers against their partners, animosities tend to develop among partners over this issue. Also, if the firm really needs working capital, the concept of taking a note does not solve the problem. "Funny money" is not the solution to working capital needs.

- Determine the level of capital and require immediate payment using bank financing. We feel that this is a method that should be considered seriously since it puts the business relationships of the partners at "arms length." Simply stated, the firm enters into a capital financing program with its bank. Most larger banks generally will lend the individual partner the necessary capital funds, and if the firm is willing to guarantee the note, will offer very favorable terms.

Another issue to determine once the decision is made on the overall amount of capital is in what manner each partner will contribute. There are two basic approaches.

- Have each partner contribute equally to the capital account. Some firms require contribution upon admission while others allow a graduated payment schedule over a period of years.
- Have each partner contribute according to his interest in profit and adjust annually on some regular basis. This method is preferable since it requires the partners with the larger financial return to carry more of the financial burden.

One last consideration concerning capital. A firm that is considering a merger with another firm should have a clear understanding of the terms of capital and its allocation among partners. Many firms that have not "cleared the air" on the subject of ownership of assets and paid-in capital sometimes find that their internal problems create an obstacle in formulating a professional corporation or in considering a merger. Some typical contractual language concerning capital follows:

PARTNERSHIP CAPITAL

The capital required to operate the firm shall be determined from time to time by the Management Committee. Each partner shall contribute his proportionate amount thereof based upon his Units of Participation, and required adjustments shall be made as additional Units are issued to existing or new partners. No partner shall be entitled to receive interest on his capital contribution.

At the end of each fiscal year the amount of such capital and each partner's contribution to such capital shall be reviewed by the Management Committee and fixed in accordance with the firm's needs.

The Management Committee is specifically empowered to establish the terms and conditions of the payment of the capital contribution of each partner. If payment of any such contribution is deferred, interest at rates fixed by the Committee may be charged on deferred amounts in the discretion of the Committee.

An individual capital account shall be maintained for each partner. Such accounts shall reflect the adjustments to be made under Section _____.

For the purposes of this Agreement no value shall be attributed or given to goodwill, the name of the partnership, fees billed but uncollected, work in process but unbilled or client costs advanced but uncollected.

From time to time the partnership may be indebted to the partners in varying amounts for sums loaned to the partnership for use as working capital. Interest at rates fixed by the Management Committee may be paid on such amounts.

Partner Withdrawals

If agreements cover no other circumstance, it is essential that they deal with voluntary and involuntary withdrawals from a firm. In pursuing this discussion, the philosophy of your law firm will play a significant role in determining the nature of your agreement. A firm that is attempting to instill an institutional attitude among its partners will down-play any withdrawal rights of partners other than for retirement, death, or disability; a firm that is more like a group of single practitioners sharing space will emphasize the individual ownership aspect of the firm.

Death of a Partner

Since no situation is quite as traumatic and emotional as a partner's death, it is essential that firms develop plans for such circumstances. Regardless of the relationship that exists, a firm of any size is well advised to have pre-set agreements concerning payments and interests of partners at the time of death.

> Case in point: CDE firm had fifteen partners who had been practicing law together for many years. The partners prided themselves on the fact that they never required a partnership agreement, and always took good care of each other.
>
> A forty-five year old partner was vacationing in Florida in December 1980. He was driving back to the airport at the end of his vacation when a large tractor trailer crossed the road and struck his car. He died instantly.
>
> Emotions ran very high in the months that followed, and the firm went out of its way to try to assist the family. As time passed, however, the widow became disenchanted with the "lack of attention" and the fact that none of the partners seemed to be willing to arrive at some type of settlement with her.
>
> She finally visited a single practitioner, in a nearby small town, who advised her that she could claim interest in work in process and accounts receivable of the firm. In fact, since the firm did not have an agreement, it could be legally dissolved and she had an interest in the assets.
>
> The widow sued the firm, asking the court to declare a dissolution and forcing a distribution of assets. The firm had forced upon itself a judicial accounting and was required to retain counsel and outside consultants. Two years later, with expenses in the six figure range, the matter was finally concluded with a cash settlement.

The point is clear! All of this could have been avoided with rather simple agreements. Here are several approaches.

NON-INSTITUTIONAL METHOD

Provide that a partner's percentage of profits at the time of death (or some average percentage over a period of years) be applied to the current work-in-process and accounts receivable at the time of death and that this be paid to the partner's estate if and when the firm collects for the work. The advantage of this method is that it is rather simple to calculate and seems to satisfy many partners as a fair determination of their equity interest in the firm. This advantage, however, is also its greatest disadvantage since such "soft equity—i.e. not cash or cash–related assets" is always subject to debate and manipulation.

No arrangement is made on the theory that each partner should be paying his own way and it is not the firm's responsibility to take care of personal situations or worry about a partner's estate planning. This is an old fashioned concept of a law partnership and not realistic. Many older partners, however, still cling to this idea and in so doing strain relationships with their younger partners.

INSTITUTIONAL METHOD

Determine that no partner has a continuing interest in the firm or any of its assets. In lieu thereof, provide a payment based upon past compensation. For example:

(1) Highest annual dollar compensation in any one year during the five years prior to death.
(2) Average annual dollar compensation of the five years prior to death.
(3) Average annual dollar compensation of any five years out of the 10 years preceding death.

Having decided to use one of the above methods or some other basis for the calculation, multiply the result of 1, 2, or 3 by a percentage. For example:

Average of highest compensation for 5 years	$100,000
Multiply by a factor	300%
Total retirement benefit	$300,000

The $300,000 death benefit is then paid to the deceased partner's estate over a period of time, usually five to ten years and may be reduced by any insurance the firm carries on the partner's life. Most firms should consider insurance to protect themselves against this obligation and can arrange coverage at rather inexpensive rates. Indeed, the proceeds of life insurance would come to the partnership tax free and the payment specified in the above example would, under present law, be an ordinary business deduction. We recommend that all partners have a minimal level of insurance (regardless of compensation) of at least $250,000.

There are almost an infinite number of ways to arrive at the desired result, but regardless of the method or of the insurability of the partners, a plan, institutional or non-institutional, should be adopted.

It is interesting to hear the partner who is "anti-insurance" argue about what a bad investment insurance is and how he does not need any additional coverage. When it comes to a firm's obligation to a deceased partner's family, however, the views of such a partner cannot be allowed to prevail. If he predeceases his partners, the firm's obligations have little to do with his own uninformed approach to insurance protection.

Protecting a firm from disruption when a partner dies is extremely important to the ability of the firm to move ahead. Such protection may not erase the moral obligation to families of deceased partners, but such obligations will at least not terribly disrupt the relationship of the living partners.

Disability

More firms are beginning to recognize the difficult financial burden that can be placed on a firm by one of its partners becoming disabled. There are a number of ways to handle this situation.

NON-INSTITUTIONAL METHOD

1. If a partner becomes disabled, the firm ceases to owe him any obligations after possibly some initial period of time when he will continue to be compensated.
2. Each partner should handle his own insurance since the firm does not believe in buying insurance for its partners. It is non-deductible anyway, and each partner has different needs.
3. If a partner becomes disabled and withdraws from the practice, he receives his percentage interest in work-in process and accounts receivable.

The same advantages and disadvantages exist with disability as were explained earlier under death of a partner. Generally speaking, a firm that does not provide for disability arrangements will not include any provisions in its partnership agreement. This is a matter of leaving the responsibility in the partners' hands, the firm believing that it should not be liable for any obligations, and that insurance for disability should be paid for by individual partners.

The problem with this approach is that while it might seem sound initially, when a disability occurs, certain moral obligations present themselves, and most partnerships find themselves faced with difficult issues concerning their obligations.

INSTITUTIONAL METHOD

When a firm is going to provide disability protection for a partner, it must be certain to cover all aspects of a probable situation. Defining disability in the usual situation is easy enough and can usually track the language found in a disability policy, provided that policy carefully defines disability so it is not too broad. (There are disability policies written for professionals which define disability down to a specific area of practice, for example, trial lawyer.)

More important, however, is to provide for disability should emotional, alcoholic, or drug-related conditions exist. Unfortunately, the percentage of lawyers who collect disability benefits for typical physical disabilities is rather small while the conditions arising out of emotional disability are much higher than is generally known.

The firm should also consider stipulating a period of time during which a partner will be fully or partially compensated before a declaration of total disability is made. This is vitally important when integrating with an insured plan.

Lastly, some voting criteria should be established for declaring a partner disabled. Such criteria should include a vote not including the disabled partner and should be set at a high enough percentage of the active partners to ensure that there is a strong feeling concerning the issue. The reason for this requirement is to prevent a small number of partners from forcing out a disabled partner when, in fact, most partners feel that individual can still be useful.

There are several methods of writing specific clauses concerning disability:

1. Provide for a non-funded arrangement similar to the type outlined for death. In fact, some firms arrive at a disability benefit as if the partner had died upon being declared disabled.
2. Provide a non-funded benefit offset by the amount of insurance protection.
3. Provide for a totally insured benefit by purchasing a policy for each partner and including in the partnership agreement language that, in effect, makes such a policy the only benefit.
4. A combination of the above.

A typical clause in a partnership agreement might be as follows:

> A partner will deemed to be disabled when he is unable to perform the functions of a partner in the firm as provided by this agreement. A declaration of disability will require a 75% vote of the active partners not including the disabled partner and will be effective 180 days days thereafter, although the firm may authorize the managing partner/executive committee to instruct the partner to cease active practice at anytime pending a partnership vote.
>
> Upon becoming disabled, a partner will receive his pro-rata share of firm profits for 90 days from the date of disability. Thereafter he will receive a benefit as if he had died on the date of disability offset by any disability payments received from the firm's insurance carrier.
>
> The above mentioned benefit is in lieu of any interest in the firm other than return of the partner's capital account, assets, good will, work-in-process, or accounts receivable.
>
> The firm reserves the right to allow a partner to return to the practice on a full or part time basis to be determined at the appropriate time and approved by 75 percent vote of the partners.

Retirement

Many firms fail to agree on the retirement of a partner simply because they believe that most lawyers never retire. This is simply not realistic. Unfortunately, many firms also wait to come to grips with this issue until there are a number of partners near the retirement age, thereby making the situation difficult to deal with in an objective manner.

There are two major aspects of the retirement situation that should be addressed in the firm's agreement. First, there is the question of when and how a partner retires and second, the issue of compensating a retired partner.

RETIREMENT PHASE OUT

Many larger firms have adopted some type of "forced" retirement by which a partner at a specific age begins to take less money from the firm until he reaches an age at which he is deemed retired for compensation purposes. The definition of retirement is a vital point, since partners often confuse the concept of reduction for the purpose of retirement with their desire to remain active. Indeed, in many situations a partner who is beginning a phase down works as hard as he did prior to his reduction and even continues to practice after the specified mandatory retirement date.

Nevertheless, it is very healthful for the continuing law firm, and smaller firms would do well to consider this concept seriously, and to require a reduction in income of senior partners as a way of encouraging a redistribution of income. It is, in many ways, an investment by seniors in the future of the firm. Additionally, it would be healthful if, during this phase down, partners were not permitted to be active in firm management, except as advisors.

Many seniors take this as a slap and will accuse the authors of not realizing that it is they who built the firm and who in many ways provided the clients. In many firms this is the indisputable truth. The concept of phase out, however, really forces the seniors to transfer clients and power to other partners if they are interested in seeing the firm continue beyond their lifetimes. Furthermore, if they have done their jobs in choosing their partners carefully, they should desire a reallocation of income to recognize the development of younger partners.

It is important that seniors in most firms, especially small developing firms, consider that they can achieve a smooth transfer of power and leadership; or it can be achieved by younger partners simply removing older partners in very unpleasant and uncharitable ways. Younger partners owe a secure retirement to those who have contributed to the building of a firm but are, likewise, entitled to know their future liabilities and to plan for the development of the firm beyond the lifetimes of the seniors.

Firm XYZ had 14 partners, three of whom were age 68, 69, and 71 respectively. The three seniors had been responsible for building the business base of the firm and had over the years hired a number of good, working lawyers. The seniors had managed the firm and had not done a very good job of either communicating with or teaching the young partners the art of managing the practice. They had no written agreement and refused to discuss retirement benefits.

After the other partners began to show their unhappiness with many of the seniors' decisions, the seniors became very defensive and felt that the younger partners were attempting to drive them out of the firm. Under pressure, they entered into an agreement on compensation that, as one partner reported, was shoved down the throats of the other partners on threat of breaking up the firm. The agreement called for a phase down to retirement over three years and a very rich payment for life. The payment would have an adverse effect on the remaining partners and was hard to justify on any real basis.

The result of this "quick fix" was that a few of the younger partners withdrew from the firm and eventually left only a small number of partners to try to meet the retired partners' demands, and so the firm dissolved.

Lesson: A retirement plan must be fair not only to the seniors but also to the partners who must pay for it.

RETIREMENT COMPENSATION

There are numerous ways to approach retirement compensation. The nature of the firm and existing relationships among the partners such as historical agreements, unwritten understandings, and initial contribution to starting the firm, should play an important part in determining the method chosen by the firm.

Unfunded agreements are still very common in many firms. The unfunded agreement calls for the firm to pay to a retired partner an amount of money out of current earnings. Such payments can be for specific times, i.e., five or 10 years after full retirement, or for the life of the retired partner.

There are two common approaches to the unfunded arrangements, although many alternatives exist.

One is a payment based on a wage base determined from earnings received by the partner before retirement. For example, the formula might call for a calculation of the wage base to be determined by picking the five years out of the 10 years before a partner's full or phased retirement with the highest income, analyzing that number and applying a percentage, possibly the partner's highest percentage of profits prior to retirement--and then calculating a yearly retirement benefit. Some firms adjust such benefits for cost of living, although you must be careful that such an adjustment does not get out of control.

In any event all unfunded payments to retired, disabled, withdrawn, and deceased partners' estates should be subject to a limitation, keyed to the net income of the firm, to prevent a problem for the ongoing firm in a year in which economics may not support the payments.

Another approach is to tie the retired partner more closely to the compensation of the active partners. As an example, you might calculate the average compensation of all partners in a given year and then apply a percentage for each retired partner to that amount. In this way the retired partner has a stock in the ongoing firm (which may help him to understand the need for turning over client control), but there is an automatic reduction in retired partner income with the changing economics.

In either case it should clearly be understood that unfunded payments are compassionate to retirees, subject to the ability and willingness of active partners to pay them, and should therefore be reasonable in nature.

Some typical language concerning partnership retirement follows.

RETIREMENT

Upon reaching age 65, a partner will be considered a transitional partner and will begin a gradual reduction of interest in the Firm until he reaches the mandatory retirement age of 70.

The partner's interest in profits during the transition period is as follows: The partner's average annual percentage of the Firm's net profits (including basic draw and units of participation) for the prior five years shall be determined. Fifteen percent (15%) of that amount will be deducted to determine the percentage of net profits for the partner for the year in which his 66th birthday occurs. A similar amount shall be deducted in each of the succeeding four (4) years so that in the fifth year of the transitional period the partner's share will be twenty-five percent (25%) of the average annual percentage determined pursuant to this Section. During the transition period the partner shall devote time to Firm matters at least in proportion to his reduced share of net profits.

Upon reaching mandatory retirement at the end of the transition period, the partner will receive in monthly installments, annual payments equal to seventy-five percent (75%) of the amount received in the last year prior to mandatory retirement. Such payments will be subject to a cost-of-living adjustment at the end of each five year (5) period of retirement, determined by applying fifty percent (50%) of increase or decrease in the CPI index for (name city) during such period.

At the Firm's sole discretion, a retired partner may become "of Counsel" to the Firm and, to the extent that such partner is active in the practice, a compensation agreement over and above his retirement benefit may be mutually agreed upon.

A partner may elect early retirement as of the end of a fiscal year with the consent of seventy-five percent (75%) of the remaining partners, provided the partner has been with the Firm at least ten (10) years and has attained the age of 60.

Upon commencing early retirement, the partner shall receive annual payments calculated on the assumption that the partner has reached his 70th birthday during the year prior to the commencement of the early retirement and is commencing mandatory retirement.

Retirement payments shall continue for the life of the retired partner, provided that if the partner dies within ten years after retirement and is survived by a spouse, such payments will continue to be made to the spouse for a period ending ten (10) years after the date of retirement.

Within 90 days after commencement of mandatory or early retirement the Firm shall pay the retired partner his capital account including his share of income earned to the date of his retirement.

A partner does not have to retire at age 70 or to become a transitional partner at age 65 if so agreed to by more than fifty percent (50%) of the remaining partners.

Funded agreements. An entire book could be written on the funded retirement benefits of partnership and professional corporations, but we will comment briefly. Needless to say, having funded retirement plans accomplishes two major goals:

- It relieves the partnership from substantial current liabilities.
- It reduces the risks to retired partners.

When a firm adopts funded plans for retirement, a problem often develops for older partners who have an unfunded arrangement and not enough time left to practice for developing substantial funded benefits. In this case, adopting or using an unfunded arrangement with an offset for payments from funded plans can be used to integrate the older partners into the system.

Also, it is sometimes just plain impossible to integrate an older partner into a new retirement system. In such a case, the firm should try to move ahead with a plan that is best for the majority of the partners and simply structure a separate arrangement with the seniors. It is astounding that many firms without any plan blame this on the presence of one or two lawyers now at retirement age.

Never tie any retirement payment to a direct interest in work-in-process or accounts receivable. Such arrangements almost never work and are often subject to dispute and unnecessary negotiation.

Withdrawal Prior to Retirement

While there may be times when a partner leaves a firm under favorable circumstances, such as taking a judicial appointment, relocating, or joining a corporation, a great majority of the withdrawals that a firm will face will not be pleasant. The partners of a firm must decide whether they are going to encourage or discourage withdrawals and how to deal with them when they occur. Small and evolving firms should pay particular attention to this problem, since many of them are breeding grounds for other firms.

NON-INSTITUTIONAL METHOD

Establish an agreement under which a withdrawing partner has an interest in work-in-process and accounts receivable. Such an arrangement would usually provide for the partner's percentage in income at the time of withdrawal to be applied against the assets of the firm. There are several important things to remember when taking this approach:

1. Define the exact nature of assets and be sure there is a provision offsetting bad debts when considering work-in-process.
2. Provide for payment of work-in-process and accounts receivable only when collected.
3. Remember that without specific definitions the withdrawing partner may have an absolute right to an interest in accounts receivable and work-in-process.

The problem with this arrangement is that a partner may find it financially attractive to leave a firm, and the firm may find itself financing other lawyers' practices.

INSTITUTIONAL METHOD

Simply provide that a partner never under any circumstances has a continuing interest in work in process or accounts receivable and upon withdrawal from the firm receives nothing more than the return of his paid-in-capital and earnings to the date of withdrawal. Any other types of compensation are reserved for partners who leave because of death, disability, or retirement, or under other special noncompeting situations. Suggesting such a clause in your agreement will surely test the strength of your relationship with other partners.

Some typical language concerning partnership withdrawal is as follows:

WITHDRAWAL

A partner may withdraw from the firm at any time, provided that he give 90 days' written notice of his intention to do so. The firm, at its sole discretion, may accelerate such notice to the date it is received by the firm.

Any partner voluntarily withdrawing from the firm shall be entitled to the following:

(a) His pro rata share of profits to the date of his withdrawal;
(b) The balance of his capital account less any loans owing the firm.

All payments set forth in this section represent the partner's full interest in the firm, and he or his estate will have no further interest in assets, accounts receivable, work in process, or goodwill of the firm.

A partner who withdraws because of retirement or disability and subsequently practices law in the State of _____will forfeit all payments except payments that represent his pro rata share of profits at his date of withdrawal and return of his capital.

A withdrawing partner agrees that he will not solicit or cause or permit others to solicit on his behalf any of the firm's active clients or accept engagement from such clients without first notifying the firm. If such active client or clients owe fees to the firm, the withdrawing partner shall cooperate with the firm in effecting payment of such accounts. He further agrees that upon departure from the firm, he will not take with him any client lists, schedules, files, or other property of the firm.

Expulsion of a Partner

More and more firms are including, in writing, the basis on which a partner may be forced to leave the firm. Usually the expulsion of a partner is automatic—"for cause"—if one of the following occur:

- Disbarment
- Fraud or theft
- Tax evasion
- Indictment
- Entering into private business arrangements with clients without the consent of the partners

Many firms provide that a partner may be removed if it is felt that most other partners simply do not want to practice with that individual and, under analysis, such a position would seem prudent. Too many firms have made partners of individuals who should never have been considered for partnership and, because no removal procedure exists, continually have internal disagreements with or about these individuals.

There are two broad methods of dealing with expulsion, one being that under expulsion for cause, the partner is asked to leave immediately and receives nothing but the return of his paid-in capital. Even if a firm does provide some type of payment to a withdrawn partner, it is usually forfeited under expulsion for cause. The other method is to consider whether such a non-compensation arrangement is prudent. Indeed, it would seem much sounder to have a payment requirement to an expelled partner, both in fairness for such an arbitrary act as well as to make it somewhat costly to the partners to undertake to expel a partner. Often such payments are keyed to the partner's draw or to some percentage of annual compensation. We believe the "covenants not to compete" are generally a waste of time and unenforceable.

Some expulsion language might be as follows:

> A partner will be expelled with cause from the partnership under the following conditions:
>
> 1. Disbarment
> 2. Fraud or theft
> 3. Tax evasion
> 4. Indictment for a criminal offense
> 5. Entering into private business arrangements with clients without the consent of the partners

Furthermore a partner may be expelled without cause if 85 percent of the partners vote for such an expulsion.

A partner expelled for cause will be paid his pro-rata share of profits to the date of his expulsion and be entitled to the return of his capital.

A partner expelled without cause will be entitled to be paid his pro rata share of profits to the date of his expulsion, the return of his capital account, and six months additional draw.

General Guidelines on Partner's Withdrawals

Regardless of the reason for a partner's withdrawal from the firm, certain general guidelines should be followed.

Under all circumstances a partner should receive a return of his share of paid-in capital.

A notice period of some type, usually 90 days, should be required (except in death obviously), but the continuing firm should have the right to accelerate the actual date of physical departure from the firm to the date the notice was given.

The agreement should provide for protection of the files. Examples of how to deal with files include:

- *Non-institutional method.* A withdrawing partner may take the files of "his clients" and, except for settlement of payment to the continuing firm, all clients belong to the individual partners who brought them to the firm.
- *Institutional method.* All clients and their files are the property of the continuing law firm and will be released only under written authorization of the client and after satisfactory arrangements with the withdrawing partner have been made concerning payments of fees.

The property of clients and their files are difficult problems under any situation, and the aforementioned suggestions can serve only as an outline for purposes of defining the general relationship of the partners in the firm. Such an agreement does not replace common sense in handling the situation on a case-by-case basis.

If the agreement calls for a withdrawing partner to receive a pro rated share of profits to the date of withdrawal, the actual accounting for determining that amount should wait until the end of the calendar or fiscal year. To do otherwise could be grossly unfair to either continuing partners or the withdrawing partner. Having an agreement that calls for "closing the books" every time a partner leaves is costly as well as unworkable.

Reasonable time periods should be established for all payouts. It is recommended that return of capital be made relatively quickly, at least within ninety days. Other payments might well be stretched over a longer period of time generally in the range of three to ten years, depending on circumstances. It is wise to give the firm the option of ascertaining any and all payments at its discretion.

A limitations of payment clause should be written into every agreement under which any unfunded payments to withdrawn, retired or disabled partners, and deceased partners' estates, except return of paid-in capital, are subject to an annual cap. Such a clause might provide that the total of all such payments in one year cannot exceed ten percent of the firm's net income, or in a professional corporation, five percent of gross income, and to the extent the total of payments are in excess, all individuals receiving such payments will take a pro-rata reduction and have the time for such payments extended so as not to lose any actual dollars. It might be wise to require an interest payment on such deferrals to protect the value of the payment should it be deferred.

A sample limitation of payment clause is as follows.

> LIMITATION ON TOTAL RETIREMENT, DISABILITY, AND DEATH PAYMENTS. Notwithstanding any provisions herein contained to the contrary, it is specifically understood and agreed that the total of all disability and fixed retirement income payments and death payments, as provided for herein, payable to all partners shall not exceed in any one fiscal year a sum equal to twelve and one-half percent (12-1/2%) of the net income of the partnership for the prior fiscal year (computed before the deduction of retirement and disability income payments and death benefits), plus one hundred percent (100%) of the proceeds received by the partnership from any insurance or other funding against the payments of the obligations above described. The cost of any insurance or other funding of such obligations, whether by way of premiums or other charges, shall not be considered an expense in computing the income of the partnership for the purposes of this paragraph. In the event that such payments do exceed such limitation, they shall be proportionately reduced so as to be consistent with the limitation herein expressed. Such reduction shall not reduce the total obligation of the partnership to each individual partner, his widow, personal representative or estate, but the period of time within which such payments would otherwise have been made shall be extended in order to permit the payment of any balance so remaining.

The handling of contingent fee practices raises a set of problems that is somewhat different from the traditional problem of work-in-process.

It can be argued that the individual partners have a substantial stake in contingent fees and that each one in theory took less money each year in order to finance the cases and that if a successful result is achieved after a partner withdraws from the firm such partner or his estate should receive some payment.

This is not just a question of institutional and non-institutional methods, and a firm must examine the agreements and its own practices to determine its desires. A few possible alternatives are as follows:

- Take the totally institutional approach and decide that a withdrawing partner has no such interest.
- Arrive at a dollar settlement discounted for lack of success and "buy out" the withdrawing partners interest.
- Undertake an annual evaluation of the potential value of cases each year and apply the partners' interest for that year against the total valuation. Whenever a new case is accepted, add it to the evaluation and when one is settled remove it from the evaluation. While this may seem like a burdensome task, this procedure should be followed each year as a matter of good management, regardless if any payout is contemplated. All economic interests of the partners calculated by such a method should be "off-balance sheet" notations.

Other Important Issues

There are other important issues that should also be part of the understandings between partners and made a part of the basic agreements. These include:

Definition of Fees

The partners should have a clear cut definition of what constitutes partnership income. Generally, it is advisable to include all income related closely or indirectly to the practice including legal fees, income from trustee or guardian situations, directors' fees, salaries paid by clients, and items in lieu of fees such as stock, paintings, and the like. A gray area is one in which an individual partner may be earning finders' fees for putting deals together. Generally, one will have to examine whether the partner was involved primarily through his own investment or because it was related more to his ability as a lawyer. Decide this issue based on the particular set of circumstances.

Generally speaking, however, the more that can be tied to the partnership, the less divisive the relationship among the partners will be.

A sample clause relating to fees might be as follows:

> Fees shall constitute all payments for legal services whether paid in cash or in kind. Additionally, it shall include all payments for executors, trustees, directorship, or any salary paid by a business or government agency including legislative posts.

Management

In Chapter I we fully discussed management principles for all types of firms and suffice it to say that whatever management style is selected, a broad definition should be put in the agreement, including the procedure to be followed in determining partner compensation.

Continuation of the Firm

It is wise to have a clause in the agreement that calls for the continuation of the firm in the event of death or other withdrawal of a partner. This is not to say, however, especially in some smaller firms, that it might not be prudent to require a dissolution if one of the partners withdraws from the firm.

A sample clause might be as follows:

> Subject to ethical considerations, the firm may continue to use the name of a disabled, retired, or deceased partner in the name of the firm.

Profit Distribution

It is important for the agreement to state the broad definition of the system so partners will understand the overall approach and then rule on it.

Some typical language concerning profit distribution is as follows:

DISTRIBUTION OF PROFITS AND LOSSES

- The net profit/loss of the partnership shall consist of the gross receipts of the firm from the practice of law less all expenses of the firm incident thereto.

- Profit or loss will be shared among the partners as determined by a Compensation Committee.
- The Compensation Committee will consist of five partners, three of whom will be members of the Executive Committee and two of whom will be elected by the partners who are not members of the Executive Committee.

The Compensation Committee will review objective and subjective factors in determining the distribution of net profits. The objective factors to be considered are as follows:

(a) Hours worked.
(b) Hours billed.
(c) Contributions in bringing in new clients.
(d) Responsibility for Time and Disbursement Write-offs.
(e) Effective hourly rate of each partner.
(f) Non-billable hours approved by the Executive Committee. Examples are:
   1. Firm Management
   2. Client Development
   3. Professional Activities
   4. Continuing Legal Education
   5. Longevity

Some of the subjective criteria that the committee is expected to review are personnel reputation, contribution to the firm's reputation, effective use of associates, and other activities that might have a positive effect on the firm.

The Compensation Committee's decision will be considered final and not subject to review by the partners.

Name

Provision should be made for continuing use of the name of a retired, disabled, or deceased partner as part of the firm name. Some typical language concerning name is as follows:

DURATION/USE OF NAME

- It is the intent of the partners that the partnership shall continue from this date until dissolved in accordance with the terms hereof. The firm will not automatically dissolve upon the death, retirement, withdrawal, removal, or addition of a partner.

- The firm may continue to use the name of a partner who is deceased, disabled, retired, or on leave of absence from the firm without compensation to the partner or his estate.
- The name of a partner will be deleted from firm name if:

  (a) he permanently withdraws from the firm;
  (b) he becomes a judge, legislator, or public executive and is either by law or ethics precluded from the practice of law;
  (c) he is expelled from the firm.

Note that many states and state bar associations have rules and laws governing the use of firm names. These should be checked if a name change is being considered.

Outside Activities

It might be helpful for the agreement to make a statement concerning the partner's participation in outside activities, as well as related financial support to such activities. Clauses of this nature will become more common as firms increase their efforts in business development.

A sample clause might be as follows:

> Any partner desiring to engage in business activities outside of the law firm, except for family business enterprises, or any partner who wishes to participate in any way either as an investor, advisor, or stock purchaser of a client must receive the approval of the firm. Additionally, any partner who wishes to engage in stock transactions for publicly held corporations represented by the firm must advise the partner responsible for the client of his intended transaction.
>
> (**Note:** While it would not appear in a partners' agreement, a rule covering the buying and selling of stock in clients' companies should be a part of the firm's office procedures and applied to all employees.)

* * *

It has not been our intent to have this chapter become a model partnership agreement. Rather its purpose is to define the various issues that firms of all sizes must address to help insure a stable future. There will be enough pressure from outside the firm that will affect its ability to practice without the partners generating internal pressure that can also affect its ability to deliver a service.

Split-offs, withdrawals, changing life styles, differences in management philosophies, and other causes are more common today than they have ever been (and not just because there are legal-oriented newspapers to report them), and this trend will continue. It is more important than ever to protect the law firm and assure the continuation of the institution.

CHAPTER IV
Investments

The subject of law partners investing with each other either within the law firm or independently has long been a controversial subject. The purpose of this chapter is to explore investment opportunities as part of a law practice as well as for individual lawyers.

A basic question to be asked is whether lawyers as an investment group are different from the rest of us. Though there are similarities, lawyers (and other professional groups), as investors, have certain special needs that must be accommodated in accordance with their own idiosyncracies.

To help the reader understand some of the investment options and pitfalls, we will redefine the practice of law from an economic standpoint.

Law firms are still service businesses requiring capital investment—either directly or indirectly—from the partners/shareholders. This capital investment is modest, however, compared to the revenue produced. Remember that most law firms operate on a cash basis and distribute virtually all of their income to their principals on an annual basis.

Most lawyers are finally beginning to realize that a law firm like any other business requires some plant and equipment in order to help deliver a service, and that this equipment depreciates in value. In other words, the capital assets of a law firm, like any other business, are consumed as the cost of doing business. Once the lawyer understands this basic fact of business, he begins to realize that borrowing from banking institutions to provide the funds to purchase such support is the most sensible way of acquiring capital.

Conversely, lawyers who think they are going to get rich by holding a lasting interest in such assets and then attempt to have younger partners buy them for such an interest are simply deluding themselves and are diverting investment opportunities.

Another important aspect of the tax laws as they affect

most lawyers is that partners are taxed on a proportionate share of profits earned by the partnership—whether or not they actually receive an equivalent cash distribution. Because of poor financial planning, many attorneys in higher income brackets will actually end up paying 43-45 percent of their gross income in federal taxes, not to mention state and local obligations.

Many lawyers have an inflated and unrealistic self image concerning their investment ability. Their lack of under-standing has resulted in lawyers, as a group, being way down the investment ability scale. Much of this problem comes from a perception that lawyers develop because they often counsel individuals who are sophisticated investors and, therefore, rationalize that somehow the ability to counsel such individuals enables the lawyer to gain the same invest-ment expertise.

Given the general understanding of the economic plight of many attorneys, we will now examine the various options available to help alleviate this problem. This discussion can be broken down into two major categories—individual invest-ments and shelters and investments as part of the profession-al practice.

INDIVIDUAL INVESTMENTS AND TAX SHELTERS

Ordinary Investments

We will not spend much time discussing the vast number of investments such as stock, bonds, and savings certificates, since we are not investment advisors, and we assume most readers are reasonably capable of sorting these options for themselves.

Tax Shelters

Although we will not make any specific recommendations concerning individual tax-sheltered investments, a discussion concerning their nature is in order since, as with most other professionals, lawyers tend to be attracted to what they perceive to be "quick fix" solutions to tax liability through shelters.

Since a majority of attorneys are in higher tax brackets, they are targets for a myriad of tax shelters. Lawyers are usually poor planners when it comes to their own individual needs and, therefore, they are usually not focused on tax shelters until year end and again on April 15th. Therefore, tax-sheltered investments take on an added appeal as last minute cures for tax liability.

Entrepreneurs (a number of whom are attorneys) recognize the poor planning habits of most lawyers and offer schemes to accommodate last minute needs. (Is there anything quite as comical as a litigator trying to understand a tax shelter?) Many of their "quick fix" shelters have little chance of ever being profitable from an economic view, but do offer high current deductions and tax credits that may appear to be a long term attractive investment.

Factually, however, most tax-sheltered investments allow for the deferral of income tax by projecting current deductions, but somewhere down the line, these deductions usually become income. Therefore, in order for the highly paid professional to maintain his leveraged tax position, he must pyramid his tax-sheltered investments, by sheltering the additional income generated by other investments with new deductions from current tax-sheltered investments. This can be a never–ending vicious cycle and have such complications that only the very knowledgeable investers can truly understand the ramifications.

Since the subject of tax-sheltered investments has become so popular in recent years, Congress has been taking three steps forward and two steps backward in this area. To stimulate the business economy, laws were passed not long ago allowing investment in such enterprises as cattle breeding, cattle feeding, production of motion pictures, and the production of art lithographs.

The Internal Revenue Service found that many of these investments had little economic value and that many investors were attracted strictly for the current write offs afforded by Congress. Under the Economy Recovery Tax Act of 1981, therefore, most of these types of investments were declared "non-grata," and the loopholes were closed.

This narrowed the type of investments lawyers could avail themselves of and still be on safe ground. Today, however, Congress is scrutinizing all tax-sheltered investments viewing them all with a certain skepticism and challenging their authenticity. It would be helpful to discuss a few of the investment vehicles and show what they offer.

INVESTMENT TAX CREDIT AND BUSINESS ENERGY CREDIT

If a business invests in business property which is personal (as opposed to real estate) known as Section 38 property, with a life of 5 years or more, the business is entitled to an investment tax credit of 10 percent. Three-year qualifying property is entitled to a 6 percent tax credit. This is not a deduction, but a dollar-for-dollar credit against the tax, and therefore much more advantageous.

To spur investments in new types of business energy or equipment, which is equipment that will conserve energy or uses new fuels such as "gasahol," Congress passed a law a few years ago, allowing the investor to claim (in addition to the 10 percent investment credit) an additional investment credit known as the business energy credit.

For qualifying investments related to business energy, an investor gets a 20 percent credit or more (10 percent for the investment tax credit and 10 percent or more for the business energy credit).

Usually in these types of investments, only a fraction of the purchase price of the equipment is required in cash, the balance being financed by notes. The credits mentioned above are based upon full purchase price. Furthermore, if the equipment placed in service remains in service for five years or more, there is no recapture of these credits.

Congress as part of the 1981 Economic Recovery Act passed rules known as "Safe Harbor Rules" and "At Risk Rules," which make the proper structuring of this type of investment very difficult. Congress is still scrutinizing this area of investment. This type of investment allows the lawyer to reduce his taxes, without recapturing income later on, provided the "business energy" equipment remains in service for at least five years.

OIL AND GAS INVESTMENTS

This type of investment for lawyers is still one of the most popular because lawyers understand it and accept it as a genuine investment. It provides for large write-offs in the first year, some as high as 100 percent. But is it a good economic investment? The lawyer–investor must ask himself this question first. It does no good to invest in highly speculative deals only for the sake of the write offs. Due to changes in the laws over the last few years, the lawyer-investor must acquaint himself with those items subject to minimum tax (tax preference items) including "intangible drilling costs," "depletion" and "dry hole costs." By deducting over a certain minimum amount (about $10,000) of these expenses in any one year, the investor is actually incurring or creating additional taxes.

Congress wants to encourage investment, but at the same time wants to curtail abuses. The effect is to give with one hand and take back with the other.

It is becoming exceedingly more difficult to choose the proper oil and gas investments. Since political forces outside the country control the supply of oil and prices, your investment is subject not to the normal fluctuations of supply and demand but to an artificial market, created by political maneuvering, which can change at any time.

This type of climate does not lend itself to a stable environment. Extreme caution must be taken by the investor, and his investment must be viewed as highly speculative.

REAL ESTATE

During the 1970's lawyers as well as doctors and other professionals invested heavily in real estate. In fact, many lawyer groups formed their own real estate partnerships and purchased residential homes, office buildings (including offices in which to practice law, which will be discussed later in this chapter), as well as participating in larger syndications. To a lesser extent this type of investing is still going on today. It offers the lawyer rapid write-offs (15 years under ACRS), an investment in something tangible, with utilitarian value.

But what has happened to the real estate market? Due to high interest rates and limited mortgage money available, the market of some real estate has in fact gone down. Is this just a correction due to the rapid increases in market values in the 1970's or will real estate grow at a modest rate from now on?

EQUIPMENT PARTNERSHIPS

In the lawyer's quest for tax shelters, he has stumbled upon the equipment partnership. Those lawyers who have formed professional corporations gave up the benefits of having investment tax credits, depreciation, and other deductions passed directly to them. These deductions now go to the corporation. To have the best of both worlds, individual lawyers (principals) have formed equipment partnerships.

The equipment partnership buys the equipment that the professional corporation needs and leases that equipment to the corporation. By following this procedure, the individual partners get to deduct the investment tax credit, depreciation, etc.

There are specific IRS rules governing this type of transaction. The IRS is closely scrutinizing the facts pertaining to such an arrangement and is looking to "substance over form." They are asking such questions as, "is this an arm's length transaction," and "are the parties who are principals in the equipment partnership also principals of the professional corporation?" Great care must be exercised in undertaking such an arrangement. There are countless other types of investments which lawyers have ventured into in search of tax shelters. Most of these are dangerous especially with Congress and the IRS closely scrutinizing all of them.

Investment objectives should constantly be reexamined and reevaluated with these questions in mind:

1. What are my long range goals?
2. Is safety or preserving my capital important to me?
3. How do I plan for a changing economy?
4. How do I preserve my liquidity?
5. How do I plan for a downturn in the economy?
6. Are tax shelters right for me?
7. How do I pick my investment vehicles?

8. Should my investments be balanced?
9. Have I given thought to an emergency fund?
10. Is my family adequately protected against disaster?

Investments as Part of the Professional Practice

The investments that lawyers make with each other, especially inside the same firm, have been constant sources of friction and indeed, have caused some firms either to ban all such activities or put very stringent rules on the partners concerning such activities. In some firms, investments by partners have led to withdrawal of individuals from the firm and in some situations have been one of the reasons for firm dissolutions. Some of the reasons for problems arising out of investments are:

1. Individual partners have different investment objectives.
2. If an investment goes sour, the partners tend to blame each other.
3. Exclusion of some partners from investments causes friction ("there are really two partnerships here").
4. Trust in a lawyer's legal ability is not the same as trust in his investment judgment.
5. Accommodating the liquidation of some partners' interests and adding new partners to the investment can be burdensome.

Despite all of these problems partners will continue to find ways to invest as part of their professional practice. We will, therefore, examine various investment opportunities and discuss their "pros" and "cons."

Deferred Compensation

If ever there was an area where law partners should invest, it is in the qualified retirement plans now offered on an equal basis to both partnerships and professional corporations. Deferred benefit, defined contribution, target benefit, profit sharing and IRAs are still the best long term, constant tax shelter available. It is amazing how lawyers search for a tax shelter without having fully utilized the one right under their noses. It is not so much the total amount of money that can actually be sheltered each year, although that is very attractive, but the astronomical accumulation of tax deferred earnings that makes these plans so attractive.

As with any complicated investment, competent outside advice from pension planners and actuaries should be sought. Incidentally, some of the worst designed plans are those developed by the firm's own tax lawyers who simply do not have a grasp of this particular area of tax law. Since deferred compensation tax shelters are conservative by comparison to other potential risks, a liberal and imaginative approach should be taken in their design. Besides, objectivity is hard to achieve when a partner is trying to advise his law partners on something that affects them personally.

Real Estate Investments

During the last several years a great deal of interest has developed by law firms in building or taking an equity interest in their own building. The basic reasons for this interest were:

    a. An astronomical increase of rentals in major cities.
    b. "Sweetheart" leases held by some firms that became major assets of the firms and either could be "sold" back to the landlords or subleased at current market rates.
    c. Tax shelter needs.
    d. The concept that it was better to pay rent to yourself and take the finance cost as a deduction.

Unfortunately, at the time of this writing many firms that decided to get involved in their own buildings have had some second thoughts.

Overbuilding in most major cities, coupled with the recession, has created excess office space at reduced costs. This development has two major impacts:

• The asset that was held by the firm in terms of its lease lost a great deal of its value, sometimes almost overnight. Therefore, the profit that was to be realized through sale of the space, which in many cases was to be used for financing of a building, was not

available. It is one thing to rent space at $12.00 a square foot where the present market value has risen to $24.00, it is another problem if there is no one to rent it.
- The cost of financing skyrocketed, thereby eroding the rental leverage that was expected because of the firm's equity position. In other words, what was planned to be a relatively low rent in the equity position turned out to be market or worse with substantial cash flow problems in the early years.

Aside from the financial aspects of this type of investment there are other substantial questions associated with an equity position in a building to be used for the firm's practice.

Who owns the building? Will all partners own the building at the time of the investment and if so on what basis? What happens when a partner leaves the firm? Will new partners be admitted in the future and on what basis? There are no "right or wrong" answers to these questions, but there are certain dangers inherent in the methods used to structure the relationship of the partners.

Try to avoid "two partnerships" from developing. This may not be a significant problem initially, but ten years after the transaction there may be as many partners who do not own the building as those who do. Unhappiness over this issue, incidentally, usually first appears in partnership compensation issues. Such statements as "you are taking it both ways" or "the capital structure needs adjustment" are a sure sign of developing unrest. While it may not be feasible or desirable to admit every partner to the real estate ownership when they are admitted to the law partnership, some right of purchase of interests of departing partners to those who do not own interests might help delay the problem. Some firms take a "snapshot" of the firm when they enter into an equity arrangement and allow all partners and associates (when they become partners) to buy into the equity at the initial offering price. Other firms offer units of participation in the real estate venture and require every partner to have at least one unit. This is based on the assumption that ownership, no matter how little, defuses the "landlord-tenant" issue.

Other firms have taken quite a different approach to the problem. Rather than give any partner an individual interest, the equity is held for the purpose of funding a heretofore unfunded retirement benefit and, therefore, there is no "buy-in" or "buy-out" in the partnership. In lieu thereof the individual partner who is retiring receives a retirement benefit paid out of the cash flow of the real estate partnership. This replaces, or at the very least offsets, any other unfunded arrangement. Such deals are usually structured to allow the tax advantages to be passed on to the partners. This approach requires the law firm or rather its partners, to be institutionally-oriented in terms of the law firm, for this is truly a long term investment situation.

The question of buy-out should a partner leave the firm can also be a serious problem if the above concept is not used. Some firms simply buy out a partner at his interest of an appraised value and generally admit partners in a similar way. If the real estate investment appreciates considerably, such an arrangement can be onerous for both the partner coming in, and to the firm in its obligation to a departing partner.

Another unrelated problem is the question of how much space is available in the building where the equity is being taken. It is one problem to move into a space and outgrow it under normal leasing situations. It is quite another to have an ownership interest in a building and run out of space. The firm must plan ahead and will likely have to take more space than is needed with all the associated risks that such a situation entails.

In summary, a law partnership embarking on an equity arrangement for office space must operate a second business, that of landlord and real estate entrepreneur, with all of the dangers and complexities that such a business presents.

Investing with Clients

When situations that offer investment opportunities with clients arise, the firm should examine its policies to avoid internal conflicts.

The most common problem is what to do when an investment opportunity is offered, assuming the firm agrees to some participation. The safest situation is to offer the opportunity to all equity partners in accordance with their profit participation. For if interest in investments is offered only on a selected basis to specific partners conflict between partners is sure to arise.

More complex, however, is the situation in which a partner invests his own funds as an entrepreneur with businesses that later become clients of the firm. Here no general rule can be applied, but it is clear that entrepreneurial activities of lawyers will continue to increase as firms search for new business opportunities. Very often specific arrangements that fit the structure have to be developed for such a partner. As clients become more difficult to find, however, entrepreneurial activity is almost unavoidable. A firm should never be so complacent as to cut itself off from business opportunities through arbitrary and inflexible rules.

Investment Pools

Some firms establish investment pools within the partnership for the purpose of investing and as a vehicle for pooling the partners' resources for investment opportunity. This is not unlike a "closed" mutual fund.

The major problem with such activities is the lack of trust that seems to be common the first time the fund has a poor performance. Another problem is the determination of who joins the fund and on what basis as well as what to do with the partner who cannot affort to join. Readers might, when reading this, take a rather hard "tough luck" position, but that does not help the possible harm done to intrapartnership relationships. Again allowing each partner to join in accordance with profit interest may be the answer. It is interesting to note that some of the larger banks are providing funds to such partnerships to form investment opportunities.

We feel that unless extraordinary circumstances present themselves, most law firms are advised to leave investment opportunities outside the law practice.

Buying and Selling of Stock

The only real issue that the law firm has to deal with concerning the buying and selling of equities by individuals is the possible SEC violations that can occur by untimely transactions with listed company clients.

For example, a firm is assisting a company with an acquisition which is heretofore unannounced, and one of the partners unaware of the firm's activities buys or sells stock during the acquisition activities. Such an incident could be quite embarrassing for the firm.

It would be advisable for all firms to have a policy that anyone employed by the firm (including partners) who plans an equity transaction with a client company alert the responsible partner for that client before making the transaction.

The purpose of this chapter is basically to outline the various ramifications of investments by partners either individually or in conjunction with their firm for the sole purpose of pointing out the issues that should be examined. There is no right or wrong concerning any of the various examples given herein. The danger lies in not understanding the ramifications of investment activities and in not providing clear guidelines wherever possible. Remember that whenever a law firm's partners embark on any type of investment program within the confines of the partnership, they dilute the effort of the firm to the degree that they now operate a secondary business. Unfortunately, experience tells us that many of these ventures have more problems directly affecting the professional relationship than benefits that enhance it.

CHAPTER V
Profit Distribution

The subject that creates the greatest amount of debate, animosity, and upheaval in a large number of firms is profit distribution. Though it is often first on lawyers' complaint lists when we talk with them, questioning often brings out issues really unrelated to the dollars. These issues include:

- a feeling the firm is not managed or administered properly;
- a lack of communication from management;
- little or no opportunity to give input or discuss compensation prior to determinations being made;
- a lack of articulated criteria; and
- a feeling that unproductive partners are being overcompensated.

Interestingly, when actual dollars are mentioned, there is seldom any complaint about the income the individual lawyer received, but rather that the firm is not earning enough; that while the dollars are really satisfactory, ("I never thought I would earn this much money.") they are not when compared with what certain other lawyers in the firm earn; or that there are problems in the systems used to make the determinations.

Of course, there are a number of systems used to compensate partners. Since there is often no relationship between the stage of the firm's evolution and the system of compensation, systems normally used in smaller firms are explained first, followed by a discussion of methods used as firms grow, and concluding with suggestions on some good approaches for institutional firms.

Criteria used in determining compensation are often referred to in terms of "objective" and "subjective". By objective we mean dealing with something real or actual, without bias or prejudice, and minimizing or eliminating subjective factors. Subjective means including thoughts and feelings as opposed to just rigidly dealing with areas capable of measurement. An example of an objective compensation system would be a formula that deals only with things that are measureable, such as hours worked, hours billed, business originated, and write-offs of time or fees. A subjective system might include some of the objective measurements just mentioned, but would also include people's feelings on a lawyer's reputation, the quality of the work, ability to teach and train, cooperation with other lawyers and staff.

Democratic Compensation Systems

Firms in the 10 to 20 lawyer range and relatively new law firms often select unsophisticated compensation systems in order to foster and continue the team approach, to hold down internal competition, and to simplify the distribution of profits. Many feel that such systems are quite successful in the early stages of a firm's development because they foster the building of the firm. This is done by avoiding any real study of objective or subjective criteria, as well as by eliminating the measures of individual performance. Perhaps small groups of partners work better together, or maybe by the effort being directed at building the business and dealing with the external competition, the attention is directed away from individual performance. But these systems seem to center on the theory that since the partners are making fairly equal contributions, they should receive equal compensation. Equal contribution does not relate to a specific set of criteria (though many firms do outline minimum requirements), but rather to the overall perception that in one fashion or another, all are carrying their approximate share.

These "democratic" systems include the following:

1. *equal distribution*—all partners equally share in the profits
2. *lock step*—groups of partners (usually in the same age group or with like experience) receive increases as a group, i.e. the same increase at the same time
3. *seniority or longevity*—distribution is based on how long the lawyer has been with the firm.

The following discussion covers these plans together since, though they are not identical, the basic premises are nearly the same. (Incidentally, although they are common in smaller firms, they certainly are not limited to them.)

As an example of equal distribution, partner A works 1600 chargeable hours, and has a good billing and collection record. Most of his work is done for clients of other lawyers in the firm. Partner B works 1100 chargeable hours, but is a rainmaker and brings a good deal of work to the firm. Partner C works 1100 chargeable hours and devotes several hundred hours to firm management. Partner D works 1300 hours and is the tax expert for the firm. Each partner is contributing something different to the firm, but all the contributions are meaningful and benefit all the lawyers as well as the firm. Generally, this group will have little problem with a system that distributes income evenly.

A common "lock-step" system would include groups that became partners at the same time or within a year or two of one another. As an example, the firm admitted two partners in 1968, three in 1974, five in 1976, seven in 1978, and three in 1981. This firm might have six groups; partners in practice with the firm prior to 1968, the 1968 partners, and groups for 1974, 1976, 1978 and 1981. Partners within the various groups would be compensated identically; in other words no distinctions would be made between partners in the particular group. For example, presuming other things are relatively equal, but one of the 1974 partners worked 300 more billable hours in 1982 than the other 1974 partners, his compensation would still be the same.

A seniority system is similar to the lock-step. Under a true seniority plan, the longer you are with the firm, the more you earn. Many lock-step plans start phasing down particular groups at a certain age, for example 60, while seniority systems usually continue to increase compensation unrelated to the work being performed. The simple theory behind the seniority system is that "you pay your dues" for many years and then reap the rewards.

These systems are all effective in the early stages of a firm's growth, and the lock-step continues to work effectively for many firms, no matter what their age or growth. These approaches seem to work best when the firm does not keep (or does not publish) lots of statistics which might draw attention to differences or create arguments on the value of various contributions. The systems also fare better under management that has an institutional mentality and works to instill this in the lawyers in the firm.

We have seen many firms go to another compensation approach when the democratic approach ceases to satisfy a number of partners, or even one partner, if that partner is important enough to the firm to cause the change.

The major reason for a change in all of these systems is that they do not accommodate the "superstar." Though there are many exceptions, most partners who not only charge the hours but also bring in substantial business and devote time to the firm are unwilling to work under any system that does not provide some form of individual "reward." Once an exception is made, the system breaks down so the law firm must decide whether keeping the system intact or keeping the star is more important.

All three systems often break down if the firm does not have a phase down retirement policy, or a policy that while it may not discuss retirement, covers drops in income at a particular age. In a young, growing firm the system starts to create problems when the more senior people reach 55 or 60 years of age. The younger partners feel the seniors should then start taking less money, and the seniors feel one of the reasons they took less money during the height of their careers was to insure a good income as they got older and started to slow down.

Some firms have solved this problem by allowing for exceptions to the general system. In other words, the firm might base income on longevity, arbitrarily deciding on three classes.

One firm determined that new partners would be in Class 3 for 8 years, in Class 2 for 10 years, and then in Class 1 (Class 1 earning the most money). When a partner's performance obviously seemed to indicate that he was ahead of the class, he would be accelerated into a higher class. In this firm exceptional performance really related to client development. Another partner might be moved back to a lower group because his performance (here often related to hours worked) seemed to warrant it. This succeeded since such moves rarely were made and the reasons for them were apparent to most of the partners.

We like all of the democratic systems (if the seniority system has some phase-down) and feel they work well in many firms. One major advantage is that internal competitiveness

is held to a minimum, and lawyers do not spend time worrying or arguing over what they earn in relation to others of the
same age and experience. Competition is directed outward, to
other firms, rather than inward.

The major advantage to the aforementioned democratic
systems is that they promote the concept of *firm* as opposed
to the individual. Firms operating under one of these systems
are usually institutionalized, with good delegation and specialization, and a team approach to client service.

It is important to remember, however, that the aforementioned systems have two basic requirements:

1. Continued economic growth
2. Selectivity in partnership admission

Buying and Selling Time *usually distasteful*

This system has exactly the opposite result of democratic
systems in that it promotes individualism and works against
institutionalization. Though a few larger firms use this system, it is more common in the smaller (5–25 lawyers) firms.

Under this method, each lawyer is assigned an "inside"
hourly rate and an "outside" rate. Time is charged to the client at the outside rate, and internal records are maintained
on the inside rates.

EXAMPLE

	Hourly Inside Rate	Hourly Outside Rate
Partner A	$50.00	$100.00
Partner B	$50.00	$100.00
Partner C	$40.00	$ 85.00
Associate D	$30.00	$ 55.00
Paralegal E	$15.00	$ 30.00

Partner A brings a client to the office and time is put in one
the matter as follows:

	Hours	Inside Rate	Outside Rate
Partner A	3	$150.00	$300.00
Partner B	4	200.00	400.00
Partner C	2	80.00	170.00
Associate D	4	120.00	220.00
Paralegal E	2	30.00	60.00
	15	$580.00	$1,150.00

The bill to the client is $1,150.00. Since partner A is the originator, he will be charged with the inside rates paid to everyone who worked on the matter or $430 and will realize $720 in his own column ($300 for his own time and the $420 excess on the outside rates). Various methods of charging overhead are used, including dividing it equally or applying the percentage of net income the partner earns against the overhead.

This system, which might be perfect for space sharers because it measures individual performance and does nothing to build or foster the firm, has many dangers. Almost all of them lead to less quality and service than the client should have.

The first example points out the problems of lawyers working on what is most profitable for them, rather than on what would be best for the client:

Partner A does little litigation work, but brings in a litigation matter. He goes to partner C who specializes in litigation. Partner C has several small matters of his own and is working on them because he is not terribly busy. Partner A will need 10 hours of Partner C's time, for which Partner C will receive $400 (his $40 inside rate times ten hours). Partner C turns the work down and puts the hours in on his own small matters, for which he received $850 (his $85.00 outside rate times ten hours). Partner A must now handle the litigation matter himself or shop for other help. In either case, the lawyer best able to serve the client is not doing the work.

Another alternative is to start internal bargaining. Partner C indicates he can somehow find time if he is given $70 an hour. Partner A agrees. Partner C delegates his own work to associate D. Associate D does the work for which he receives $300 credit and partner C receives $250 (the difference between the associate's inside and outside rates). He also receives $700 for his work for partner A, so ends up with $950 rather than $850.

Though the first consideration should be the quality of the service to the client, in most firms using this system, client service is secondary. Work when delegated is done by choice of the originating attorney, and often it is delegated to the lawyer or paralegal who will provide the most profit to the originator as opposed to the lawyer best qualified to do the work.

This system impedes departmentalization and specialization, creates internal strife, fails to recognize time devoted to office governance and management, and as shown in the following example, often stifles business developers.

One young partner in a 16 lawyer firm had developed something of a specialty in a particular area of health care, and had a few matters come his way. He had been invited to speak at several seminars and to write a book on the field, but felt forced to turn these down. The lawyer was married with four children. In order to support them he had to work enough hours to provide a decent income.

All partners agreed that with enough time and exposure, their partner would generate a good deal of work and that in two or three years this would benefit the firm. Their profit distribution system, however, did not allow them to say, "John, we will guarantee your income for the next two years while you develop this field, since we will all benefit in the long run." The sentiment was, "Why should we help him. If he develops the area, he'll get most of the profit, so why should we support him while he does it?"

Granted, there are some firms using this system successfully. Generally they have more business than they can handle and have many business developers so that all lawyers can earn a good income delegating to those best able to serve the client. But those are the rare exceptions. This system emphasizes the individual as opposed to the "team," and we believe any system that does this will ultimately either destroy the firm or will prevent it from the growth it would otherwise achieve. In other words, the system is usually a disaster.

A Better Approach—Compensation Committee

Many firms, both large and small, use a compensation committee to determine income distribution, while others leave this to the executive committee. Some compensation committees are appointed, others elected. Some firms force rotation under the theory that committee members will be fair when they know that next year others will determine what they earn.

The firm just starting with a compensation committee for a few years will probably be more comfortable with an elected committee. Though they may also want rotation, we do not feel this should be forced—a member should be able to be elected indefinitely.

In some cases the determinations of the committee are final, in others the executive committee has approval, while in some the partners vote on the recommendations. Some firms have an appeal board, while others do not. There are firms in which the committee assigns points or percentages, and others in which they deal in actual dollars. Both prospective and retrospective systems are used. Needless to say, the compensation committees may be structured and may operate in a myriad of ways.

There is no "best way" to make up the committee. Our experience indicates that a separate committee appointed or elected for this purpose has greater acceptance with the partners than having the executive committee also act as the compensation committee. We do not like appeal boards, since they often undermine the authority of the committee who make the determinations. A vote of all partners on the recommendations, on the other hand, seems to ratify the findings of the committee and to hold down internal bickering.

One firm has taken an interesting approach that has merit and has worked successfully for many years. The committee makes a written recommendation, and this is submitted to all partners. Ten days are then allowed for any partner to discuss any of the recommendations with one or more members of the committee. The committee then either confirms its prior recommendations or arrives at new ones, and again submits these in writing. A vote is then taken, in this firm by voting interest as opposed to per capita, and two thirds is required to adopt the recommendations. If not approved, the committee reconsiders its recommendations and interviews any partner requesting an interview. They then present a second recommendation, which may or may not be the same as the first. On this second vote, a simple majority in interest of the partners adopts the recommendation. If the second vote is not sufficient, the percentages remain the same as they were for the preceding year.

Most compensation committees will examine any objective data available and will also take subjective factors into consideration in arriving at their determination. Assuming the goodwill of the committee members, the success or failure of this approach is often dependent on two major factors: an enunciation of the criteria to be considered and whether particular factors are weighted more heavily than others.

Perhaps the major complaint from partners dissatisfied with the compensation committee's determination is that no one knows what the criteria are, or more commonly, that the criteria change without notice. For example, one year, a partner was told his distribution was a little lower than certain others because his chargeable hours were below what the firm considered standard, though in other areas he did very well. The following year he was told that though his hours came up and exceeded the standard, this year the firm was placing more emphasis on business origination. Though in some cases this is a "line" used to justify the amount a particular partner receives, in most cases it is a glaring example of poor communication, creating unnecessary morale problems. The complaint is normally not the dollars, but the way in which it was handled.

Input from all partners on their thoughts on their own contribution and that of other partners is essential to the success of any compensation committee. Partners want and are entitled to some say in compensation determinations, both as related to themselves and others. In the smaller firm the committee may divide up the partners and talk to them on an individual basis, or may set times at which they are available to talk to those partners who desire to do so. When possible, personal contact is better and gives the committee member better insight into the thoughts of his fellow partners.

Firms of twenty partners or more may follow the same procedure or may design a form to be filled out by each partner. We have examined several forms and list a few examples of the type question asked:

(a) If you served as a member of the Executive Committee, Recruiting Committee, or as a Department Head (or in a like position), please estimate the number of hours devoted and any significant accomplishments in such position.

(b) Please describe any community activities, speaking, teaching, writing (or related) that you have done in the past year and which you believe should be called to the committee's attention.

(c) Do you feel there are items on the statistical information (provided by the computer reports) that need special explanation, i.e., high old receivables, high or low hours, write-offs of time and disbursements, or other matters.

(d) Other than the areas covered in this questionnaire, are there other factors you feel the committee should take into consideration? Please explain.

Obviously the questionnaire would be tailored to meet the specific firm and those areas considered important. Though these forms work well, we would add a last question asking whether the partner would like to meet with the committee to discuss compensation in more detail. This would allow for face-to-face communication which is important to many lawyers. An example of another type of form follows:

ALLOCATION OF PROFITS

TO: All Partners
FROM: Chairman, Compensation Committee
DATE:

Please apportion percentages in profits to each partner, including yourself, on this form. For purposes of this exercise, assume that available profits, including draws are $ _____.

NOTE: ASSIGN PERCENTAGES, NOT DOLLARS. THE PERCENTAGES SHOULD EQUAL 100%

The form should be returned to me in an unmarked envelope on or before _____. The completed forms will be destroyed after tabulation.

PARTNER	% OF PROFITS
Abelman	_____
Brantoff	_____
Wilshire	_____
Riverton	_____
Losston	_____
Total	100.0%

Point and Percentage Systems

Many firms use a point or percentage system to distribute net income. In order to determine the number of points or the percentage particular partners have, again either an objective system, a subjective system, or a combination of both might be used. From a psychological standpoint the point system seems to make a great deal more sense to us than does the percentage system.

For example, under the percentage system, presuming equal partnership, five partners each have 20 percent interest in the net income of the firm. In 1982 the firm's net income is $1,000,000. Applying the 20 percent, each partner would earn $200,000. The same fact and conclusion would result under a point system with each partner having 20 points. The problem, albeit a psychological or imaginary one, arises when another partner is added. The sixth partner is to come in on an equal basis with the others. This means that six partners must now have percentages adding up to 100 percent. The result of this is that all partners now have 16.66 percent and though they realize that these percentages are equal, the original five have all given up something. Under a point system the addition of an equal partner would merely mean adding another 20 points to the system, so the original five partners would remain at 20 points and the new partner would come in at a new 20 points. Again, all are equal but the original five do not feel that they have given up anything to admit the sixth. Applying this to an actual dollar amount under both systems you come out with the same result. The percentage system gets even more complicated when partners do not have equal percentages (which would be the more common occurrence). Then the addition of a partner involves convoluted mathematical calculations which are unnecessary under the point system.

Formula Systems

Many firms use a formula system either to determine or assist in determining income distribution. This is done under the theory that no one can argue with objective standards and that determining income in an objective manner is "fairer" and takes less time and fewer individual judgments. In the material that follows, we will explain why we disagree with this theory and its results, as it applies to many firms while we do admit it takes less time and fewer individual judgments. There are firms in which the formula systems work, but such firms are often ones in which certain partnership problems, including lack of trust, exist.

Formula Features

Over the years, dozens of formulas have been developed. The formulas most commonly in use credit a partner with some percentage of fees received on matters he originated and credit for hours billed. For example, a partner originates $250,000 of work in 1982. He is credited with 20 percent of this, or $50,000. In addition, 1400 of his hours have been billed at an hourly rate of $120 per hour, or $168,000, and he is credited with 80 percent of this, or $134,000. These are added together, totalling $218,000 and an overhead factor is applied. Presume this is 10 percent, making the total $196,200. The $196,200 is the basis on which his income is determined. There are so many permutations that as a practical matter it is impossible to list them all. However, we will give some historical background and also some of the most common areas of measure found in these formulas.

HALE AND DORR

Many of the formula systems started from a system devised by Reginald Smith who practiced with the Boston law firm of Hale and Dorr. This formula looks primarily at the objective factors of hours worked, origination, profitability, and weight them. The formula is applied to monies collected. A weight of six is applied to the work done (the worker's share), a weight of three for origination of the business, and a weight of one for the profit (to the originator). Approved management time and other work performed for the law firm is given the same six weight as the work done. Articles written on this system indicate it was Smith's intention to look at several years in order to arrive at a fair compensation for the partners.

What confuses many people is that some systems allocate actual dollars while others simply create an index. The weighting factor has no allowance for overhead. The information creates an index which is a number applied against the total net income to be distributed. Most of the formula systems in use now take in some of the factors and weighting in the Smith system but make substantial modifications. We believe a great many of these modifications were made because firms recognize that some judgmental rather than strictly objective factors were necessary to distribute firm income properly. It should be noted that Hale & Dorr continues to use their formula successfully.

BUSINESS ORIGINATION

This gives a "credit" on fees received to the lawyer who originated the business—the lawyer who can say, "This is *my* client." The credit usually ranges from 15-30 percent of the receipt. Almost without exception, it does not matter whether or not the "originator" of the business works on the case.

HOURS BILLED AND/OR HOURS WORKED

The worker normally gets credit for the number of hours he has worked on a matter or for those hours on the matter that have been billed. This would usually be from 50-80 percent.

In most cases, it is more equitable to look at the hours worked, since the workers often have no control over the billing. This would mean that a billing attorney could decide to delay billing on a matter. Presume partner A worked 300 hours on a matter in 1982 at a $100 an hour billing rate. In June the billing partner bills the work to date, which includes 50 hours of partner A's time. Partner A is credited with $5000. The work is nearing completion at year end, but the billing partner decides to hold the bill until the matter is closed. Partner A has 250 hours that have been worked, but not billed. He will not get the credit for the $25,000 in figuring his 1982 income. True, in 1983 this will be billed, but this might mean partner A has a poor 1982 and a good 1983. On a straight objective system this might create a large swing in income.

Should the firm require, at a minimum, quarterly billing, it would not really matter whether the figure considered was hours worked or hours billed.

USE OF OTHER LAWYERS AND PARALEGALS

We have recently run across a few formulas that "reward" the originator for using associates, or "penalize" him for using other partners. For example, partner A originates a matter, works on it for two hours and has the rest of the work done by associates B and C. When the fee is received, partner A is credited for his own time and all of Associates B and C's time (less an overhead factor for the associates). However, if partner A works on the matter for two hours, has four hours work done by partner G, and eight hours work done by associates B and C, partner A will receive credit for associate B and C's time only to the extent he worked on the matter, and partner G (who worked eight hours) will receive four times as much of the credit. This makes it much more beneficial to partner A not to use another partner.

We wish we could say that this formula feature does not present a problem, because lawyers will delegate work to appropriate persons, be they partners or associates. Unfortunately we have talked to associates in firms with this system who tell us they are given work they should not be doing, and/or are told not to ask another partner if they have any questions. In these same firms we find partners who are underutilized because it "costs" their fellow partners something to delegate to them.

OTHER CREDITS

Some firms add an additional credit to origination and hours. This might be a longevity credit or an office management and administration credit. Some consider approved nonchargeable time as though it were time at the partner's regular hourly rates, and others may figure it into the equation at a lesser rate.

PROBLEMS WITH FORMULA SYSTEMS

We believe formula systems, if used as the sole measure of compensation, do not properly measure the contribution each lawyer makes to the firm, and foster "playing the numbers" to make the lawyer concentrate more on his own compensation than on what is good for the client or good for the firm. Formulas seldom credit meaningful management time, training of associates, team spirit, and attitude. In addition, they usually cause serious side effects within the firm including hoarding of clients, internal competition, and under utilization of partners.

Though the Hale and Dorr formula started a trend to these systems, in recent years formulas have been less popular. We believe this is because firms recognized that objective systems did not really reward the contribution certain lawyers made and started making exceptions or found ways around the formula, finally realizing that the formula was a minor element in determining compensation.

While we do not totally dismiss formula systems based solely on objective criteria, we have a great deal more problem with them than we do with systems which look at both objective and subjective factors and criteria. Perhaps there is an objective system that can measure the lawyer's total contribution to the law firm, but we have not yet seen it. Interestingly enough, many firms with a supposedly objective system have found ways around it, though they continue to call it objective.

One firm went to a profit center system in order to eliminate subjective criteria. Even with this objective system, administrative responsibilities, authoring articles, and "nonproductive" items are compensated out of the firm's "discretionary" fund.

The treatment of individual lawyers or departments as profit centers is usually divisive and destructive both to individuals and to the long term success of a law firm. This does not mean that statistical information relating to profitability should not be maintained, since this is useful in such things as long range planning, staffing, and budgeting. If, however, it is a major measure of compensation, it will create internal competitiveness, will hamper delegation, and will hamper institutionalization. As an example, a firm with a corporate department and a good corporate business had a two-lawyer tax department working almost exclusively for the corporate clients. They did all work delegated to them, each working approximately 1400 hours in a year. Profit center figures showed them to be a marginally profitable department, yet they were directly responsible for holding many of the corporate clients. If subjective factors had not been considered, on a profit center basis they would not have been compensated properly.

Later in this Chapter we discuss other problems with formula systems.

Origination Credit

Origination credit is usually the portion of a formula that creates the problems. The workers feel they should be given all the credit, and the person who brought in the business feels his is the major role. Often the originator loses contact with the client (i.e., the litigation lawyer brings in the client but all the work is in the corporate area), yet gets "credit" for fees received. This might be compounded if a new client comes in on the recommendation of the first. The litigation lawyer gets "credit" for this also, yet it is the quality of the work done by the corporate department (or a particular lawyer in it) that probably brought in the business.

The origination credit in itself does not motivate a partner to obtain more business, nor does it give him the ability to attract clients. Partners who have the ability to be originators would not only have the same ability, but would use it regardless of the origination factor. Partners who do not have that ability, no matter what the firm might do to encourage them, would be unsuccessful in their origination efforts. A well-managed law firm understands the need for both individuals and establishes policies that reward each of them. Law firms cannot substitute good business judgment with an arbitrary formula that emphasizes competition from within and de-emphasizes a joint effort as a firm to deal with external competition.

The very theory that origination of business in an established law firm can be credited to any one partner is subject to a great deal of challenge. Is not group dynamics an acceptable reason for a client coming to the firm or even sending more business to the firm? As firms attempt to attract more and more high-quality business, they have to realize that clients, while they may be attracted by a particular partner, are more often attracted because that partner has a firm providing a multitude of services and support to him.

Origination can be, and often is, very indirect. If a firm is progressive, it will attempt to develop that type of client contact as much as possible. The combined efforts of a partner's reputation and the work of a number of others in the firm should be and probably is developing most of the business. As a firm grows in size and reputation, this proves even more common.

In this day of "business development," some firms are heading away from compensation concepts that encourage institutionalization and going toward concepts that give more credit to origination. Interestingly enough, some of these same firms do not recognize unusual legal skills of particular partners, or for that matter partners who for whatever reason make the firm "what it is."

We are not suggesting that the issue of business origination be ignored, but caution that in encouraging business development, the firm make sure that the possibility of abuse and the likelihood of lawyers working toward the wrong goals are kept at a minimum. Some firms prohibit sharing of credit for origination under the theory that this will hold down disputes. Group efforts at development are often more effective than those of individual lawyers, and lawyers who *assist* in developing business must also be recognized.

A firm that does not know who its "rainmakers" are and does not reward them, under any system, is headed for problems. The overemphasis on origination, however, detracts from the law firm as an entity and encourages the "my client syndrome".

Reevaluation and/or Declining Credit

Firms that now use business origination as a major part of a formula should consider some system of reevaluation.

For example, at the end of five years, a committee reviews all credits. Where it is clear that the "originator" no longer is either supervising the work of the client or is holding the client because of a personal relationship, origination credit should be discontinued and the client considered a firm client. Since this system is quite subjective, it can create hard feelings and arguments and can encourage originators not to delegate work for fear of losing credit.

Many firms have solved the problem by using declining origination credits. In this situation Lawyer Brown brings the client to the firm. Under the formula system he gets credit for 25 percent of the fees received. The second year he would get 20 percent, 15 percent the third, 10 percent the fourth, 5 percent the fifth and none after that. Though there is a reward and an encouragement for bringing in business, this concept does not allow the lawyer to slacken either his business development efforts nor his work since his clients gradually become firm clients.

We cannot overstress the dangers in credit for origination, since we have probably seen more splits, dissension, and problems created by the origination credit issue than any other. The goal of any firm, large or small, should be to assure that clients become firm clients and to insure that joint efforts at both obtaining new business and keeping it are the mode of operation and not subject to a determination of whether the compensation formula will properly reward such efforts.

Other Formula Problems

Most firms with very objective formula systems become associations of lawyers, with each individual more concerned with his clients and his compensation than in the overall success of the firm. In short, such firms find "the tail wagging the dog." The net result will be the substitution of a daily discussion of who should get what credit, rather than a yearly discussion on profit distribution.

It is important to recognize the fallacy with most formula systems is not so much in how they actually divide profits but rather in the effect they have on each lawyer's attitude toward the firm as a whole.

Another very serious ramification of a formula plan is that it de-emphasizes leadership and may create a weak management structure. When a firm faces problems with a weak or non-producing lawyer, it is easy to say, "Let the formula deal with it," rather than to have the partners face the issue head-on. The eventual result of such an attitude is a weak firm with disgruntled partners.

Another major fallacy in the formula approach is the belief that such a system is, indeed, objective. In truth, it may turn out to be less objective than a so-called "subjective system." The reason for this is that a formula system will invite manipulation in order to have the numbers "come out right." Typical of such manipulation would be the splitting of origination credits to "encourage" another partner to assist the originating partner in handling work.

Another manipulation is the control one partner has over another by refusing to delegate work, and thus, through the "objective formula" can create a situation in which a partner's "numbers" look bad, eventually forcing a reduction of his income.

Nor does the formula say to a partner, "The time you spend supervising, billing, and directing other partners and associates is as valuable, whether billable or non-billable, as the time of a partner who seldom uses or trains any other attorneys and who works, bills, and collects for as many hours as are available."

Note the following illustration:

PARTNER A
DOES ALL WORK HIMSELF
ONE HOUR WORKED = 1
TOTAL 1 HOUR

PARTNER B

| ATTORNEY C | ATTORNEY D | ATTORNEY E |
| ONE HOUR | ONE HOUR | ONE HOUR |

TOTAL 3 HOURS

Which partner is more valuable to the firm? A formula system really encourages partner A and does not recognize the economics of partner B.

A good law firm, while obviously needing the partner who directly originates business, also desperately needs those lawyers who not only can perform an outstanding service, but are directly instrumental in retaining and, perhaps, indirectly responsible for a great amount of unreported "origination." Also, the lawyer who spends his time training is as non-fungible as the business originator.

Is a formula really more objective than a compensation committee or the partners as a whole dealing directly with the unproductive lawyer? Substituting leadership and management by formula rather than by common sense is not the answer.

Before considering a formula system if you do not have one now, or in any discussion of a formula, you should carefully examine the reasons for it and make sure it is not a cover-up for much deeper problems, i.e., distrust among the partners, mismanagement, or just not enough income. If these are really the basic issues, a formula will not solve them.

Total Contribution Systems

The determinations related to income distribution should be based on the total contribution the partner makes to the firm. Systems of this nature are also called "rough justice" systems. There are many approaches to making these determinations, one as simple as a group sitting down, talking about it, and coming up with figures, to another that uses a formula but only to come up with guidelines as a place to start in their deliberations.

One approach to this involves the use of a compensation committee (and in a small firm this may be all the partners), a set of criteria to be considered, and (in some firms) a discretionary fund to be used in particular circumstances.

The primary duties of the compensation committee would be:

- To set up a schedule of monthly partner draws for the coming year. (This is often based on 75% of the partner's prior years earnings.)
- To set the units of interest that will be allocated to the partner for the year. (Many firms allocate units for two or three years rather than going through the process every year, and we think this is a good idea even though occasional adjustments may have to be made.)
- To make the determinations regarding any special allocations, or use of any discretionary funds.

The compensation committee works with a set of criteria. (This is not a contradiction of our comments relating to formula systems.) Records of the economics of the practice and of the partners must be maintained and considered, but we do not believe total contribution (both past, present, and anticipated for the future) can be formulized. Many firms include the criteria in their partnership agreements, and often the criteria are fairly broad and simple—for example, "the criteria include a review of the following: cooperation with other partners, quality and quantity of the legal work, leadership ability, dedication and efficiency, training and effective use of associates, ability to satisfy and bring clients continually back to the firm and to attract new clients, attitudes and cooperation in dealing with problems, and historical contribution." A more detailed list might include the following:

- Billable hours *worked*
- Hours billed
- Effective hourly rate
- Business generation
- Client responsibility
- Non-billable hours in categories approved by the partners, including but not limited to: firm management; client development; and professional, charitable, and political activities;
- Effective use of other lawyers
- Timekeeping and billing efficiency;
- Accounts receivable control (including a review of time and disbursement write-offs)
- Collections
- Longevity
- Reputation
- Quality of legal work.

Tier System

A two- or three-tier system would then be used.

Tier one. Each partner will receive a fixed monthly draw which will represent the first level of income distribution. The draw will apply against the partner's participation in the profits of the firm as to tiers one and two. The draws should not be considered as expenses in determining profits and losses. Normally, firms should not set salaries exceeding 70 - 80 percent of each partner's prior year total compensation, excluding pension and profit-sharing contributions.

Tier two. Net profits or losses in tiers one and two will be shared among the partners on the basis of units of participation. Annually, (or less often) each partner will be allocated a certain number of units which will be determined by the compensation committee. The committee in its deliberation will consider the criteria outlined previously. It will not be necessary to adjust the units of participation when a new partner is admitted. Simply assign the new partner his units.

Units are easily transferred to percentages, but percentages require change when partners are admitted or depart.

If you use a prospective system, and we recommend you do so, you will have to assign the units at the beginning of each year. Except in unusual circumstances (gradual retirement as an example), a partner's units should not decrease. You might also consider a maximum number of units for each partner, say 100.

Each partner's share in the firm's net profit or loss will be in direct proportion to the ratio of his units to the total number of units of all of the partners. Should a partner's draw and periodic distributions during the year exceed his interest in the year's profits, he will be charged for the deficiency during the next fiscal year.

We recommend quarterly distributions if the funds are available.

Under a two-tier system, what we have just outlined would determine partners' compensation.

How it works. Say the firm has seven partners and their draws and units of interest for 1983 are as follows:

	DRAW	UNITS OF INTEREST
Partner 1	$ 85,000	25
Partner 2	85,000	20
Partner 3	75,000	20
Partner 4	70,000	15
Partner 5	65,000	15
Partner 6	50,000	10
Partner 7	50,000	10
TOTAL	$ 480,000	115

Net income for the year is $850,080. Each unit is therefore worth approximately $7392. In addition to the monthly draw, each partner has taken four distributions (at tax time).

Draw & Distribution

	Income	Previously Received	Distribute
Partner 1	$ 184,800	$ 85,000+ 40,000	$ 59,800
Partner 2	147,840	85,000+ 40,000	22,840
Partner 3	147,840	75,000+ 40,000	32,840
Partner 4	110,880	70,000+ 35,000	5,880
Partner 5	110,880	65,000+ 35,000	10,880
Partner 6	73,920	50,000+ 10,000	13,920
Partner 7	73,920	50,000+ 10,000	13,920
	$ 850,080	$ 690,000	$ 160,080

Modifications

This approach has many modifications. For example, many firms add a third tier. They may say that they are budgeting $850,080 for the year and that anything over this, up to a set amount (say $100,000) will be split equally. Net income is $927,080 or $77,000 above budget. Each partner would get an additional $11,000. Were net income $1,000,000, each partner would share equally in the first $100,000 over $850,080 and $49,920 would be distributed based on units of interest.

Other firms use the amount set in the third tier to reward unusual performance or seniority or another factor. In some firms it is used to handle the extraordinary fee, so that both the lawyers involved and the firm as a whole (often including associates and staff) benefit.

If the third tier is used, the dollar amounts allocated to Tiers One and Two should be set high enough so that Tier Three comes into play only in a very good year.

Some firms do not allow fixed monthly draws but base the draw on the net income for the month, believing that this puts more pressure on the partners to bill.

Other firms ignore the units of interest or percentage concept, wait until year end, and then make an allocation of dollars. This system is less popular because partners have no way of projecting that their incomes will be based on budgeted results.

System Specifics

We believe that under total contribution (rough justice) systems, there are some very specific things that should be done:

- *Each partner should receive a fixed monthly salary.* This assures a partner of money to live on each month, makes personal budgeting easier, and avoids buildup of hostilities because there is not enough to take home in a particular month.
- *Excess distribution should be made quarterly.* This has two advantages: the first is practical—the partner has money to make income tax payments; the second is psychological—once a year distribution deals with greater dollars, calling more attention to differences in income among partners.
- *All calculations are always against net income after*

all expenses and a reserve determined by the partners.
Firms that distribute based on gross income often
find themselves without enough money to pay their
bills or to deal with any emergencies that might
arise.

• *The compensation committee should spend time get-*
ting input from all partners. They may even want to
have each partner submit suggestions for the assign-
ment of points, percentages, or dollars.

As we stated earlier, under any system the opportunity to
discuss and give input holds down the complaints and unhappiness.

As a matter of interest, we believe more and more firms
have switched to more subjective systems in recent years,
probably noting the success of firms that are institutionalized
and recognizing that members of the firm bring different talents and abilities to it, and all of these must be recognized
and rewarded.

It is much easier to convince partners to agree to a new
management structure than to a new compensation system.
Often firms try to accomplish this at the same time, which is
normally a mistake. You must have good management in
place, operating under a mandate from the partners, before
you attempt to change the method under which profits are
distributed.

Should you be considering a change, keep the following in
mind:

Relate to the stage of your evolution and to your management. Make sure there is a reason to change, and this is not
being done to placate a minority group.

Do not use a monkey-see, monkey-do approach. Many firms
have tried to adopt a system that works beautifully in another
firm—either having read about it or having discussed it with
lawyers in such firm—only to have it fail. That goes for some
of the systems suggested in this chapter, also.

It is helpful to have outside experts work with you on any
change. Nothing will stir the emotions more than this subject. Consultants can be dispassionate, have no ax to grind,
and are more likely to arrive at systems with a chance of acceptance, or with compromises that could work. The same
systems or compromises suggested by a partner could be cast
out by fellow partners feeling there must be something self-
serving in the proposals.

Under any system, avoid small differences in income. They are divisive, meaningless, and create problems that are unnecessary. It is fairly easy to explain why one partner earned $100,000 and another $70,000. There is not, however, much rationale for one earning $70,000 and one $72,000. Some firms do this thinking it delivers a message, but the message seldom gets across. Neither lawyer understands it. Note: We would also eliminate minor differences in associates' salaries.

Just as you should avoid minor differences in income, you should avoid major swings from year to year. If a partner has an exceptional year and is compensated on that basis, should the next year be average or below, you are going to have a difficult time making a substantial downward adjustment. Consider looking at at least three years in making your determinations.

As best you can, when considering making any change in the system, should there be complaints or accusations, make sure you are dealing with a profit distribution problem and not a lawyer problem before backing down or away.

Be prepared to explain the system, with examples if possible, so that all partners understand it. If the change requires a vote of the partnership, do not rush it. You are better off taking more time, or agreeing to a gradual implementation than you will be by adopting a system people aren't sure they understand or aren't yet convinced rewards partners properly.

We have covered many compensation systems and have discussed some and shown a bias for others. Many of the systems will work for different firms, at different stages of their development. Most of them work well when the firm is prosperous and each year is substantially better than the year before. Normally it is in the stagnant or poor years that problems surface and that searches for a new approach begin.

It is important to remember that the compensation system not only allocates dollars, but also determines the type of relationship that will exist between partners.

Though it is not easy to arrive at a system, and any system may have to be changed based on the evolution of the firm, every attempt should be made not only to reward total individual effort and contribution, but most important to insure that the guidelines for partners' compensation stress the building of a solid, profitable, and enduring institution.

CHAPTER VI

Business Development and Marketing

Marketing has become one of the most talked-about topics in law firms today. The emphasis is on developing ways to educate clients and the public about the total capabilities of individual lawyers and the firm as a whole. Formal marketing plans, including every imaginable tool, are being developed with special emphasis on the care and feeding of present and future clients. Major changes in firm philosophy relating to advertising and public relations are more evident than ever before, and it is common for some firms to budget from 1-4 percent of gross fees for the marketing effort. Firms that continue to neglect this area, either because of inertia or a "sense of distaste," probably are going to feel the pressure from losing clients to more aggressive firms, and perhaps will find that developing new clients may be more difficult than in the past.

Many lawyers believe, unfortunately, that all of the talk and emphasis on marketing is not worthwhile and a waste of time. The delivery of a quality product on a timely basis, they believe, will satisfy their present clients and foster the development of enough new business to sustain the firm in this decade. These lawyers must be educated to face reality that "once a client always a client" is no longer something firms can count on, even those firms that have provided quality products at reasonable fees.

The firm description indicating that it has the "best lawyers" (whatever that means) is always amusing. Simply stated the law firm that believes it can rest only on the self-serving premise that because it has the "best lawyers" and turns out a quality product it will always have business, will find itself at a disadvantage in the new legal environment. This chapter explores most of the tools contained in a marketing plan and gives some helpful hints as to how each tool can be utilized as part of a master plan for marketing.

Marketing and Partner Compensation
Plans

Attempts by many firms to increase the emphasis on marketing have been stymied because their compensation plans do not reward this activity. It is almost impossible to develop a marketing plan unless time devoted to this activity is considered one of the criteria for determining partner interest in profits. Those firms utilizing the objective formula approach to partners' compensation have found it very difficult to develop the marketing activity since the formulas have no way of measuring each partner's total contribution (see chapter V). Some firms believe that the answer is to reward business origination. But the marketing area is another reason direct origination credit tied to a formula should be avoided. As a firm attempts to attract more and more high-quality business, it will have to realize that clients, while they may be attracted by a particular partner, are more often attracted because that partner *is a member of a firm providing a multitude of services and support to him.* Every partner will have a role in the firm's marketing plan, and the compensation plan must be flexible enough to recognize marketing time as productive time.

Insure a Quality Product

A firm must continue to produce a quality product at reasonable fees. A marketing plan must include a method for showing the clients they are receiving quality work. Clients assume they are receiving quality products, but lawyers must be encouraged to "blow their own horns" on the quality of service. If a client received a saving of $100,000 in his tax case, tell him about it and show him how it was accomplished. Timely completion is a requirement of a quality product. Clients that have to remind the lawyers about their commitments will take their business to a competitor.

Some states have initiated mandatory continuing legal education requirements, and other states are exploring the advantages of this program. Every firm should establish a mandatory continuing legal education policy for all lawyers and strictly enforce it in order to make sure the clients are receiving quality products. Advise the clients you are doing this to improve both quality and service.

Keep the Clients Informed

In the past several years, lawyers have been severely criticized for escalating fees for their services and not keeping the clients informed on the status of their cases. This is partially the result of a lack of diligence in the handling of client matters and a belief by lawyers that winning is everything. Some lawyers also believe that the more the client knows, the more of a problem he will be for his lawyer. The end result is that clients are changing lawyers because there was little, if any, *evidence of effort*. Communicating with clients is essential.

Present clients are one of the best sources for spreading the word about the firm. Lawyers must learn to work with their clients and to keep them informed. One way to do this is to send a copy of everything, except work papers, to the client with a stamp, "Client Copy." The client is made to feel important and is kept current. This also illustrates effort by the lawyer. Regular billing also indicates effort. Many clients believe that they will receive a bill whenever the lawyer has worked on their files. Regular, imaginative billing techniques represent one of the best public relations tools available to lawyers. This is another area where the lawyer can blow his horn about the great job he did for the client.

It is important for the client to receive something with the firm name on a regular basis. This might include copies of correspondence, loan documents, depositions, announcements of new lawyers, or a move to new offices. Special tickler files for regular review of certain matters, such as wills and corporate upkeep, should be maintained so that regular contact with clients is guaranteed. Regular contact indicates effort. The value of staying in touch with the client is motivation for the client to return for all needed services and to spread the word to friends and acquaintances.

Long-Range Planning

The development of a marketing plan is often considered with long-range planning. A long range planning questionnaire (See Chapter VIII) could then include subjects related to marketing such as geographic diversity, nature of the practice, specialization, firm revenue, attorney time utilization, individual income, management structure, and business development. These are closely related, and an organized business program is a major part of this planning process. Some of the questions relating to business development include:

- State briefly and in order of importance, what you think are the four best ways of developing business (in addition to doing excellent work).
- State the one method of developing business, other than doing excellent work, which you personally would like to pursue.
- Describe briefly how much time a month should be devoted to business development by senior partners, junior partners, older associates, and younger associates.
- Describe in order of importance three approaches to business development which could be pursued by the firm as an organization, rather than by individual lawyers.
- State your views as to the manner in which expense allowances should be provided to maximize business development.

An analysis of the information received from the completed questionnaires will allow the firm to establish objectives for the business development plan. The primary objective should be to produce results while at the same time guaranteeing that the advertising, business development, and public relations are handled in a professional manner so as not to hurt the firm's reputation for ethics and integrity.

Marketing Coordinator

Since there are many facets to the marketing plan and various portions will be delegated to lawyers, staff, and outside consultants or market researchers, someone must act as a coordinator. The firm should appoint one of the partners to head up this effort and to coordinate all aspects of the plan. If he wants help, he should select other partners to work with him as a committee. The lawyer acting as marketing coordinator has a major assignment which could take several hours a week. This effort must be rewarded and considered a vital contribution to the firm. Once the plan is completed and in effect, the coordination and follow-up may be assigned to an employee who reports to the firm's administrator or the partner in charge. Some larger firms are hiring marketing coordinators from the outside, and other firms are looking for administrators with backgrounds in marketing, advertising, and public relations. Not enough time has passed to make a judgment on how effective these administrators have been in the marketing effort, but it is an indication of the emphasis being put in this area.

Strategic Objectives

Strategy must be developed. Some sample objectives include:

- To remain the premier labor firm in your area.
- To maintain and enhance the firm's reputation in energy matters.
- To broaden awareness among clients, potential clients, and referrers of the firm's expertise in tax, securities, and related matters.
- To increase the revenue of the corporate department by 10 percent within one year.
- To increase the number of labor clients by 10 percent within two years.
- To achieve billings growth at the rate of 15 percent per year, and a gross fee income of $20,000,000 within five years.

The strategy will be effective only with the development of a plan to carry it out.

Tactical Objectives

Tactical objectives should be designed toward fulfilling the strategic plan. Some are:

- To develop and implement a formal marketing plan for business development and public relations.
- To broaden the awareness of the firm's full range of capabilities.
- To develop two budgets—one for the expenditure of dollars and one for the expenditure of time.
- To establish internal communications and involvement to guarantee the active participation of each partner. Some of the more effective tools are circulation of a list of new clients and matters on a weekly basis and biweekly meetings of the lawyers to discuss new clients, how they were developed, the loss of clients and the circumstances causing the loss, and a report on progress with targeted clients.

Once the objectives have been established, the next step is to establish specific goals, set timetables for completion, and assign responsibility for each activity to one or more partners. Some of these goals should be:

- Develop and implement a formal marketing plan. This is a key step, and many firms have found that the employment of marketing consultants specializing in research, planning, and program implementation in this area is beneficial.
- Support the marketing plan with activities designed to expand service to clients and to referrers.
- Develop a formal public relations program.

Profiles of the Partners and the Firm

One of the first requirements is to analyze the capabilities and philosophies of each partner and to recognize the style of the firm. A questionnaire should be completed by each partner including at least the following items:

- Business development strengths
- Business development limitations
- Specific skills (writing, speaking, teaching)
- Current club and organization memberships
- Targeted club and organization memberships

- Client targets
- Program role

Partner strengths must be recognized and utilized in the activities where they will contribute the most. The "rainmakers" must be identified and their efforts channeled toward this activity. The achievers must also be identified and exploited since a great deal of business development is the result of the lawyers who are responsible for delivering a quality product and directly responsible for client maintenance. Every partner will have a role. It may include responsibility for getting articles written and published, handling speaking engagements, and coordinating all luncheon and entertainment activities.

Every department must be analyzed. A questionnaire for departmental analysis must be developed and completed by each department. The questionnaire should include:

- Growth trends—up, down, or static.
- Negative trends and client losses—how to reverse.
- Steps to be taken to equip the firm to handle the projected growth.
- Amount of new business anticipated during the next 12 months from present department clients, present firm clients in other departments, and new clients.
- Steps to be taken to achieve the projected growth.

The civic and social exposure of the partners and the firm are also very important. A simple questionnaire should be developed and completed showing where the firm is represented and by which partner(s):

- City, country, and other social clubs.
- Civic organizations, Chambers of Commerce, politics, etc.
- Schools and colleges, hospitals, churches, cultural, etc.
- Other relevant exposures.

A similar questionnaire should be completed showing where the firm is not represented and partners to be considered for representation.

More Business from Existing Clients

Every effort should be made to develop additional business from existing clients. There is a tendency to forget that the smaller client may need an estate plan, may consider incorporation of a business, may need a pension or profit-sharing plan, or have other legal work he would have done if someone called this to his attention.

This project will require an analysis of who the existing clients are, what work is being done for them, what fees are being billed, and who has the major client contact. In some firms this will require manual compilation of the information. In others, much of the information is, or could be, available from the data in the computer.

Though you might expect it to be common knowledge to the lawyers in a firm (small or large) that certain work is being done for a client, and that this should send up a flag that other work could be generated, this is seldom the case. The majority of lawyers work on their own projects and do not think of the bigger picture. A practice management committee will recognize opportunities for additional business, since they meet regularly, discuss work being done in all departments, and talk about client development (see Chapter I for more on this committee).

Every partner should have a role in business development and marketing. Many lawyers who find the entire subject distasteful or "unprofessional" will be willing to work on ways in which more business can be obtained from existing clients, since this concept seldom offends them. It is probably wise to place the emphasis on marketing to existing clients on the practice level. If the firm is departmentalized, one of the functions of the department leader should be marketing.

Targeted Clients

A marketing plan should include a "hit list" of targeted clients, and one or more partners should be assigned to each desired client. Do not be bashful about using a straightforward approach in telling clients you want referrals. A report should be given on each targeted client at the biweekly meetings held to discuss all aspects of business development.

Business Entertainment Policy

A budget must be established for business entertainment and guidelines for reimbursement adopted. Such things as expense allowances, payment of club dues, tickets to sporting and cultural events, and dinner parties at partners' homes are the norm in today's law firm. The policy should not be so restrictive as to discourage partners from participation in these activities. Many firms use the honor system for reimbursement, except they normally exclude bar tabs and excessive amounts for certain events. Another method is to establish a fixed budget for each partner for the purpose of entertainment.

Client Evaluation Service

Many firms are asking their clients to evaluate the services rendered. They are using a questionnaire containing some of the following questions:

- Were you kept informed as to the status of your case?
- Why did you choose our firm to represent you?
- Were your telephone calls returned promptly?
- Were you treated courteously?
- Was the fee reasonable?
- Were you satisfied with the results?
- Would you recommend our law firm?

Case Acceptance

An organized business development program may result in the firm's having to evaluate its case acceptance policy. An effective policy requires all business to have approval unless it meets the following criteria:

- The firm's hourly rate schedule is observed and there is no contingency. Contingency means both payment based on recovery and likelihood of getting paid.
- There will be regular billing, at least quarterly.
- There are no violations of sensitive issues such as political ramifications.
- The affected department chairman must approve. For example, if a litigator brings in a real estate matter,

it must have the real estate department chairman's approval.
* There must be a signed fee agreement specifying billing rates in effect at the time the service is rendered.

Traditional Devices

Entertaining, writing, and speaking are excellent business development activities. A partner should be assigned the responsibility to coordinate luncheons. The two-on-one lunch should be encouraged. A partner who is the contact for a particular client should take one of his partners from another department to lunch with the client to spread the word about additional expertise in the firm. This process should be continued until the client has been exposed to a partner in each department. This approach sells the firm's total capability.

It is common for a firm to lose a corporate client if there is only one individual known to the firm and he leaves the client's employment. His replacement may not know the firm and may employ a different firm. One-on-two lunches will help alleviate this possibility. A partner goes to lunch with his contact and suggests that they have an additional employee of the client join them. This continues until there is a broad awareness of the firm by several employees of the client.

Writing articles is also an excellent business development tool, but it is important to monitor this activity very closely. Lawyers have the tendency to agree to write articles but with their heavy practices never find the time to do the writing. These articles must be scheduled well in advance of publication, and the partner charged with this responsibility must be strong enough to push the authors to meet their writing commitments. These articles should be placed in strategic publications such as trade journals and newsletters, bar association journals, newspapers, and technical magazines and pamphlets. It is important that the articles be written in laymen's language. A public relations firm can be helpful here.

Some firms are establishing speakers' bureaus with speakers being made available at no charge to civic, church, veteran, bar, and trade groups. The program should stimulate speaking opportunities, and it is very important to maintain quality standards for both the content and delivery of such speeches.

Partners and associates should be encouraged to participate in specific civic activities, PLI, bar association, and other educational activities that will demonstrate professional capability, however, such activities usually don't directly result in new clients.

Newsletters

Client newsletters are one of the more popular marketing tools. The primary motivation in producing a newsletter, in addition to constantly keeping the firm name on view, is to inform the clients and prospects of the total capabilities of the firm. They are also published to:

- Update changes in the law.
- Highlight unknown problems to the clients.
- Summarize highlights from each department.
- Announce new programs.
- Highlight sweeping changes in the law in specialized areas.

Most of the newsletters are published four to six times per year. But there are numerous problems associated with the production of the newsletter, such as:

- Who will write the articles?
- Who will do the proofreading?
- How will lawyers receive credit for writing and editing?
- Who will develop the mailing list?
- Who will monitor and control costs?
- Who will be responsible for graphics?

The editor should be a senior partner with clout. Another person must have responsibility for coordinating the project. Some firms are using professional writers to edit and rewrite the articles produced by the lawyers. A newsletter is costly to produce, and the firm must be selective as to the recipients. Most of the firms that are producing newsletters believe they are effective and plan to continue with their production.

There appear to be no ethical problems with sending the newsletter to present and prior clients, friends, and acquaintances. However, there is a question about the direct mailing of a newsletter to a random list of potential clients unknown to the lawyers in a firm. When considering the development of a newsletter, it is a wise practice to review your approach with the appropriate state bar association before going beyond your client, friend, and acquaintance lists. (See Appendix B for sample newsletter.)

Client Seminars

Many firms believe that client seminars are the best tools for business development. These seminars require a great deal of care in organizing and must be promoted very professionally. Many firms have conducted seminars for selected clients on new tax laws and have found these meetings very successful and responsible for the development of a substantial amount of business. These seminars have been popular for years for the firms representing financial institutions, and it is common for these meetings to lead to additional seminars for some of the larger clients of the banks and savings and loan associations. If only one or two partners are conducting the seminars, it is important for some of the other partners to attend so they can be introduced to those attending. This is an excellent way to highlight the total capabilities of the firm.

Learn the Business of the Client

Some firms are encouraging the lawyers to spend time at each corporate client's place of business studying his operations and products. The client is told there is no charge for this study and it is being done in order to better represent the client. Clients love this and will spread the word to potential clients.

Firm Brochure

A few firms have developed brochures for business development purposes. While brochures have been produced by many firms for several years for recruiting purposes, these business brochures are produced for different purposes, and it is difficult to develop a single brochure for both purposes. If you read 25 recruiting brochures (firm resumes) you will have a difficult time distinguishing one firm from another. Few of these documents sell the firm as well as describing it. Only a few of the state bar associations have approved the use of brochures except for existing clients, friends, and acquaintances. There is still a question as to the future of brochures, but the firms that have produced them believe they are an excellent marketing tool.

The brochure outlines the capabilities and accomplishments of the firm and introduces its personnel. Some general guidelines are:

- Present a thorough and factual appraisal of the kind of issues and problems the firm deals with.
- Avoid generalities.
- Provide information on all departments.
- Provide high graphics standards.
- Consider the employment of a company that has produced brochures. It would be helpful if they have worked previously in the legal environment.
- Avoid the yearbook approach.

Public Relations Program

A formal public relations and publicity program is also a major ingredient of a marketing plan. This activity requires outside expertise, and it is a good policy to interview several companies before reaching a decision on which one to employ. The public relations counsel should assist in media decisions and preparation of publicity releases. Some of the goals of the program should be:

- Spread the word about the firm's activities and expertise.
- Spread the news about accomplishments of the firm and the individual lawyers.
- Educate the press as to the capabilities of the firm and the individual lawyers and the firm's agreement to serve as a source of information.
- Seek exposure on talk shows and appropriate panels.
- Meet with client public relations programs.

Defining Your Market

Definition of the market segments to be targeted is very important. This will require a great deal of research and can best be handled by a company working with law firms in the marketing area. This preliminary research will cause the firm to focus on a realistic market size and mix and keep the firm from going in all directions and accomplishing very little.

Presentations

When a corporation is considering utilizing or changing advertising agencies, it will ask for a presentation to give it an idea of the creativity and personality (as well as costs) of the people who will handle their account, should they be hired. The successful advertising agencies do a good deal of research, both on the corporation, its product, management philosophy, image and on the people who will attend the presentation and make the decisions. It will become more common for corporations to request presentations from law firms they are considering retaining. Until recently these "presentations" (often just a lunch, but really a show and tell) were limited primarily to a corporation moving to a new location or wanting local representation for a branch office. This is going to change now that lawyers are asking for (soliciting?) business, and requests to come in to discuss the law firm will occur frequently.

This is an area in which public relations counsel can help serve and educate the firm.

Though some of the ideas presented here might have been considered "unprofessional" a few years ago, recently there has been a shift in approach with more awareness of the law firm as a business. In the future, there will be more aggressiveness and more competition, and law firms will have to adjust to the requirement of marketing their services. It is time to put this entire topic on the table for discussion and action—effective promotion does not cost—it pays.

As a matter of interest, an outline summarizing some of the material in this chapter follows and can be used as a starting point for the preparation of a marketing plan.

MARKETING PLAN OUTLINE

I.   INTRODUCTION:
     Prepare a description of your firm and its practice to include:
     A. Location and facilities
     B. Size including composition of personnel
     C. Type of practice
     D. Structure
         For this internal document prepare an honest appraisal of strengths and weaknesses and competitive position. Define your growth goals. Try to develop a one sentence description, almost a slogan, for your firm's claim to fame.

II. STRATEGIC OBJECTIVES (Developing the five year plan)
     The strategic objectives of the firm are:
     A. To provide clients with a product of excellence
     B. To maintain and enhance the firm's reputation among clients, referring sources, other lawyers, and the community at large.
     C. Broaden awareness among clients, potential clients and referrers of its area of expertise.
     D. To achieve billing growth at the rate of X% per year and a gross fee income of X% by 1990.

III. TACTICAL OBJECTIVES—1984
     The tactical objectives designed toward fulfilling the strategic plans are:
     A. To develop and implement a formal marketing plan, including systematic programs for business development and public relations.
     B. To broaden the awareness of the firm as an institution, as well as of the full range of its "product" capabilities.
     C. To develop a budget—covering both the expenditure of dollars and the expenditure of time—consistent with the growth and profit goals.
     D. To generate a program of internal communications and involvement, to assure the active participation of each partner in the program.

IV. SPECIFIC GOALS, TIMETABLES, AND RESPONSI-
    BILITIES
  A. Develop and implement a formal marketing
     plan
     1. Systematic program for business develop-
        ment.
        a. Recognize the actual capabilities, philoso-
           phy and style of the firm in its partners;
           build on your strengths.
        b. Analysis of present situation, department
           by department; set departmental goals.
           (1) Is the department growing? Shrinking?
               Static?
           (2) How much new business will come
               from:
               (a) Present clients
               (b) Present clients of the firm new to a
                   department
               (c) New clients
           (3) Are there any negative trends? Client
               losses? Why?
           (4) Are the departments' current resources
               adequate for the projected growth?
        c. Analysis   of   business   development
           strengths of each partner
           (1) Who are the rainmakers? Who can be?
               Are their efforts being channeled?
           (2) Who are the "achievers"? Whose re-
               sults can be exploited?
           (3) What role can each of the others play?
           (4) What is the present exposure of the
               firm to the social, civic, philanthropic
               network? How can this be meaningful-
               ly expanded?
               (a) Develop for each partner potential
                   for some work within the frame-
                   work of the individual personality.
               (b) Are there organizations, clubs, ac-
                   tivities where business opportuni-
                   ties exist where the firm is not
                   represented? Who has an affinity
                   for the work of this organization

and can be encouraged to get involved.

d. Identify a list of desired prospective clients and of business referrals to be cultivated.

   (1) Don't be bashful about telling clients you want referrals.

   (2) Assign specific individuals to specific targets

e. Develop a plan for systematic business entertaining.

   (1) Have guidelines for entertainment. Partners should not feel inhibited nor should they require prior approval, but shouldn't use these moneys for random dinner parties or "to pick up tabs." Guidance can be provided through organized programs of:

      (a) Two-on-one client luncheons, where a client of one department is exposed to a member of another department. Conversations at such luncheons should be goal oriented to acquaint the client with this additional dimension of the firm. This is an activity in which all partners should participate.

      (b) One-on-two client luncheons to acquaint additional people at client companies with the firm's expertise.

      (c) Luncheons with bankers, accountants, and other referral sources.

2. Develop a firm brochure outlining the capabilities and accomplishments of the firm, and introducing its personnel.

   a. Thorough and factual appraisal of the kinds of issues and problems the firm deals with.

   b. Avoid puffery and generalities

   c. Be explicit about what you do and, equally important, what you do not do.

       d. High graphic standards.

       e. Also useful as a recruiting aid

    3. Conduct regular meetings devoted specifically to business development activities for all partners.

       a. Review on an ongoing basis ongoing activities

       b. Include an instructional component

    4. Assign specific management responsibilities for goal setting, monitoring, and evaluating the program and its results.

B. Activities designed to expand service to clients and to referrers and pro bono work will in the process enhance the firms' reputation for service and expertise and increase its visibility.

    1. Encourage partners and associates to participate in specific civic, pro bono, PLI, and other educational activities that demonstrate professional capability. Note the time devoted to such activity should be rewarded, not penalized, in determining compensation.

    2. Establish a speakers bureau, available at no charge, to civic, church, veteran, bar, and trade groups.

       a. Develop a program to stimulate speaking opportunities

       b. Maintain quality standards for both the content and the delivery of such speeches.

    3. Develop a regular program to advise clients of changes in the law, or on interpretation and the implications

       a. Establish a newsletter to be published at least quarterly

          (1) Each issue should contain:

             (a) Appropriate news about the firm, new associates, new partners, awards, honors, elections, specific office, etc.

             (b) News about current cases and accomplishments of the firm and of its clients.

(c) At least one brief update item from each department.

(d) relatively thorough note or comment per issue, each issue spotlighting a different department.

(2) It may be desirable to have the newsletter done outside, since this establishes discipline, assures timeliness and (crisis situations will not cause it to be put aside).

(3) Develop a mailing list of clients, potential clients, referrers, etc., for the newsletter.

b. Plan a quarterly seminar or client update meeting on an appropriate area of law. The same basic material perhaps can be presented in separate sessions to a variety of audiences.

(1) Existing clients—invite them to bring a friend.

(2) Bank and savings and loan officers, accountants—the forwarders.

(3) Lawyers not in competition with you.

c. Prepare documents in a uniform style for general distribution and as a handout in specific situations.

4. Assign specific management responsibilities for goal setting, monitoring and evaluating the program and its results.

C. Develop a formal public relations/publicity program

1. Make your activities and expertise known through appropriate use of media.

2. Recruit public relations counsel to assist media decisions and preparation of publicity releases.

3. Regularly disseminate news about specific activities and accomplishments of the firm and its shareholders.

4. Acquaint the press with your capabilities

and your willingness to be called upon as an information source.

5. Aggressively seek (through knowledge of your own staff capabilities and efforts of public relations counsel) exposure on talk shows, panels, etc.

6. Systematically determine opportunities for future type articles: Assign responsibility for writing and placement.

7. Interface with client public relations programs.
   a. Whose story is it, yours or theirs?
   b. Screen copy for all legal related releases; make sure the firm receives appropriate credit.

8. Keep clients informed of your activities.
   a. Mail interesting clippings, reports.
   b. Report in the newsletter or obtain press coverage.
   c. Advance notice of broadcasts when possible.

9. Assign specific responsibility to periodically measure results, progress, and contribution toward overall goals.

CHAPTER VII
Mergers, Acquisitions, and Branch Offices

Motivating Factors

The rapid growth of firms during the last several years has created a myriad of management problems. Firms have historically built their practices by hiring law school graduates who work their way to the partnership level. While this aspect of growth should still be a part of the growing firm's overall plan, factors are now at work that may require a firm to re-think its approach to growth.

Crisis of Leadership

There is a virtual crisis of leadership in many of our nation's law firms, and very few firms, regardless of size, seem to be immune from this problem. The days when senior partners could manage without communicating with their partners is long past (see Chapter I). There is no other issue that can raise more questions about the firm and its leadership than a merger with another firm or the acquisition of a lateral partner. To accomplish a successful merger or be able to integrate a lateral partner, the firm requires strong and consistent leadership.

There are some firms that, for whatever reason, have lost those people who historically provided leadership to the firm. When such a situation exists, a merger or acquisition may be the only way to acquire this leadership. A true case in point may help illustrate this.

Smith & Jones was a 40-lawyer firm in a moderate size city. The firm was founded by several entrepreneurial partners and grew rapidly. As the nature of the firm changed, the methods employed by the founding partners began running into trouble. Part of this problem stemmed from a compensation system that overrewarded the entrepreneurial partner and set up a relationship between the partners that was overly competitive. Additionally, the firm's rapid growth had required the hiring of many other partners and associates who were good working lawyers, but lacked any real entrepreneurial skills. Compounding the problem were the attitudes of the seniors running the firm as a self-perpetuating dynasty, while at the same time, telling the other partners that they did not have to worry about business development.

As time went on and the management methods of the founding partners began to alienate the other partners, a slow but certain withdrawal of partners began. This withdrawal caused a revolt of the younger partners who tried to take the management role away from the seniors. The revolt triggered the withdrawal of several more of the senior partners who took a number of clients with them.

The result was a firm consisting of a number of rather "happy" young partners with little or no business base or experience and very little leadership.

The firm eventually merged with a larger firm which had strong senior partners who exercised a degree of enlightened leadership.

If this situation had been recognized and handled when it first started to develop, steps could have been taken to develop a management and compensation plan that would have settled the complaints of most of the partners returning the firm to a reasonably viable relationship.

Firm Evolution

The above case also addresses the issue of firm evolution. Virtually all law firms during their history move from an entrepreneurial type operation to a more structured, institutionalized firm. This evolution is often painful and very often causes the withdrawal of partners. The failure to recognize, however, the changing nature of the firm and to adapt to its needs can be the death of the firm.

A change in nature of the firm requires a re-examination of the roles of the partners, the admission of partners, and the methods of compensation. (See Chapter I for a discussion of firm evolution.)

Client Base

One of the most significant reasons for the wave of mergers that is sweeping the profession is the need to broaden client bases as well as to protect erosion of clients. Often the firm, because of its past hiring practices, finds that it does not have the appropriate entrepreneurial and/or working skills in-house.

One has only to read the professional journals as well as some business publications to see that the movement toward corporate in-house legal staffs is aimed primarily at only one objective: to save money by reducing the use of outside counsel. Sometimes mergers and acquisitions can sufficiently broaden a firm's base to allow it to withstand the loss of business from some major clients.

This change in relationship between business clients and their outside law firms requires a reexamination of the nature of a firm's business and the type of law practiced.

The only effective and expedient method, generally, to develop skills that the firm does not possess in-house is through adding such skills. More and more firms are turning to acquisitions and mergers for this purpose.

Correct Recruiting Mistakes

Most firms of any reasonable size should have an ongoing recruiting plan for the purpose of building the future firm. Unfortunately, many firms have looked at the recruiting effort as a major and dispensable overhead item and in years when the firm may be experiencing less than desirable economic growth, the recruiting effort is cut back or eliminated.

The damage done by this mistake is long term and expensive. There is no question that a firm should continually adjust its recruiting policies to respond to the economic circumstances it faces, but recruiting is not a short-term project. The real effects of a bad or eliminated recruiting year will be felt 3-5 years later when the firm is forced into lateral hirings to make up for poor planning. Many firms have gaps in their practice ability because the leadership of "depression mentality" partners has prevailed.

The reluctance to invest properly in the future creates difficulties for the firm long after the partners who created the problem of poor recruiting have retired. Merger can sometimes correct this situation.

Geographical Expansion

The movement to broaden the operating base of many firms by reaching to other geographical areas of practice is creating a great deal of merger activity. Typical of this are branch offices in places such as Washington, D.C., Florida, Texas, California, and elsewhere.

One of the principal motivations to expand from any given city is that the firm has obtained a reasonable market share of the legal business in a community, such as Detroit, Cleveland, Pittsburgh, Philadelphia, or San Francisco, that is relatively stagnant.

Unfortunately, many firms undertake the opening of a branch office with the same lack of planning that existed before the concept of another office was introduced.

In one case, a firm in a major metropolitan area determined that it should have a branch office in Boca Raton, Florida. The rationale behind the decision (forgetting that one of the partners has a condominium there) was that many of the clients who had come to the firm for estate planning would eventually relocate to the area and unless the firm established a presence, it was apt to lose the estates (in which, incidentially, it had invested a substantial amount of money).

The firm did the following in establishing its office:

- It found a partner-level individual from the New York area and sent him to Florida. The partner's expertise was in general business practice.
- The firm felt that it would support the practice from its home base and, therefore, provided no local associate assistance.
- It allowed the partner to handle all financial transactions, such as billing and expense approval, on a local basis.
- The local partner designed an office that was much more lavish than generally provided other partners in the firm.

- The firm did not involve the Florida partner in over-all management, nor did it provide for regular meetings and communications between the two offices.
- The home office partners continually referred to the Florida office as a "branch."

In short, all of the things that would ultimately lead to a failure were systematically adopted by the firm.

The number of firms which have opened unsuccessful branch offices based on this rationale are staggering. The reasons for the lack of success emanate from the lack of a clear plan and the failure to consider the following:

- The estate planning and probate practice in many firms is not very profitable. Why then should it be profitable in a remote location with added overhead?
- The argument that there are no good Florida firms that can service such clients is unfounded.
- The rationale that a single partner with back-up support a thousand miles away can provide service just as good as the local lawyer is without merit.
- There was a failure to recognize that even long-standing clients change relationships when they enter retirement years and move, and that some of those relationships are often with local lawyers.

This is not to say that a firm should not open a Florida office but rather that the reasons and the expectations for an office should be carefully examined.

Economic Problems

A merger can be a solution to the economic problems of a law practice. General economic conditions over the last few years have placed a severe strain on many law practices. These pressures have been especially acute in poorly managed firms, which have found that while their gross incomes may be increasing, the rise in expenses has stagnated or even lowered the compensation to partners. Mergers of such firms with economically strong ones can in some cases save the weaker firm while adding a new dimension to the stronger one.

Specialization

In this era of specialization, many firms find that their clients are demanding a broader range of specialized services. If the firm cannot perform a specific service, the client will look elsewhere. Obviously, there is an ever present danger that a client who takes one type of business to another firm will begin referring other business as well.

Firms have also realized that extreme specialization can be very dangerous economically. Talk to the real estate firm in Florida, the securities firm in New York, or the regulatory firm in D.C., and you will quickly see how a downturn in a specific business area can have a devastating effect on the overspecialized firm.

Dynamics of a Merger

Economics, while important in evaluating merger candidates, is almost never the reason why a merger is not successful.

While it might be agreed that the best merger would result from the combination of two economically strong firms, the problems arising from such a match can result in the most difficult problems. There is little doubt that the compromises that have to be made when two such firms attempt to merge are much more difficult to settle than when a stronger and weaker firm are negotiating.

Recruiting a Merger Prospect

For those firms handling the merger process themselves, the recruiting of a merger prospect can be time consuming and frustrating. In some cases, this is easier if a firm is recruiting another local firm. There are, however, the troublesome decisions of how to approach the other firm and who should make the contact. Most firms do not want other firms in the city to know they are looking for a merger. Confidentiality is difficult to maintain unless a firm employs a third party to make the initial contact with the understanding that the name of the firm will not be released without prior approval. This can be one of the major roles of a consultant.

Prior to recruiting, you must think through the entire process and put a plan together which should include:

1. The purpose of a merger;
2. The localities to be considered;
3. A general profile of the firm to be recruited including size, specialties, clients, etc.;
4. A merger committee; and
5. The role (if contemplated) of a third party consultant.

There are many sources for locating a merger prospect, including:

1. Friends and business acquaintances in other firms;
2. Advertising in bar association journals, Wall Street Journal, and similar publications;
3. Review of Martindale Hubbell and other law lists for firms with the desired expertise; and
4. Third party consultants.

Details should be spelled out: What is the purpose of the merger—is it to add a new area of practice the firm feels it needs, to broaden the base of business, or to grow to a particular size? Though portions of this master plan may change as discussions with a firm begin, it is important to have the basics down. For example, if the master plan indicates that a candidate should be no larger than twelve lawyers, there is little need to pursue discussions with thirty-lawyer firms. If the plan details an interest in a satellite office in Washington, D.C., New York, or Florida, the search time will be cut considerably.

After this master plan is put together and approved by the firm, contacts made, and preliminary discussions set to begin with a selected firm, it is mandatory that a detailed checklist (road map) be put together to guide the firm through the step-by-step process of handling a merger.

Merging a strong firm with a weaker one, on the other hand, while usually easier to accomplish, places an inordinate amount of burden and economic risk on the larger firm. Yet, in the long run, many successful mergers are based on this type of combination. One example would be the strong firm with a good business base but lack of depth in a particular area, or the need for more experienced lawyers to handle the volume. Another might be the firm with a strong management structure unwilling to cope with equally strong management, but in need of legal skills.

Evaluating a Merger

COMPATIBILITY

The first analysis of the compatability of a merger between two firms of any size should be centered on a very simple formula—$2 + 2 = 5$. Unless the combined firms have a reasonable chance to end up more successful financially, there is little reason to merge.

Financial success in itself, however, does not always mean that the partners will greatly increase their personal incomes as a direct result of the merger. In many cases the financial reason may be simply to preserve good economic performance. It should be understood that by-and-large there is no major economy of scale in the practice of law. Indeed, if the reader understands the pyramid concept, he will quickly realize that it is quite probable that operational cost as a percentage of overhead will increase as a result of a merger. In fact, if the partners are serious about making the merger truly successful, the involvement of time in developing a business plan may even have a short run negative impact on the partners.

The actual merger discussions will be difficult at best, and only if the partners remember the $2 + 2 = 5$ formula will they persist in hammering out an agreement. A fundamental question to be asked constantly during the compatability discussion is, "What are we doing for you, and what are you doing for us?"

Take a careful and initial look at the compatibility of the partners. This is the most critical of all steps. While differences in personality and style are healthy, there has to be a reasonable degree of philosophic agreement. Some of the important considerations are:

- Age of the partners —Will the ages compliment each other, or could there be problems over too many partners in the same age group or a younger-older partner split?
- Educational backgrounds—Partners with degrees from the "top" law schools may be unhappy practic-

ing with lawyers whose degrees are from schools they consider average or inferior.

- Social standing in the community—If partners in both firms have close to equal social standing in the community, they will probably adapt to each other faster, and the firms will have an easier integration period.
- Quality of practice—The firm which represents individuals and small business may be uncomfortable with a practice geared to large corporate clients, and the reverse will also be true.
- Ethnic backgrounds—Diversifying the lawyers and clients by a mix of ethnic backgrounds can be very healthy for the merged firm, but might create adjustment problems if the lawyers have little, if any, contact outside of the office.
- Outside wealth—If a large number of partners in one firm are independently wealthy, their attitudes toward fees, business generation, and effort necessary to maintain a profitable operation will be different from the other lawyers.
- Work ethic—Some firms are proud of and foster the "sweat shop" atmosphere. They work long hours and weekends and take few vacations. Other firms pride themselves on being "gentlemen's clubs" and encourage outside activities and interests, and a relaxed working environment. Unless there is some match in the work ethic, problems are sure to arise.
- Approach to business development—Do both firms encourage business development? Are there generous expense accounts, or do lawyers pay their own development and entertainment charges? Is there any conflict in philosophy on marketing tools such as newsletters, brochures, public relations agencies?

(We will comment further on some of these considerations later in this chapter.)

CONFLICTS OF INTEREST

Conflicts occur in two broad areas.

- Client conflict
- Associate conflict

Client Conflict. The normal type of client conflict can usually be determined relatively easily and is an important early step in the merger discussions. The obvious client conflict occurs when firms are in adversarial roles or on opposite sides in a business counseling relationship. The not so obvious conflict can result from a number of situations.

- The merger firms have a common client, such as a bank, that prefers to spread its legal business to a number of firms. The result of a merger would be a problem in such a situation.
- A client has had unsatisfactory dealings with one of the merger partners that will affect its willingness to refer work to the merged firms.

An even less obvious conflict is one in which two potential merger candidates have taken opposing positions on issues of law. Consider, as an example, the following situation.

A medium size firm with a general business practice decides to merge with a small administrative law firm (known in the good old days as a lobbying firm). The business firm represents a number of companies in the labor relation area. The administrative law firm, on the other hand, has represented a number of unions for the purpose of getting labor legislation approved which adversely affects the companies represented by the larger firm. The conflict may not be one of law but rather of client resistance and loss.

Associate conflicts. Too many firms overlook the impact of a merger on the associates. You can be reasonably sure that associates in both will be against the merger. Such attitudes usually result from:

- Lack of understanding of firm needs;
- Lack of communication;
- Insecurity; and
- A feeling of betrayal.

Steps should be taken to advise associates as soon as possible that a merger is being contemplated and to elicit their comments. An early meeting of the associates of both firms usually dispels much of the fear. (In one recent case, however, such a meeting resulted in a break-off of discussions.)

Other points to be dealt with concerning associates are as follows:

- Compensation arrangements;
- Partnership considerations;
- Outstanding commitments;
- Quality of talent;
- Fringe benefits;
- Assignments; and
- Training and evaluation.

Getting the associates enthusiastic about the merger is a communication problem for the partners. A job well done can result in happier associates and a much smoother integration of practices. It is far better to go in the direction of early communication with the risk of leaks, then for associates to hear of the merger on the street.

ECONOMICS

It is essential to go through a careful study of the economics of each firm. The following list can be used as a guide in determining the various items that should be reviewed.

Income and expense statements for the last three years. In reviewing financial statements, it is important to look at financial trends and such things as ratios of gross income to net income, expenses, retained capital, and the like.

Balance sheets - three years. Particular attention should be directed toward such items as loans payable, loans receivable from partners, outstanding client advances, and capital accounts.

Tax returns. A comparison of the firms' tax returns to the financial statements can sometimes reveal interesting inconsistencies. In fact, in many smaller firms the only detailed financial data available for analysis might be the tax returns.

Capitalization. The capital structure of the two firms should also be closely analyzed. On what basis is capital determined? Do partners put in cash capital, or do the firms take "promises" from partners to put capital in out of current earnings? Is the difference between cash earnings and distributable funds creating large capital liabilities? These are all important questions and reflect issues that must be resolved early in the negotiations.

Work-in-process and accounts receivable. The information about these two items can tell a lot about the firm's future health. Ratios of these areas to gross income, age and turn-over, as well as billing and collection habits are all important items to compare and discuss.

Fiscal year. If the firms have different fiscal years or if a partnership and a professional corporation are merging, spe-cific tax advice has to be obtained. It is critical to seek out-side advice, regardless of in-house capabilities.

Partners' compensation. The actual and relative compensa-tion levels of partners as well as the actual compensation sys-tem and underlying philosophy should be discussed. This area can be one of major difficulties. Merging a firm that has a subjective system of compensation with one that uses a for-mula approach may be almost impossible. Incidentially, the problem in this regard is not generally the amount of com-pensation of an individual partner but the underlying philos-ophies that may go to the heart of the relationships between the partners.

For example, firm A is a 22 lawyer firm with 15 partners. Firm B is a 10 lawyer firm with 7 partners. The partners in firm B are earning substantially less individually than the partners in firm A. The following chart of compensation lev-els illustrates the problem.

	Firm A	Firm B
Partner A	175,000	150,000
Partner B	160,000	135,000
Partner C	125,000	109,000
Partner D	100,000	85,000
Partner E	90,000	75,000
Partner F	70,000	60,000
Partner G	60,000	50,000

Note: The partner levels are relatively "equal" for partners in the same firm.

The partners in firm B take the position that they are as important as their counterparts in firm A and that once the firms are merged, it would be "demoralizing" for the partners to be at different levels. The problem for firm A is the ques-tion of who reduces income to permit closer equalization in compensation levels for partners in firm B.

In this particular case the formula of 2 + 2 = 5 was so ob-vious that the partners in firm A felt that the reduction of im-mediate income was a reasonable investment in the future.

This investment was structured on a two–tier level whereby partners in firm B were awarded 1/2 of parity the first year on a specific earning level of the new firm. Once this level was reached, additional net was "tilted" toward firm A. The plan was to correct all inequities over a three year period.

Leasehold obligations. The obligations of both firms should be reviewed. In present times many firms are sitting with valuable leaseholds that may be assets that require specific treatment in the merger.

Value of assets. If partners of either firm are contributing hard assets such as furniture, books, and automobiles as capital, the ownership and value of the assets may require the evaluation of an independent appraiser.

Client revenue. It would be helpful if both firms in the merger process would prepare a list of fees received, from each client, in order of highest to lowest over a three year period. This is to determine percentages of income from any one client or group of clients, as well as to anticipate the ability of the firm to regenerate business from existing clients and the volume of work each year from new clients.

One of the problems to consider is that should a small, highly specialized firm that receives most of its income from law firm referral merge with a full-service firm, it is not uncommon for the merged firm to lose a large percentage of this referral business.

Also consider the following:

- Schedules of billable and non-billable hours, hours billed, collections, billing rates, compensation at all levels, and turnover during the last three years.
- List of clients in order of fees received for the past three years. This information will help identify trends in business development, dependence on clients, and regeneration of business.
- A current client list.
- Copies of all agreements. This is especially important because the relationship and philosophies of the partners are revealed through the provisions of their agreements.
- Deferred compensation and insurance information, i.e., death, disability, and retirement plans.
- Obligations to withdrawn partners.

General Issues

NAME

Choosing a name for the new firm should be a business decision. Even in smaller firms the tendency is to shorter names that do not change automatically based on the ego needs of individual partners. This is not to say, however, that a large institutional firm might not be well advised to make a name change based on the image that should be communicated as a result of the merger.

Some firms compromise by agreeing to a longer name to preserve the identity of both firms for a specific time, after which it is agreed that a shorter name will be adopted. The name problem is more acute in smaller firms where there is a tendency to have long names and a reluctance of partners to have their names dropped as a result of a merger.

Other firms solve the problem by immediately adopting a new, shorter name but listing the full names of the predecessor firms somewhere on the letterhead. Be careful to discuss this early in negotiations—the name can be a deal breaker!

OUTSIDE ACTIVITIES

A discussion of the philosophy of the partners in each firm concerning outside activities should be an early part of the general discussion. Specific areas to examine are:

- Political activities;
- Contributions;
- Civic and pro bono work;
- Outside investments;
- Client involvement;
- Teaching.

EXPENSE POLICY

The policies of both firms concerning the spending of money should be examined. Differences in such issues as partners business expense, club dues, business development expenses, and the like can create serious problems.

Practice Issues

A merger does not prove successful because several partners negotiate a reasonable arrangement. Rather, the success of a merger is on the practice level when the lawyers in the firm work together. It is, therefore, important as part of the merger discussions to explore the practice management of the firm and to lay the groundwork for integrating the partners in the firm. An inventory indicating the primary and secondary areas of expertise of the lawyers should be prepared. For example, one lawyer may show private placement as a primary area and merger and acquisition as a secondary area. Another may list products liability as his major expertise and general litigation as secondary. By reviewing this information, the firms discussing the merger can determine the amount of overlap, or whether particular lawyers can be used for new areas of practice, or to fill holes existing in one or the other firm, and whether specialties compliment each other.

Specialization and departmentalization are important for today's firms, for both client service and for quality control of the practice. Depending on the size of the firm, such a structure can have varying degrees of flexibility, and there is no reason to rush into a permanent structure until after the merged firms have worked together for some time.

Management Structure

It is vitally important at the onset to establish the form of management to be used in the new firm. It is important to balance the initial management makeup of the new firm with partners of both firms even if this results in a transitional management with committees that are too large.

There are a few important concepts to remember in the area of management structure.

1. Rather than arguing about which management style is the best and should be preserved, approach the management question from the point of view that neither style will probably work and that the merged firms being larger than each of the individual firms will require new concepts and structure. Obviously, the new requirement might be best served by one of the existing management structures, but the psychological

impact of approaching such a decision as just described has many benefits.

Two firms with strong managing partners merged. Since neither was happy ceding the management role to the other and because they realized they would not agree on many issues, with the approval of the partners in the merged firm, each one picked another lawyer, and the four then selected a fifth. The new firm was governed by a five lawyer management committee. This structure worked well while management by the two strong managing partners, in all likelihood, would have been a disaster.

2. There is nothing wrong with a transitional management that will later give way to a different system.

3. It is important to involve partners of both firms in the management structure even if the partners of one firm express a desire not to be involved.

Administration

There are many topics that must be addressed concerning the administration of the new firm. Here are examples of some of the most important:

ADMINISTRATOR
- Define role
- Recruit if necessary
- Assign duties in merger

STAFFING
- Current staff of both firms
- Additional staff required
- Excess staff
- Office manual

SYSTEMS & PROCEDURES
- Data and word processing needs
- Telephone system
- Timekeeping procedures
- Billing procedures
- Files

- Library
- Bank accounts

INSURANCE

All insurance coverages must be reviewed and integrated. Specific attention should be paid to professional liability and especially any coverage gaps that might develop because of a policy cancellation.

PRESS RELEASES AND PUBLIC RELATIONS

A plan should be developed for handling press releases in order to gain the greatest amount of publicity possible out of the merger. Additionally, a plan has to be formulated to handle inquiries during the merger discussions. Assume that you cannot keep the merger secret until you are ready for an announcement and plan accordingly.

Avoiding Problems

During the course of the merger watch out for danger signs that might indicate that the merger is in trouble. Examples of such danger signs are as follows:

HASTE

A merger discussion should take place when there is enough time to consider all of the issues. Unusual haste on either side is probably a danger signal of underlying problems. The worst possible result is for a firm to announce a merger without fully discussing all of the relevant issues. On the other hand, discussions that go on and on and on seldom culminate in a merger agreement.

COMPATIBILITY

As stated earlier, more important than any other factor in the merger discussions is the question of reasonable compatibility of the two firms. Arrangements should be made for the partners and associates of both firms to see and talk with each other before the merger is consummated.

In addition to the previous discussion on this subject, some of the areas that can cause compatibility problems are:

Lack of confidence in the other firm's legal ability. Very often firms that are planning to merge, especially in the same city, have had some contact with each other or are known to each other through reputation. If there is a feeling by some of the lawyers in either firm that the quality of people or work is significantly different, the merger will probably fail.

Different philosophies relating to business development, growth, type of clients, expense accounts, and the like. Many times firms with really different business styles attempt to merge. If the firms recognize a need to compromise on some of the issues mentioned here, a reasonable arrangement can probably be made. If on the other hand, a firm holds fast on some of these issues it may be a reason for reconsidering the merger.

For example, a firm that has a very aggressive marketing plan and is attempting to merge with one where a number of partners feel that having a listed telephone number is a form of advertising will probably not ultimately succeed.

Varied ethnic and religious backgrounds. Not very much should be said concerning this possible conflict except to be mindful of such differences.

Recruiting. A firm that recruits predominantly from major law schools merging with one that believes such an effort is a waste of money and time may be in store for future problems.

Once all of the major issues have been explored, a letter of intent should be prepared outlining the broad agreements that have been reached. This is the appropriate time for both firms to obtain the consent of the partners to proceed with the preparation of a detailed agreement.

There are other related issues which possibly will surface during discussions between the partners prior to, and during the course of negotiations. A few social events are also very helpful in identifying conflicts.

Acquisitions or Lateral Entries

An acquisition of an individual lawyer to fill a specific gap, be it service or client development, is commonplace. While it is always simpler to integrate an individual or a small group of individuals, some of the principles set forth in the merger discussion also apply on a smaller scale.

The most important consideration when studying an acquisition of a partner is to analyze objectively the basis on which the individual will join the firm and to document these arrangements carefully. Consider such things as, among others, what his capital contribution will be, how he will be compensated, his interest in the firm's work in process and accounts receivable, where he will appear on the letterhead and in legal directories. Also spell out what he brings in the way of clients, receivables, hard assets, and things of that nature. Additionally, do not oversell the positive aspects of a potential acquisition to your partners as they are sure to be disappointed when their expectations are not precisely met.

Also, be sure to advise all partners and associates that someone new is joining the firm. There is nothing worse than having a new partner or senior associate walk through the halls being introduced when no advance notice was given.

One of the most important pitfalls that occurs when analyzing a lateral entry is the support staff that will be needed to support that individual. If the need for an acquisition is real and if the individual being considered has a client base, then the firm should be looking not only at the individual but also the legal staffing that will be needed to support him.

It is also important to analyze carefully the promises made by incoming partners concerning the amount of business that they expect to bring to the firm. *In more cases than not, these promises are overstated.* There is nothing wrong with the firm acquiring a business-getting partner to request a meeting with prospective clients to seek reassurances that the promised business will be forthcoming.

It is also wise to examine carefully a partner who is coming from a political career. The number of ineffective lawyers who are former politicians, even at the highest levels of government, far outweigh the ones that can deliver a small fraction of their promises. The same caution is offered for individuals who have served in the judiciary for a good part of their careers. Judges seem to have an exaggerated view of their public image and their ability to attract clients.

There are, of course, exceptions to all the rules, and no doubt there will be a number of offended readers because of the above statements. Nevertheless, the experience of the authors on this issue clearly indicates the need for a higher degree of caution should be exercised in this type of acquisition.

Branch Offices

Nothing brings more concern to the minds of many managing partners than the problem of opening and/or managing a branch office.

There is little doubt that the tendency to open branch offices will continue. It is also safe to assume that the unhappiness surrounding many branch office operations will also continue.

Let us explore some of the most common reasons for branch offices.

Protect a shifting client base. With the mobility of corporations and individuals today, it is often necessary to have lawyers available where the client is located or where the services are performed.

Expand business base. Sometimes a branch office is a product of a merger and is undertaken for many of the same reasons as a merger, especially the broadening of the business base.

Competition. There are many large cities in which medium and small firms have continued problems attracting clients and competing with larger firms. Washington, D.C., is an example. Many medium and smaller size firms are looking for mergers to offset a limited client base and a reduction in the amount of work that is being sent to the D.C., firm from other parts of the country.

Structuring the Branch

There are many steps that should be considered carefully in setting up a branch office. The most successful branch offices are a result of a careful plan. The plan should address the following issues.

PURPOSE

What is the reason for the branch? This question must be answered as objectively as possible. Some of the reasons firms open branch offices are:

- to follow a client that is moving all or a part of its business to a new location
- because a client requests the firm to open a branch office
- to serve existing clients
- to develop business in the branch location
- to attract new business, primarily in the headquarters location, in the belief that a branch will make the firm more attractive to them
- because they believe they need the status that a branch office in a particular city might give them
- to serve the needs of lawyers in the firm who travel to another city on a fairly regular basis and spend a good deal of time there.

Any or all of these might be the reason for a branch office, but it is still important to articulate it. If a firm votes to open a branch because it feels this gives them status (perhaps other firms in their city have done so), there will be much less discussion on profitability or on what the lawyers in the branch are "really" doing, than if the firm says the branch is to develop business or to hold business it might otherwise lose.

STAFFING

Many firms have opened a branch office in a distant city and in order to hold down start-up costs, or because they believe it will take some time to develop the business to keep a lawyer or lawyers busy, support the branch by sending in lawyers from the "main office." This might mean a lawyer spending two or three days a week in the branch office, or two lawyers alternating weeks. Some firms have one lawyer in the branch, but send in additional help on a temporary basis to cover the work. In most cases, this does not work.

Clients and prospective clients in the branch location quickly see through this arrangement, and if they don't, competitive law firms will often call this to their attention. Interestingly enough, many firms that have tried this approach do not permit part-time arrangements in the "main office," under the theory that clients need their lawyers on a full-time basis. Staffing from the main office might also indicate that the firm has not made a real commitment to the branch operation.

If the branch office is going to be successful, long-range staffing questions should be considered. This should also include projections for space, equipment, and non-lawyer personnel. The plan should be based on the goals set for the branch operation and on a set budget for the first year and then projected, presuming progress proceeds as per the plan. Going through this exercise will educate the firm on the cost of the operation and certainly is preferable to the "we'll send partner X there, and if he needs help, we'll send someone else in," which is the extent of planning done by many firms.

COMPENSATION

Most firms that operate in different cities quickly learn that they have to adopt different compensation levels for partners, associates, and staff depending on local market conditions. There are several ways in which firms make the adjustments. The most common is to adjust compensation (upward or downward) based on cost of living in the branch location. Some firms do this scientifically, using the C.P.I., or Department of Labor statistics, while others make "an educated guess." Should a lawyer transfer back to the headquarters, his income would be adjusted accordingly. Most firms take a different approach in hiring associates. The most commonly used system would be to compensate associates based on the going rate in the cities in which they are located. The differences in salary between headquarters and branch associates decreases after approximately five years. Firms that do not make adjustments for partners, associates, and staff are asking for problems.

ROTATION AND MANAGEMENT

If at all possible the firm that is opening a distant branch should transfer a partner to manage the branch even if the branch is a result of a merger. The addition of associates is also a good concept. Often the extent of integration is a determining factor in the success of the branch operation. If a branch is opened ab initio, a transferred partner can impart the philosophies and practices of the headquarters to the lawyers hired. He is there to insure continuity and to prevent "we-they" attitudes from forming. Occasional visits from headquarters management does not accomplish the same thing. Integration is equally as important if the branch is a result of a merger. Unless there is some transfer of personnel, the branch will continue to operate as it has in the past, and in most cases this will be in a different style from headquarters. There will be little sense of loyalty to the institution and more probability that the branch will split off.

The branch will require local management supervision, but there should be one overall management structure for the firm at large with specific delegation of duties to branch offices. Often the manager of a branch office that is of sufficient size, either in numbers of lawyers or in production, will sit on the firm's Executive Committee. Many firms rotate Executive Committee meetings, so that it is not always the branch manager who must do the travelling.

Firms that have a practice management structure have lawyers assigned to a particular department, which helps integrate both the lawyers and the practice. Depending on the mix of lawyers at the various locations, a Section Chairman might be located in either the branch or the headquarters location.

The important thing to remember is that there will be a greater chance of long term success if there is enough integration of the practices to make one law firm out of the two.

ECONOMIC EVALUATION

Many firms do not do any specific analysis of the operation of the branch office, under the theory that this could be divisive or that it is impossible to determine what business belongs to the branch, what came to the branch through headquarters, or what business the branch generated because of the reputation and capabilities of the headquarters. However, if the firm is opening a branch in another city for the sole purpose of attracting local business and where there is little or no integration of the two offices, a profit center approach may be desirable.

On the other hand, when a business firm opens a branch for the purpose of serving clients at large, then a profit center may be actually encouraging the branch to become an independent firm. *A true case in point!*

A large city firm with a general business practice representing corporate clients who have the need for a Washington, D.C., presence opened an office to solidify further its client relations. The accountant advised the firm that it should keep a detailed profit and loss statement reflecting the branch office operation. Because much of the work handled in Washington, D.C., was part of the firm's overall practice, the branch never showed much economic promise. In fact, it often operated in the red. Because of the constant complaining of a number of headquarters partners, the partners in Washington eventually left the firm. There was an outcry against the firm's management and a demand to close the branch. "After all we can be in Washington in an hour, so who needs the office?"

A number of the partners who were concerned about the Washington presence decided to discuss the situation with their client, against the wishes of some other partners. The partners were surprised to learn that the clients felt very strongly about the Washington presence, telling the partner that if the office were closed they would have to reconsider their relationship. A question to the firm's accountant—Did the branch really operate in the red, or was it simply a part of the overall firm profitability?

Lastly, though we have used the terminology, we strongly recommend that the term "branch office" not be used. Far better you establish the mentality that the law firm has various offices, not branches.

We have attempted in this chapter to examine as many of the important issues on the subject of expansion and growth through merger and acquisition, as was possible.

The best advice we can give when you are thinking of attempting such a move is to do so carefully in a well-planned manner. Branch offices, mergers, and acquisitions of experienced lawyers are not usually short term fixes to a problem, but rather long term investments in firm growth.

CHAPTER VIII

Long Range Planning

Many issues in managing, administering, and operating the legal firm concern problems that occur over and over again that can be avoided by long range planning. Unfortunately, until recently, such planning has been considered either a luxury that the busy firm felt it could not afford (either in time or money) or something done by a "business organization" (and until recently law firms did not put themselves into this classification), or by those firms that might have had someone who saw the importance of long range planning, understood the concepts, and could lead the effort.

Beginning in the late 1970's and early 1980's, long range planning became a key issue. The majority of legal organizations undertaking such planning do not fully understand it, but they are going at it full speed. Both the interest and speed can be attributed to the fact that the considerable growth of law firms in the past ten years or so seems to have frightened management to the point that they are beginning to think about coping with future expansion and its inherent problems. The subject of long range planning has, therefore, become one of the major topics under discussion at partners' meetings, in management committee sessions, and at retreats. Some of the "Big Eight" accounting firms are starting to market programs, and there has been a proliferation of material on the subject in legal and management publications. Though all of this material will help serve the needs of the many committees being formed—calling themselves such things as The Long Range Planning Committee, Committee For Future Legal Planning, Committee on Economics and Management in the 80's and similar sobriquets, it addresses the issue of why long range planning should be done, rather than how to do it.

This chapter will cover approaches to long range planning, including computer projections (to show, for example, how the growth of the firm will affect such things as space, finances, salaries), and its importance, along with a discussion of how the firm can approach the investigation and analysis necessary to arrive at a plan.

Planning or Projection

Unfortunately, there has been more discussion geared to projection and less to planning. Though the terms can be used synonymously (and Webster shows them as such), they are being used quite differently in the legal environment today. Many lawyers consider running the numbers to be planning. This is actually the projecting, and the results of this may give the firm important data to consider when it gets to the actual plan. The results may convince the firm that certain practices or policies should be changed in order to improve the economics, or if no change is made, what the costs of continuing as in the past will be.

The difference between the terms as used can be explained simply. Based on past historical data, and making a few future assumptions, *projection* is what the firm will look like (in numbers and dollars) in 1987 and 1992. When a firm *plans*, it is saying that "Based on our decisions of what we want the firm to be in 1987 and 1992, here are our plans to reach these goals."

Combining Planning and Projection

The first step is planning, with projection to follow later. It is the planning that tells you what you want to project. Essential elements are the philosophy and direction in which the firm wants to go, which can be determined only by extensive work by the firm, either on its own or with the assistance of consultants with experience in the field. With proper input to a manual or computer program, the law firm can then determine not only where it might be in five or ten years, but also how to get there, and how to reach the goals that have been formulated. With both planning and projection, done in the proper order, meaningful results can be obtained.

PROJECTION

In order to make the projections, the firm gathers a good bit of current and historical financial information, data relating to ages of partners and associates, the policies relating to partnership (most specifically number of years), and other detail depending on what it considers to be the significant issues. With this information it can do the projecting, either manually (which is time consuming) or through designing computer software or having the projecting done by a company that has the software designed and available. As an example of some "projecting" (looking at what the firm might look like in 1993), we are including long range planning quantitative models for one firm with seventy-five lawyers (30 partners and 45 associates) and another firm with thirty-five lawyers (18 partners and 17 associates). The examples include brief comments on what the figures tell the law firm to help it in any decision making necessary when it starts to plan.

LONG RANGE PLANNING
75 Lawyer Firm

I. Personnel Growth

In this model we are analyzing both legal and administrative personnel growth over the next five years. Growth projections are calculated by evaluating the firm's past average personnel growth trends and extending them out an additional five years.

From this analysis a firm can determine what area of personnel growth needs improvement or what area should be reduced. For example, in reviewing the model we can see that the attorney to secretary ratio was about even (1 to 1 ratio) in 1982. Projections indicate that this trend will continue over the next five years if present hiring practices continue.

From this model the firm might decide to attempt more secretarial sharing arrangements (1 to 2, cluster, etc.) while possibly increasing other areas of utilization, such as word processing as a result.

Of course, other areas can be analyzed from this model for the purpose of reducing personnel and related expenses and increasing firm profitability and operational control.

LONG RANGE PLANNING PERSONNEL GROWTH

Legal	1982 BASE	1983	1984	1985	1986	1987
Partners	30	33	36	39	42	46
Associates	45	51	58	67	76	87
Paralegals	11	12	14	15	17	19
Totals	86	96	108	121	135	152

Administrative						
Administrative Personnel	4	4	5	6	6	7
Secretaries	71	79	89	100	112	125
Accounting Personnel	5	5	6	7	8	8
Word Processing Operators	4	4	5	6	6	7
Computer Personnel	2	2	2	3	3	3
Library Personnel	4	4	5	5	6	6
File Clerks	4	4	5	5	5	6
Messengers	2	2	3	3	3	3
Other Clerks	5	5	5	5	5	6
Totals	101	109	125	140	154	171

II. Secretarial Salary Expenses

From our personnel growth model we can now evaluate salary expenses related to particular positions. For example, our model for secretarial salary expenses indicates expenses the firm will encounter in the secretarial area if the firm's present hiring practices continue. Also projected is the cost to the firm for additional secretaries hired each year over the next five years.

SECRETARIAL SALARY EXPENSES

	1982 BASE	1983	1984	1985	1986	1987
Number of Secretaries	71	79	89	100	112	125
Average Secretarial Salary including Benefits (10% growth per year)	25,000	27,500	30,250	33,275	36,602	40,262
Total Salary Expenses	1,775,000	2,172,500	2,692,250	3,327,500	4,099,424	5,032,750

ADDITIONAL SECRETARIAL HIRING EXPENSES/YEAR

	1983	1984	1985	1986	1987
Number of Secretaries	8	10	11	12	13
Secretarial Starting Salary Including Benefits (10% growth per year)	21,000	23,100	25,410	27,951	30,746
Total Expenses	168,000	231,000	279,510	335,412	399,698

III. Client Growth

The client growth model analyzes past client growth and projects this out over the next five years in accordance with a firm's past history in this area. It indicates to the firm how much client growth it should expect in the future if past and present trends continue.

From this model the firm can formulate various "what if" assumptions by projecting client growth at a 10%, 15%, 20%, etc., growth rate per year, as opposed to its past average growth rate. This can provide the firm with a forecasting model used in conjunction with a strategy for increased client development.

CLIENT GROWTH

	1980	1981	1982	INCREASE %
Number of Clients	1,180	1,250	1,349	14%
Total Number of Matters	4,700	5,100	5,567	18%
Average Number of Matters/Client	4	4	4	—

PROJECTED CLIENT GROWTH OVER NEXT FIVE YEARS
BASED ON PAST AVERAGE GROWTH/YEAR

	1982 BASE	1983	1984	1985	1986	1987
Number of Clients	1,349	1,443	1,544	1,653	1,768	1,892
Total Number of Matters	5,567	6,040	6,553	7,111	7,715	8,371
Average Number of Matters/Client	4	4	4	4	4	4

IV. Billable Hours/Rates/Gross Income

From this model we can evaluate past trends in the areas of gross income, billable hours, rates collected, writeoffs, etc. It can be used as a model for projecting future gross income for the firm and to indicate growth in these areas over the last four years.

This particular example indicates the disparity between average gross billing rates and average rates collected. It reviews firm writeoffs for both billable hours and accounts receivable over the last four years and indicates at the bottom what additional percentage of gross income was lost as a result of write offs.

	BILLABLE HOURS/RATES/GROSS INCOME				INCREASE (DECREASE)
	1979	1980	1981	1982	1979–1982
Gross Income	7,770,000	9,234,500	10,500,000	12,558,000	62%
Billable Hours	111,000	126,500	140,000	161,000	45%
Average Rate Collected	70.00	73.00	75.00	78.00	11%
Average Gross Billing Rate (Assuming 1500 Billable Hours per Attorney)	75.00	77.00	79.00	82.00	9%
Write offs of Billable Hours	543,900	461,725	525,000	627,900	15%
Write offs of Accounts Receivable	275,000	450,000	575,000	636,250	131%
Total Write offs	818,900	911,725	1,100,000	1,264,150	54%
Total Write offs % of Gross Income	10%	10%	10%	10%	—

V. Gross Income Projected

From our previous model (Billable Hours/Rates/Gross Income), we can now create a projected model for a firm's growth in the area of gross income, billable hours, rates of collections, and write offs.

GROSS INCOME PROJECTED

	1982 BASE	1983	1984	1985	1986	1987
Gross Income	12,558,000	14,573,850	16,642,994	19,244,908	22,226,504	25,640,952
Billable Hours	161,000	179,676	200,518	223,778	249,736	278,706
Average Rate Collected	78.00	81.00	83.00	86.00	89.00	92.00
Average Gross Billing Rate	82.00	85.00	88.00	91.00	94.00	97.00
Write offs of Billable Time	627,900	578,165	614,590	653,309	694,467	738,219
Write offs of Accounts Receivable	636,250	852,575	1,142,450	1,530,883	2,051,384	2,748,854
Total Write offs	1,265,150	1,430,740	1,757,040	2,184,192	2,745,851	3,487,073
Total Write offs % Gross Income	10%	10%	10%	11%	12%	14%

Taking the past average growth in each area, projections can be made for the next five years.

A firm could experiment with this model employing "what if" assumptions for estimating additional improvement in gross income for each year. For instance, growth can be projected at a 10%, 15%, 20%, etc., rate per year.

This model could be extremely important for indicating the requirements for additional income for a firm.

VI. Average Starting Salary Information

This model examines past starting salary trends and indicates increases (or decreases) for both legal and administrative staff. We can see from this model how much of an increase has occured in each position over the last three years.

This can be an important criteria for a firm in evaluating additional starting salary increases and for evaluating personnel expenses.

AVERAGE STARTING SALARY INFORMATION
1980–1982

Legal	1980	1981	1982	INCREASE % (DECREASE) 1980–1982
Associates	27,600	31,400	34,200	24%
Paralegals	14,200	15,000	16,500	16%
Administrative				
Administrative Personnel	24,000	26,500	30,000	25%
Secretaries	14,200	15,000	16,500	16%
Accounting Personnel	14,800	15,500	17,000	15%
Word Processing Operators	14,000	15,200	16,800	20%
Computer Personnel	12,000	13,200	15,500	29%
Library Personnel	12,000	13,200	14,500	21%
File Clerks	9,500	10,000	11,500	21%
Messengers	8,000	8,500	9,200	15%
Other Clerks	8,500	9,300	10,000	18%

VII. Projected Average Starting Salary

This model indicates a five year projection of starting salaries for both legal and administrative staff. Based upon the average percentage increases indicated from our prior model, we can project future salary increases.

This is important for a firm in its budgeting practices. It enables a firm to compare personnel expenses with related legal and administrative hirings.

PROJECTED AVERAGE STARTING SALARY
1983–1987

Legal	1982 BASE	1983	1984	1985	1986	1987
Associates	34,200	38,133	42,518	47,407	52,859	58,938
Paralegals	16,500	17,820	19,245	20,785	22,448	24,243
Administrative						
Administrative Personnel	30,000	33,450	37,296	41,585	46,367	51,700
Secretaries	16,500	17,820	19,245	20,785	22,448	24,243
Accounting Personnel	17,000	18,275	19,645	21,118	22,702	24,404
Word Processing Operators	16,800	18,312	19,960	21,756	23,714	25,848
Computer Personnel	15,500	17,592	19,967	22,663	25,722	29,195
Library Personnel	14,500	15,950	17,545	19,299	21,229	23,352
File Clerks	11,500	12,650	13,915	15,306	16,837	18,520
Messengers	9,200	9,982	10,830	11,751	12,749	13,833
Other Clerks	10,000	10,800	11,664	12,597	13,604	14,693

VIII. Partnership Retirements

This model projects the number of partners retiring over the next five years and related accumulated expenses incurred as a result of it. It is based on partnership agreements regarding the future retirement provisions for partners.

PROJECTED COST FOR PARTNERSHIP RETIREMENT

	1982	1983	1984	1985	1986	1987
Number of Partners Retiring (Accumulated total)	2	3	4	6	7	9
Payments due in each year under terms of partnership agreement	148,512	227,965	312,979	494,910	592,243	800,535

IX. Partner Admission Policy

This model evaluates the number of associates attaining the partnership level over the next five years based upon the estimate given in our Personnel Growth model.

Taking into consideration the firm's policy regarding the average time for attainment to the partnership level, we can project partnership growth over the next five years. In our example, partnership attainment is roughly eight years.

We can use a "what if" assumption to project partnership growth if the firm increased the average number of years required before the attainment of partnership. This can be used as an example of curtailing partnership growth and maintaining the balance between partners and/or associates.

PARTNER ADMISSION POLICY

	1982 BASE	1983	1984	1985	1986	1987
Number of Partners	30	33	36	39	42	46

If the policy were changed to nine years partnership growth would look like the following:

	1982 BASE	1983	1984	1985	1986	1987
Number of Partners	30	30	33	36	39	42

If the policy were changed to ten years partnership growth would look like the following:

	1982 BASE	1983	1984	1985	1986	1987
Number of Partners	30	30	30	33	36	39

X. Projected Future Space Requirements

This model analyzes the firm's space requirements over the next five years as the number of legal and administrative personnel grows. It enables management to get a clear idea of what the space requirements of the firm will be over the next few years and whether they could be accommodated under current space conditions.

In this example, we can see that the firm will be required to add approximately 63,000 square feet by 1987, to the existing 60,000 square feet in order to compensate for growth. In our example, approximately 600 square feet per lawyer at a lease rate of $30.00 per square foot is required. The firm will have to relocate in 1984 to accommodate growth at a lease rate of $37.50 per square foot, and represents a substantial increase in the annual cost in the projection model.

PROJECTED FUTURE SPACE REQUIREMENTS

1983–1987

	1982 BASE	1983	1984	1985	1986	1987
Present Square Footage	60,000	70,000	81,000	93,000	107,000	123,000
Per Lawyer Square Footage	600	600	600	600	600	600
Annual Cost (including Taxes, Maintenance, etc.	1,800,000	2,100,000	3,037,500	3,487,500	4,012,500	4,612,500

XI. Profit & Loss

Our last model projects distributed net income based upon gross income minus the firm's expenses. Projected expenses are based upon the average percentage increases for each expense over the last four years.

In this example we provide a detailed breakdown of all expenses with regard to their related areas.

We can see from this example that the percentage of distributed income from 1983 to 1985 has decreased. Part of this decrease was caused by the increase in occupancy expenses (see space requirements section), due to the firm moving to accommodate its growth requirements.

Many "what if" types of comparisons can be made from this model. It represents an important picture for the firm's future profitability.

PROFIT & LOSS

	1982 BASE	1983	1984	1985	1986	1987
Gross Income	12,558,000	14,573,850	16,642,994	19,244,908	22,226,504	25,640,952
Expenses:						
Legal						
Associates	2,475,000	2,747,250	3,049,447	3,384,886	3,757,224	4,170,518
Paralegals	286,000	308,880	333,590	360,277	389,099	420,227
Sub-Totals	2,761,000	3,056,130	3,383,037	3,745,163	4,146,323	4,590,745
Administrative						
Ad. Personnel	180,000	199,800	221,778	246,173	273,252	303,310
Secretaries	1,775,000	1,917,000	2,070,360	2,235,988	2,414,867	2,608,057
Acct. Personnel	182,000	196,560	212,284	229,257	247,608	269,417
WP Personnel	100,000	108,000	116,640	125,971	136,048	146,932
Comp. Personnel	46,000	49,680	53,654	57,946	62,582	67,589
Library Pers.	88,000	95,040	102,643	110,854	119,722	129,300
File Clerks	68,000	71,400	74,970	78,718	82,654	86,787
Messengers	26,000	27,300	28,665	30,098	31,603	33,183
Other Clerks	75,000	79,500	84,210	89,326	94,685	100,366
Sub Totals	2,540,000	2,744,280	2,965,204	3,204,331	3,463,021	2,744,941
Occupancy	1,300,000	2,100,000	3,037,500	3,487,500	4,012,500	4,612,500

195

PROFIT & LOSS (Continued)

	1982 BASE	1983	1984	1985	1986	1987
Equipment						
Typewriters	137,500	151,250	166,375	183,012	201,313	221,445
Word Processing	75,000	82,500	90,750	99,825	109,807	120,788
Data Processing	100,000	110,000	121,000	133,100	146,410	161,051
Photocopiers	17,500 (Lease)	19,250	21,175	23,292	25,621	28,183
Telephone System	100,000	110,000	121,000	133,100	146,410	161,051
Others	254,000	279,400	307,340	338,074	371,881	409,069
Sub-Totals	684,000	752,400	827,640	910,403	1,001,442	1,101,587
Other Expenses (Supplies, Travel, Food, etc.)	487,000	535,700	589,270	648,197	713,016	784,318
Depreciation	152,000	167,200	183,920	202,312	222,543	244,791
Payments to Retired Partners	148,512	227,965	312,979	494,910	592,243	800,535
Net Income Distributed	4,485,488	4,990,175	5,343,444	6,552,092	8,075,416	9,761,535
Net Income as a % of Gross	36%	34%	32%	34%	36%	38%

I. Following are just the figures for the 35 lawyer firm (without the commentary).

35 Lawyer Firm
PERSONNEL GROWTH

Legal	1982 BASE	1983	1984	1985	1986	1987
Partners	18	20	22	25	27	30
Associates	17	19	22	25	29	33
Paralegals	4	4	4	5	5	5
Totals	39	43	48	55	61	68

Administrative						
Administrative Personnel	2	2	2	3	3	3
Secretaries	31	34	37	39	41	44
Accounting Personnel	3	3	3	3	4	4
Word Processing Operators	2	2	2	2	3	3
Computer Personnel	2	2	2	2	3	3
Library Personnel	1	1	1	1	1	2
File Clerks	1	1	1	1	1	1
Messengers	1	1	1	1	1	1
Other Clerks	2	2	2	3	3	3
Totals	45	48	51	55	60	64

II. Secretarial Salary Expenses

35 Lawyer Firm
SECRETARIAL SALARY EXPENSES

	1982 BASE	1983	1984	1985	1986	1987
Number of Secretaries	31	34	37	39	41	44
Average Secretarial Salary including Benefits (10% growth per year)	21,600	23,760	26,136	28,749	31,623	34,785
Total Salary Expenses	669,600	807,840	967,032	1,121,211	1,296,543	1,530,540

ADDITIONAL SECRETARIAL HIRING EXPENSES/YEAR

	1983	1984	1985	1986	1987
Number of Secretaries	3	3	2	2	3
Secretarial Starting Salary Including Benefits (10% growth per year)	16,740	18,079	19,525	21,087	22,774
Total Expenses	50,220	54,237	39,050	42,174	68,322

III. Client Growth

35 Lawyer Firm
CLIENT GROWTH

	1980	1981	1982	INCREASE %
Number of Clients	1,300	1,415	1,543	19%
Total Number of Matters	1,876	2,345	2,678	43%
Average Number of Matters/Client	1	2	2	—

PROJECTED CLIENT GROWTH OVER NEXT FIVE YEARS
BASED ON PAST AVERAGE GROWTH/YEAR

	1982 BASE	1983	1984	1985	1986	1987
Number of Clients	1,543	1,666	1,799	1,944	2,100	2,267
Total Number of Matters	2,678.00	3,213.60	3,856.32	4,627.58	5,553.10	6,663.72
Average Number of Matters/Client	2	2	2	2	3	3

199

IV. Billable Hours/Rates/Gross Income

35 Lawyer Firm
BILLABLE HOURS/RATES/GROSS INCOME

	1979	1980	1981	1982	INCREASE (DECREASE) 1979–1982
Gross Income	2,535,000	3,016,200	3,536,000	4,002,000	58%
Billable Hours	39,000	45,700	52,000	58,000	49%
Average Rate Collected	65.00	65.00	68.00	69.00	6%
Average Gross Billing Rate (Assuming 1500 Billable Hours per Attorney)	72.00	74.00	76.00	78.00	8%
Write offs of Billable Hours	135,000	165,000	200,000	235,000	74%
Write offs of Accounts Receivable	165,000	171,000	196,000	270,000	64%
Total Write offs	300,000	336,000	396,000	505,000	68%
Total Write offs % of Gross Income	12%	11%	11%	13%	—

V. Gross Income Projected

35 Lawyer Firm
GROSS INCOME PROJECTED

	1982 BASE	1983	1984	1985	1986	1987
Gross Income	4,002,000	4,628,400	5,427,072	6,272,817	7,347,000	8,487,224
Billable Hours	58,000	66,120	75,376	85,929	97,960	111,674
Average Rate Collected	69.00	70.00	72.00	73.00	75.00	76.00
Average Gross Billing Rate	78.00	80.00	83.00	85.00	88.00	90.00
Writeoffs of Billable Time	235,000	282,000	338,400	406,080	487,296	584,755
Writeoffs of Accounts Receivable	270,000	321,300	382,347	454,992	541,441	644,315
Total Write offs	545,000	603,300	720,747	861,072	1,028,737	1,229,070
Total Write offs % Gross Income	13%	13%	13%	14%	14%	14%

VI. Average Starting Salary Information

35 Lawyer Firm

AVERAGE STARTING SALARY INFORMATION

1980–1982

Legal	1980	1981	1982	INCREASE % (DECREASE) 1980–1982
Associates	24,000	26,000	28,000	17%
Paralegals	13,000	14,500	16,000	23%
Administrative				
Administrative Personnel	20,500	22,000	24,000	17%
Secretaries	13,200	14,500	15,500	17%
Accounting Personnel	13,500	15,000	16,000	18%
Word Processing Operators	12,500	13,500	15,000	20%
Computer Personnel	10,500	12,000	14,000	33%
Library Personnel	10,000	11,500	12,500	22%
File Clerks	8,500	9,200	10,500	23%
Messengers	7,500	8,100	8,700	16%
Other Clerks	8,100	8,600	9,200	14%

VII. Projected Average Starting Salary

35 Lawyer Firms

PROJECTED AVERAGE STARTING SALARY

1983–1987

	1982 BASE	1983	1984	1985	1986	1987
Legal						
Associates	28,000	30,240	32,659	35,271	38,093	41,141
Paralegals	16,000	17,680	19,536	21,587	23,854	26,359
Administrative						
Administrative Personnel	25,000	27,625	30,525	33,730	37,272	41,186
Secretaries	15,500	16,740	18,079	19,525	21,087	22,774
Accounting Personnel	16,000	17,360	18,835	20,436	22,173	24,058
Word Processing Operators	15,000	16,426	17,985	19,693	21,564	23,613
Computer Personnel	14,000	16,100	18,515	21,292	24,486	28,159
Library Personnel	12,200	13,481	14,896	16,460	18,106	20,007
File Clerks	10,500	11,655	12,937	14,360	15,939	17,693
Messengers	8,700	9,352	10,053	10,807	11,618	12,489
Other Clerks	9,200	9,752	10,337	10,957	11,614	12,311

VIII. Partnership Retirements

35 Lawyer Firm
PROJECTED COST FOR PARTNERSHIP RETIREMENT

	1982	1983	1984	1985	1986	1987
Number of Partners Retiring (Accumulated Total)	1	2	2	4	5	6
Payments due in each year under terms of partnership agreement	59,863	123,621	123,621	276,059	358,278	444,278

IX. Partner Admission Policy

35 Lawyer Firm
PARTNER ADMISSION POLICY

	1982 BASE	1983	1984	1985	1986	1987
Number of Partners	18	20	22	25	27	30

If the policy were changed to seven years, partnership growth would look like the following:

	1982 BASE	1983	1984	1985	1986	1987
Number of Partners	18	18	20	22	25	27

If the policy were changed to eight years, the following would hold:

	1982 BASE	1983	1984	1985	1986	1987
Number of Partners	18	18	18	20	22	25

Taking this step further, if the firm pursued a nine year associate level before partnership attainment, the following would hold:

	1982 BASE	1983	1984	1985	1986	1987
Number of Partners	18	18	18	18	20	22

X. Projected Future Space Requirements

35 Lawyer Firm

PROJECTED FUTURE SPACE REQUIREMENTS

1983–1987

	1982 BASE	1983	1984	1985	1986	1987
Present Square Footage	22,000	25,000	28,000	32,800	36,400	41,000
Per Lawyer Square Footage	600	600	600	600	600	600
Annual Cost (including Taxes, Maintenance, etc.)	572,000	650,000	966,000	1,131,600	1,255,800	1,414,500

XI. Profit & Loss

35 Lawyer Firm
PROFIT & LOSS

	1982 BASE	1983	1984	1985	1986	1987
Gross Income	4,002,000	4,628,400	5,427,072	6,272,817	7,347,000	8,487,224
Expenses:						
Legal						
Associates	650,000	757,318	935,435	1,133,813	1,357,899	1,654,120
Paralegals	70,000	77,000	84,700	121,500	133,661	147,027
Sub-Totals	720,000	844,318	1,020,135	1,255,323	1,501,560	1,801,147
Administrative						
Ad. Personnel	52,000	56,160	60,652	98,158	106,010	114,491
Secretaries	510,500	583,148	662,880	730,000	703,068	906,246
Acct. Personnel	50,000	55,900	60,500	66,550	95,205	104,725
WP Personnel	32,000	34,880	38,000	41,441	66,735	73,408
Library Pers.	14,000	15,120	16,329	17,635	19,046	40,570
File Clerks	11,500	12,420	13,413	14,480	15,645	16,897
Messengers	9,000	9,720	10,497	11,337	12,244	13,223
Other Clerks	20,000	21,600	23,328	36,194	39,090	42,217
Sub Totals	699,000	788,048	885,599	1,015,801	1,157,043	1,311,777
Occupancy	572,000	650,000	966,000	1,131,600	1,255,800	1,414,500

XI. Profit & Loss (*Continued*)

35 Lawyer Firm
PROFIT & LOSS

	1982 BASE	1983	1984	1985	1986	1987
Equipment						
Typewriters	60,000	67,000	74,000	80,000	87,000	95,500
Word Processing	36,500	39,420	42,573	46,000	70,600	75,254
	(Lease)					
Photocopiers	18,500	19,240	20,009	20,810	21,642	23,373
Telephone System	44,000	47,250	51,321	55,427	60,000	64,800
Others	90,000	100,000	110,000	133,100	146,410	
Sub-Totals	249,000	273,180	297,903	323,237	372,342	405,337
Other Expenses (Supplies, Travel, Food, etc.)	183,500	220,200	264,240	317,007	380,505	456,636
Depreciation						
Net Income Distributed	1,520,500	1,788,854	1,923,015	2,152,528	2,594,830	3,004,445
Net Income as a % of Gross	38%	39%	35%	34%	35%	35%

You can see there is no end to the number of projections you can make, and how you can use the "what if" to change these, and this can be done in a matter of seconds once you have programmed your computer and put in the basic input data.

PLANNING

Planning is concerned with what the firm *wants or plans* to be in 1993 as opposed to what the projections show it will be. While this is a much more philosophic exercise, it is more meaningful. Planning means:

- Formulating long range *goals*;
- Specifying operational *objectives*;
- Anticipating *problems*;
- Identifying and selecting *strategies*; and
- Adopting appropriate *policies*.

Though almost all legal organizations would be interested in the results of long range "projections" and many are engaged in this exercise, few have really faced long range planning. Unfortunately, time is a limited commodity for lawyers. Time grudgingly devoted to planning is used to discuss today, tomorrow, or at most next year. This is, perhaps, the major problem in long range planning. The committee members are preoccupied with the current problems of their clients and of the profession and are unable to force themselves to gain the perspective necessary to plan for the future of the firm—the future being *at least* five to ten years into the future. In addition, the committee must focus on long range trends affecting the *profession* in order to bring appropriate policies to the firm for adoption.

Topics commonly found on the agendas of long range planning committees include in-house computerization, number of associates to be hired in a given year, or contemplated merger with a Washington, D.C., firm. While these are obviously important issues and of vital concern to the law firm, they are short rather than long range issues. They should be handled by the management committee or committees designated to deal with the specific issues. If the long range planning committee has to deal with short range issues, it will never accomplish the purposes for which it was formed.

In order for the planning process to work smoothly and efficiently, the charge of what the planners are to accomplish, how they may go about it, what the timetable is to be, and what the firm intends to do with the results or products produced should be clearly outlined. Many firms have wasted a great deal of lawyer time and have delayed future planning because they were not sure exactly what it was they were trying to do and/or how to go about doing it.

In the material that follows we will discuss an orderly approach to the process, including comments on who should be involved in the planning, approaches they might take, what the timetable should be, and what results to expect.

COMMITTEE MAKEUP

Obviously, a good deal of the success (or failure) of a long range planning committee will depend on the committee makeup. Several firms have told us about the futility of their attempts to plan long range. There are many reasons for their failures.

Mix of members. Many firms have selected the more senior and influential partners to serve on planning committees. There is little junior partner involvement and no input from associates. This often results in an inordinate amount of time spent to recommend the status quo, since these same lawyers have brought the firm to where it is today and see little reason to change.

This is not to denigrate the contribution or importance of the senior partners, nor to suggest that there are not many who would be valuable members of a committee, but rather to suggest that those selected be on the committee for reasons other than seniority or status.

Since the committee may, and probably will be, discussing certain sensitive issues, and may not be as candid if there is associate representation, associate representation is not recommended. On the other hand, since the planning is for five, ten, or more years in the future, it is vital to have associate input. An associates' sub-committee could provide a forum for input and also be a sounding board for the committee.

The executive director (administrator) should be a member of the committee. He or she will bring an expertise the lawyers may not have, and also can do some of the research work required, such as financial projections. In addition, most executive directors would have more training in both the planning and projection areas than other members of the committee.

Lack of a strong chairman. Either a strong chairman or an outside resource person is necessary to keep the focus where it belongs—on long range issues. Without this, the committee usually ends up as an auxiliary management committee, which few firms want or need.

Too large a group. Without belaboring the point, it is our opinion that regardless of the size of the firm, most large committees fail, and this is certainly true in long range planning. A committee of three lawyers to a maximum of five and the executive director is sufficient in size.

Rigid management structure. Those firms with strong nonrotating management committees waste a good deal of time doing long range planning if they go outside the parameters set up by management. A long range plan that requires departmentalization or envisions fewer associates and more paralegals could prove interesting, but only if this agrees with existing management philosophy.

Lack of set deadlines. The management committee should set deadlines for reports on progress. If this is not done, the planning for 1986 may be presented years too late to accomplish the goals. For example, a goal to be reached in 1986 may require action to start in 1984.

No priorities. The planning committee must recommend specific implementation steps in priority order. It is too easy for the remaining partners to give "lip service" to the planning concept, accept the proposed plan, then do little or nothing because priorities were not established for actually getting the plan implemented.

APPROACHING LONG RANGE PLANNING

There are many ways in which long range planning may be approached. Among these are:

- Appointment of a committee that develops a plan, by discussion or in a more or less free form basis.
- Development of a questionnaire to elicit information,

with or without follow-up discussions with partners
and associates.
- Designation of committees to "look into" various long
range issues and report to the firm.
- Creation of planning documents (usually done with a
long range planning committee).

Since planning has a better chance to succeed when done
with some structure, the appointment of a committee that attempts to develop a plan by discussion or in some free form
basis seldom works. The appointment of numerous committees, even fairly structured ones, normally delays the process
by the involvement of too many people, duplication of effort,
and lack of a unified approach. The other two approaches,
the questionnaire and the creation of planning documents,
are much more effective. Projections often are used in conjunction with the information developed in these approaches.

Development of questionnaire. This approach invites input
from all lawyers in the firm, keeps them advised that the
firm is concerned with the planning process, and *most impor-
tantly*, assures that the committee is concentrating on the
long range issues articulated by the lawyers, which may or
may not coincide with their own.

For example, the members of the committee may feel
branching or the concept of a national law firm is a major issue, yet a poll of the lawyers could indicate that the sentiment is to build the practice within the city in which the
firm is located, and there is little or no interest in expansion
out of city. The questionnaire would give the committee a basis on which to start. This approach can also elicit information on policies of the firm that management assumes are
sacrosanct.

One large firm had never taken a lateral entry in its fifty-
year history and believed the majority of both partners and
associates felt strongly about continuing this policy. Its questionnaire did not ask initially about the lateral entry policy,
but did approach this in another fashion. A few of the questions were phrased as follows:

If expansion into or development of new areas of practice is
to occur, how should this be accomplished from our internal
point of view?

_____By moving present partners and associates into new areas.

_____By moving present partners into new areas with newly hired associates.

_____By bringing new partners or associates into the firm who have established expertise and/or clientele.

Other:_____ (Comment)

After a question relating to opening branch offices in other cities, the following question was posed:

> Since geographical expansion would probably mean a change in the firm's policy regarding lateral entry lawyers, do you still favor the general concept of geographic diversity?
>
> Yes_____   No _____

The answer to the questions indicated that over 50 percent of the lawyers were willing to change the policy. It was obviously important to know this before making any long range plans related to branch offices, mergers, or acquisitions.

Development of the questionnaire can be the first job of the committee, though the development of it will require extensive discussion of the issues to be included. The results will be one basis on which to proceed.

Should you use a questionnaire, be careful in its design. You may want to keep these points in mind:

1. Explain the reason for the questionnaire and how it is to be used. Who will see it? Is it confidential? Will results be shared with the partners?

2. Though the questionnaire should be brief, do not let the fear of upsetting the respondents by the length, force you to leave out important questions. Make the questions on the first page or two brief but stimulating to capture interest.

3. Questions should be relevant to the purpose in mind. If a question does not appear to relate to the subject, but really does, give a brief explanation for its inclusion.

4. Questions should cover one issue rather than two or more so that the answer is truly responsive. For example, in the questionnaire cited previously, a specif-

ic question was asked about opening branch offices, and a separate question followed on geographical expansion as it would relate to the firm's lateral-entry policy. This is the way it should be done rather than asking one question:

Should branch offices be opened and should they be staffed with lateral entry lawyers? Yes _____ No _____

The "no" answers may refer to opening branch offices altogether, or may refer to the lateral entry question.This is a double-barreled question and should be avoided.

5. Phrase the question in a positive manner but do not encourage a particular response. For example, the question, "Don't you agree that we should continue our lateral, entry policy" would elicit more "Yes" answers than "Should the firm's lateral-entry policy be continued?" Asking in a negative fashion, "The firm should not change its lateral entry policy" and having lawyers indicate AGREE or DISAGREE may create a bias and thereby affect the reliability of the answers.

6. Have the questionnaire reviewed by someone not on the committee to make sure the lawyers responding know exactly what it is the committee wants answered.

7. Do not slant the question. For example, the question, "Should we have a structured training program for associates or just let them learn by doing?" is probably slanted due to the use of the word "just."

8. Allow space for comment on questions so the lawyers do not feel their answers must be limited.

We have worked with many firms in the creation, tabulation, and analysis of the results provided by the questionnaires. Since policy changes and other sensitive issues are covered, many firms believe respondents will be more candid and will answer in more detail if other lawyers in the firm do not see their responses.

Following is an example of the headings used in one firm's questionnaire:

1. Numerical Size
2. Geographic Diversity
3. Nature of Practice
4. Specialization/Departmentalization
5. Associate Development/Utilization
6. Partnership
7. Public/Governmental/Community involvement
8. Firm Reserve/Investment
9. Lawyer Time—Chargeable and Non-chargeable
10. Business Development
11. Management Structure
12. Administration
13. General Goals

As an example of the questions used, note the following:
  1. Associate Development/Utilization
     1.1 Should new associates be assigned to a particular department as is now the case, or during the first 2 or 3 years should they rotate to different departments to obtain experience in a variety of matters in depth from start to finish? Should they, in any event, have formal rotation within a department?

     _____Departmental assignment

     _____Rotation among departments

     _____Rotation within departments

     1.2 Explain your reasons:

     1.3 Comment on the effectiveness of training of associates now being employed by the firm. What would you recommend?

     1.4 Do you think the firm utilizes associates effectively?
     Yes _____   No _____

     1.5 If your answer to 1.4 is No, please explain how you would supervise the work of associates to utilize them better.

      1.6 Should associates who it has been deter-
      mined are not partnership material be per-
      mitted to remain with the firm:
      (a)before the "normal" time for admission to
      partnership. Yes ____No ____; or
      (b)after the "normal" time for admission to
      partnership. Yes ____No ____.
      Explain.

Developing a long range planning document. Another approach is the creation of a planning document without the
use of the questionnaire previously discussed. The format
would follow the basic design of any planning document.

1. A definition of "where we are now." This is almost
   an "instant picture" of the organization, which in itself causes much soul searching and compromise, to
   get partners to agree upon these details.
2. If the statement of "where we are now" is not acceptable as a portrait of the future, then the organization
   must make a similar "instant picture" of the firm as
   it will be some day in the future. (It is very helpful
   and logical to address all of the elements in both
   "snapshots").
3. The major effort of the organizational management
   structure is to move the firm from item 1 to item 2,
   with specific and definitive action steps with related
   timetables.

One firm using this approach set the following guidelines
in advance:

1. Appoint a small (three to four partners) committee
   made up of people who have a driving interest in the
   planning process and who are not "philosophers."
2. Make the senior administrator responsible for getting
   the plan drafted and approved by the partnership.
3. Set tight time schedules for drafting and reviewing
   sections of the plan.
4. DO NOT submit the plan "piece meal" for review to
   the other partners until it is a completed document.
5. Insist that all partners review the plan, then get it
   adopted for implementation.

6. Appoint a new planning committee each year and assign it the high priority responsibility for updating the plan, to insure that it is a dynamic document and guidebook for moving the firm forward. The planning committee should also have the responsibility of recommending specific implementation steps with related priorities, to insure that the firm is moving forward as planned.

The index for one particular five year plan follows:

INDEX TO FIVE-YEAR PLAN

Assessment of Who, What, and Where the Firm is in 1982
A. Present Positioning Statement
B. Organization and Management
   1. General
   2. Organizational Chart
   3. The Partnership (Active Partners)
   4. Consulting Partners
   5. Managing Partner
   6. Distribution Committee
   7. Management Committee
   8. Subcommittees Appointed by and Reporting to the Management Committee
      a. Billing
      b. Space
      c. Marketing
      d. Planning
      e. Social Events
      f. Retirement
      g. Branch Offices
      h. Audit
      i. Investments
   9. Subcommittees Appointed by the Partnership and Reporting to the Management Committee
      a. Associates/Paralegal Committee

a. Recruiting Committee
10. Director of Administration
11. Departments
    a. Departmental Governance
    b. Assignment of Work
    c. Departmental Quality Control and Super-
       vision
    d. Departmental Education and Training
    e. Marketing
C. Legal Practice
    1. Description of Substantive Areas
    2. Allocation of Practice
    3. Work Performance
D. Personnel
    1. Attorneys
    2. Paraprofessional Personnel
       a. Paralegals
       b. Summer Associates
       c. Law Clerks
    3. Legal Secretaries/Word Processing
    4. Administrative Staff
       a. Director of Administration
       b. Controller
       c. Accounting Staff
       d. Librarian and Staff
       e. Administrative Support Supervisor and
          Staff
       f. Administrative Coordinators
       g. Summary
E. Facilities and Equipment
    1. General
    2. Main Office
    3. Branch Office
    4. Word Processing Equipment
    5. Data Processing Equipment
    6. Miscellaneous Equipment
F. Financial
    1. Budget
    2. Setting of Compensation
       a. Partners
       b. Associates
       c. Paralegals

        d. Director of Administration
        e. Senior Administrative Staff
        f. Other Administrative Staff
    3. Types of Fee Arrangements
        a. Statutory fees
        b. Contingent fees
        c. Court approved fees
        d. Miscellaneous special fees
    4. Billing Rates

II. Assessment of Who, What, and Where the Firm Wants to be in 1987
a. 1987 Positioning Statement
b. Organization
    1. Managing Partner
    2. Consulting Partners
    3. Committees
    4. Departments
    5. Administration
C. Legal Practice
    1. Types of Practice
    2. Main Office
    3. Branch Offices
    4. Legal Departments
d. Personnel
    1. Attorneys
    2. Paraprofessional
    3. Legal Secretaries/Word Processing
    4. Administrative
E. Facilities and Equipment
    1. Offices
    2. Main Office
    3. Branch Office
    4. Word Processing Equipment
    5. Data Processing Equipment
    6. Miscellaneous Equipment
F. Financial
    1. Budget and Financial Management
    2. Setting of Compensation
        a. Partners
        b. Others
    3. Fees

Though this is an effective way in which to plan, it is time consuming and probably puts most of the work on the committee and requires little from the other lawyers. If this method is used, make sure that the committee gets good lawyer input before the final plan is written and presented.

WHERE DOES THE PLANNING GO?

Though many firms have found what they call their long range planning to be an interesting exercise, after presenting the results to the partners, and perhaps even discussing them, nothing is done. The major step is designing or adopting policies to see that the plan is implemented. The plan, without a program of action which includes priorities and time tables will not accomplish the purpose.

The firm must adopt the plan, or portions of it. Management then must assign the implementation and follow through to see that action is taken. Portions of the implementation may be left to the long range planning committee, with other areas assigned to appropriate lawyers or administrative staff. Using this approach, the planning that has been done will prove to be more than just an interesting philosophical exercise.

IS IT WORTH IT?

A large law firm recently discussed drawing up a long range plan and projecting the numbers. After considerable discussion including an estimate of our consulting fees as well as lawyer time involved, the managing partner concluded that long range planning is an inexact experiment requiring periodic review and up-date which may or may not prove useful though it would certainly provide interesting information. He ended his summary by asking, "Is it worth it?"

The answer to the question he asks calls for a few questions in return.

- Are the lawyers in the firm unconcerned with the future?
- Does anyone but the management committee worry about these things?
- Has the firm done any long range planning?

Normally, the answer to these questions is "no." This leaves the major question—Is it worth the time and money to force the lawyers to participate in the process of planning for the future and to let them know that management is concerned with that future and wants them to be, too? The answer to this question is an unqualified "yes." The managing partner also answered affirmatively.

If a law firm today is in any doubt about engaging in long range planning, it should review what changes occurred in the firm between 1970 and 1980 and how well prepared it was to deal with those changes. The legal profession can expect to see as many or more changes in the 80's and 90's. Thus, even the inexact science of long range planning is preferable to the crisis management that exists in most law firms today.

APPENDIX A

A Checklist for Mergers

Delegating Tasks by Committee

A Checklist for Mergers

ONLY A SMALL percentage of law firm merger negotiations actually result in a merger. Aside from the many broad reasons for the breakdown of negotiations — such as incompatible philosophies or economic differences — failures sometimes result simply from inadequate preparation by one or both firms.

In mergers involving larger firms, the establishment of committees can greatly facilitate this preparation, particularly because of the complexity of the information that must be exchanged. Mergers are extraordinarily time-consuming endeavors, and the partners who are most actively involved can find their billable hours significantly diminished. The establishment of committees allows a few lawyers from each firm to accomplish much of the leg-work in combining the practices, thus eliminating the need for involvement by the full partnership, except for review and formal approval.

What follows is a list of the committees most commonly employed in larger law firm mergers. These committees are utilized only during the merger process and are usually terminated at some point after the merger is formalized.

(Many of these steps are crucial for mergers involving smaller firms.)

LAW FIRM MERGER COMMITTEE FUNCTIONS

I. Merger Committee

This committee is responsible for overall merger negotiations. It makes final decisions on the terms of the merger prior to submission for partnership approval.

1.01 Agree on the firm name.
1.02 Agree on the level of financial information for the partners (economic analysis).
1.03 Approve a partners' compensation plan and agree on levels of compensation.
1.04 Finalize the method of merger.

• Consider potential "vested interest" problem.
• Determine most advantageous method of combining assets.
• Develop a plan for valuation of assets.
• Determine how work-in-process and accounts receivable will be handled.
• Develop procedures and provide direction to each firm regarding billing and collections prior to merger.
• If necessary, determine most advantageous method of dissolving and /or combining the entities.

1.05 Choose members of executive committee and define their terms of office.
1.06 Define the responsibilities of the executive committee, the administrator and other committees.
1.07 Appoint a post-merger committee.
1.08 Decide on procedures for press releases and communication with news media.
1.09 Decide how liabilities to former partners will be handled.
1.10 Agree on the form of the merger announcement.
1.11 Prepare a budget.
1.12 Select an accounting firm to work on the merger.

II. Tax, Insurance and Benefits Committee

A. Tax

2.1 Select the best structure for the firm to minimize taxes.
2.2 Determine how the firm should set its compensation policy to minimize taxes.
2.3 Ascertain the local and state taxes that will be applicable to the two offices and their employees.

B. Insurance

2.4 List the insurance policies currently in effect for each office.
2.5 Select the policies that can and should be continued.
2.6 Decide whether insurance should be carried by each office or by the firm as a whole.
2.7 Determine what the firm's professional liability coverage should be.
2.8 Determine whether the firm should carry key-man life insurance for any directors/partners, and if so, how much.
2.9 Decide whether the firm should carry disability insurance for directors/partners or any employees, and if so, how much.
2.10 Determine whether the firm should carry group life insurance for directors/partners or any employees, and if so, how much.
2.11 Decide what medical and hospitalization insurance should be obtained for employees.
2.12 Determine what liability insurance the firm should have.

C. Benefits

2.13 Determine whether either pension plan or profit-sharing plan should be continued in its present form, integrated, or replaced with a new plan.
2.14 Decide what plans should be adopted by the firm and under what terms.
2.15 List other benefits that should be available to directors/partners and/or other employees, such as medical reimbursement, parking fees, business club dues, professional association and bar dues.
2.16 Calculate the financial impact of the new pension and profit-sharing plans.

III. Agreements Committee

This committee works closely with the tax, insurance and benefits committee and makes recommendations to the merger committee on legal and tax aspects of the merger.

3.1 In coordination with the tax, insurance and benefits committee, research the issues and make recommendations to the merger committee on the structure of the merger, considering all legal and tax aspects.
3.2 Based on the information from the merger committee, prepare all documents necessary to effect the merger, including:
• Merger agreement.
• Incorporation documents.
• Stock agreements.
• Employment agreements.
(The pension and profit-sharing plans will be prepared by the tax, insurance and benefits committee.)

IV. Practice/Integration Committee

A. Organization

4.1 Decide how the firm's practice should be organized and whether the firm should be divided into divisions and sections.
4.2 If the firm is organized into divisions or sections, how formal should the division organization be.
• List the functions each division should perform.
• Determine how the divisions should be staffed.
• Determine what divisions and sections should be established.
• Decide if there should be periodic divisional meetings between the two offices.
• Decide whether there should be a division chairman, and if so, what his role should be.
4.3 If the firm is not to be organized into divisions or sections, decide what other mechanism, if any, should be used to facilitate communication among lawyers in the same general area of practice.

B. Practice Capacity

4.4 Determine the specialties and sub-specialties of each lawyer and paralegal in the firm.
4.5 Ascertain how these abilities fit with the firm's current practice and manpower requirements.
4.6 Forecast additional potential requirements of the firm.
4.7 Determine what methods, if any, should be adopted to inform attorneys of the expertise and experience of all lawyers in the firm. (Coordinate with the business development committee.)

C. Practice Integration

4.8 Decide what methods should be adopted to integrate the practices of the two offices.
4.9 Determine how work assignments should be made.
4.10 Determine feasibility of staffing a project with attorneys from both offices. If it is, decide how this would best be done.
4.11 List the methods that should be used to communicate work requirements and time availability between attorneys of the two offices.
4.12 Decide whether attorneys should be transferred between the two firms on a temporary or permanent basis, and if so, how transfers should be accomplished.
4.13 Determine how lawyers can best be kept informed on a continuing basis about the work being done by other attorneys in the firm.

D. Practice Management

4.14 Determine what procedures should be adopted to handle existing (if any) and potential conflicts of interest involving clients of the two offices. (Coordinate with business development committee.)
4.15 Decide what methods should be adopted, if any, to monitor performance of legal services by lawyers in both offices.

4.16 Determine advisability of developing rules concerning rendering legal opinions, the preparation of registration statements and other sensitive documents, and supervising closings.

4.17 List procedures such as form files, legal memoranda files, etc., that should be developed to make the practice more efficient.

4.18 Decide how these matters can best be coordinated and how form documents can be used by lawyers in both offices. (Coordinate with the systems and procedures committee.)

4.19 Decide whether a practice handbook should be developed, and if so, what it should cover.

E. General Information
4.20 Formulate a plan to maintain the integration of the two offices.

4.21 Decide whether there should be periodic firm functions, and if so, how often and in what forms.

4.22 Determine whether there should be a permanent integration committee to deal with this issue on a continuing basis.

V. Associate/Paralegal Committee
This committee reviews existing personnel, hiring practices, compensation and training and evaluation.

A. Existing Personnel
5.01 List the specialties, abilities and experience of existing personnel. (Coordinate with the practice/integration committee.)

5.02 List current assignments, compensation, and work evaluations of existing personnel. Additionally, for associates determine their prospects and eligibility for directorship/partnership.

5.03 Determine whether the rotation system for younger associates should be continued, and if so, how the system should operate.

5.04 Decide how work assignments for associates and paralegals should be made.

5.05 Determine what policy should be adopted for transferring associates between the two offices. (Coordinate with the practice/integration committee.)

B. Hiring
5.06 Ascertain the current associate recruitment and paralegal hiring practices of the two offices.

5.07 Decide what the practice of the integrated firm should be.

5.08 List the firm's associate and paralegal needs for the coming year. (Coordinate with the practice/integration committee.)

5.09 Decide whether the firm should have a policy emphasizing the hiring of permanent paralegals or of paralegals who intend to enter law school in the future.

5.10 Decide how associate recruitment should be conducted this fall.

5.11 Formulate the role of the recruiting committee.

5.12 List law schools that should be visited.

5.13 Agree on how hiring decisions should be made.

5.14 Decide whether prospective associates should be given a choice of the office they wish to join. If so, determine how will this affect the firm's needs.

5.15 Determine what type of summer associate program should be developed and how should it be administered.

5.16 Decide what policy should be adopted for hiring associates during the year or for particular firm needs.

5.17 Formulate policy on hiring lateral entrants or associates with government experience.

5.18 Calculate how much "credit" should be given for clerkships and other experience.

B. Compensation
5.19 Calcuate what the starting salary for new associates should be.

5.20 Decide whether there should be a dual compensation plan for the two offices.

5.21 Determine whether the firm should pay one-time bonuses to new associates, moving expenses, bar examination course fees, bar dues, etc.

5.22 Decide if the compensation should be a straight salary or whether there should be bonuses or other incentive plans.

5.23 Decide if the compensation of associates should be on a step-seniority basis or whether raises should reflect individual merit.

5.24 Determine whether deferred compensation and fringe benefits should affect direct compensation. (Coordinate with the tax, insurance and benefits committee.)

5.25 Decide what adjustments should be made to compensation of existing associates because of increases in starting salaries.

D. Training & Evaluation
5.26 Select the type of program that should be adopted for training and supervising associates and paralegals.

5.27 Choose the evaluation systems that should be used for associates and paralegals.

5.28 Decide how often and in what form performance should be evaluated and communicated to individuals.

5.29 Determine what evaluation standards should be used.

5.30 Determine what the standards should be for eligibility for directorship/partnership in terms of time out of law school, time with the firm, etc.

5.31 Decide how the firm should deal with associates and paralegals having difficulty.

5.32 List policies that should be adopted to deal with the termination of associates.

5.33 Determine which current associates and paralegals are likely to leave the firm in the near future.

E. General
5.34 Decide whether there should be a permanent associate/paralegal committee.

5.35 Determine what policies, if any, should be developed to enhance associate morale and communication, and the integration of associates in the two offices. (Coordinate with the practice/integration committee.)

VI. Systems Procedures Committee
This committee reviews integration of systems and procedures, administrative policies and administrative personnel.

A. Integration of Systems and Procedures
6.01 Review and analyze all existing systems and procedures of both offices and make recommendations for improving and integrating those systems and procedures, including the following:

• Communications — telephone systems; direct lines between offices; accounting for toll calls; telex, Dex, and special equipment.

• Word Processing — format; use and operation; expansion and coordination of systems and communication between offices; printers and scanners; charges to clients; staffing of operators.

• Computer — terminals and printers; use and operation; capabilities (legal and non-legal work); priorities in use; expansion, coordination and communication between offices; staffing of operators.

• Billing — timekeeping methods; client and attorney codes and numbering; methods for reporting billing information to attorneys; methods for preparing and sending bills.

• Accounting and Financial — bookkeeping systems; preparation of various interim and periodic financial and operational reports; attorney expense reports and petty cash controls.

• Lexis/Westlaw — use and operation; charges to clients.

• Library — acquisition procedures; inventory of books and services; control procedures; staffing.

• Filing — central or attorney system; procedures for establishing files; maintenance, transfer, storage and disposal of files.

• Mail Room — procedures for handling mail; procedures for intra- and inter-office communications; circulation policies; charging for postage; other services (staffing); procedures for messenger and courier services.

• Duplicating Equipment — number and type of equipment; policies for duplicating and controls; charges to clients.

• Supplies — system for acquiring and dispensing letterhead and other office material; maintenance of inventories; various forms used by the office.

• Office Equipment — inventory of typewriters, dictating machines, etc.; methods of distribution; system for procurement.

• Security — physical security for offices; safekeeping practices for clients; security for client files, wills, and other instruments.

• Bank Accounts — banks with which offices do business; deposit and loan practices and procedures; client escrow accounts.

• Finance — payroll system; checkwriting procedures; taxes (withholding and payment system); investment of revenues.

• Office Furniture — inventory; procurement procedures (common areas, associates, directors/partners).

B. Administration
6.02 Determine how the administration of the two offices should be integrated.

6.03 Decide whether there should be a single firm administrator or an administrator for each office.

6.04 Make recommendations concerning the best way to integrate the administration of the two offices.

C. Administrative Personnel
6.05 List the current administrative (including secretarial) personnel of each office.

6.06 Determine what additional personnel, if any, will be needed.

6.07 Decide whether the secretarial systems of the two offices should be the same.

6.08 If they should, decide what policies should govern hiring, compensation, assignments, training, evaluation, and termination.

6.09 List the current policies toward administrative personnel and determine how they can be improved.

6.10 Decide whether the firm should adopt policies for the transfer of administrative personnel.

Mr. Akins is senior vice president and director of Bradford W. Hildebrandt & Co. Inc., a management consulting firm based in Union, N.J. He manages the firm's Dallas office.

APPENDIX B

Sample Law Firm Newsletter

LEGAL UPDATE from

MEMEL, JACOBS, PIERNO & GERSH

News of legal developments for organizations and individuals

Offices at
1801 Century Park East, Twenty-Fifth Floor • Los Angeles, California 90067 • (213) 556-2000
Suite 350, 4000 MacArthur Boulevard • Newport Beach, California 92660 • (714) 975-0244
Suite 785, 555 Capitol Mall • Sacramento, California 95814 • (916) 446-6941
TWX: 910-490-5923 • Cable: L'AVOCAT

In this issue:

Volume 1, Number 1

HEALTH DEPARTMENT NOTES

Hospitals risk tax-exempt status when partnered with private interests

In attempts to reduce costs or increase income, tax-exempt hospitals are increasingly becoming involved in partnerships and joint ventures with profit-making parties. Such projects have involved their clinical programs, for example, to construct laboratory facilities and to lease equipment, as well as real estate ventures, such as to construct medical office buildings and apartment complexes. Such involvement, however, could jeopardize a hospital's tax-exempt status.

Most nonprofit hospitals are tax-exempt under Section 501(c)(3) of the Internal Revenue Code, which for exemption requires that a hospital be operated to serve public rather than private interests and that no part of its net earnings benefits private parties. Clearly, joint ventures or partnerships with private, profit-making concerns can pose a risk to a hospital's tax-exempt status.

But the risk can be minimized by careful structuring and implementation of such projects. For example, the IRS approved a general partnership between a hospital and a commercial laboratory to construct a joint laboratory facility. And the IRS approved participation by an exempt hospital with proprietary hospitals in a shared laundry facility. In both cases, the non-exempt participants didn't benefit disproportionately because of the participation by a tax-exempt hospital.

Limited partnerships, particularly those in which the hospital is a general partner, are subject to even greater scrutiny by the IRS. In a recent case, a hospital proposed to become one of three general partners with 35 limited partners in a limited partnership formed to construct a housing project. The IRS said that by agreeing to serve as one of the general partners, the hospital would be taking on an obligation to further the private financial interests of the partners, which would be incompatible with its exclusively charitable function.

However, all participation in limited partnerships is not prohibited. In another case, a carefully structured limited partnership involving a hospital, a subsidiary of the hospital, and members of its medical staff, formed to construct a medical office building on the hospital campus, was approved by the IRS.

A hospital should be reluctant to become involved directly with a developer or members of its medical staff in a joint venture or partnership unless it is assured that the risks are borne by all parties in proportion to their investments, or unless there are compelling reasons for doing otherwise. In many cases, the prudent course of action for a hospital considering such involvement is to obtain a private ruling from the IRS on the potential effect of the transaction on its tax-exempt status. Still, of course, extreme care must be used in the implementation and operation of the project.

Medicare reimbursement expanded for hospital telephones

Because telephones for patients are considered "luxury items," Medicare and Medi-Cal don't reimburse hospitals for the expense of providing such telephones. Appeals to the Provider Reimbursement Review Board (PRRB), the federal Medicare appeal agency, based on the therapeutic value of patient telephones, have been consistently rejected.

However, as a result of recent decisions of the PRRB, hospitals may be able to receive reimbursement for some of the expenses of providing patient telephones when such expenses can be allocated to the hospital central telephone system.

For hospitals operating private branch exchange (PBX) systems—that is, through a central switchboard—the allocations developed by the PRRB are as follows:

Station costs and installation and removal costs for patient telephones connected with a PBX system are directly related to patient telephones and therefore non-reimbursable. However, remaining expenses, including operator salaries, switching equipment costs, trunk line, costs, and telephone testing costs are not directly related to patient telephones and, therefore, are reimbursable because they would exist whether or not telephones were provided for patients. Hospitals may also be reimbursed for an increased share of indirect costs (such as administrative and general expense) allocable to the PBX system instead of patient telephones.

In addition to PBX systems, the Board recently revised

its policy with regard to Centrex systems. In one case (Bethesda Hospital v. Blue Cross Association/Blue Cross of Central Ohio), the PRRB allowed a provider to allocate substantial portions of its patient telephone costs to intercom capacity for those telephones. The Board decided that because the intercom portion of the telephone system would not be used by the patient for personal convenience, it was related to patient care. The hospital was able to substantiate the amount reimbursable because its local telephone company billed it separately for telephone costs for the intercom portion of the system and the out-call portion. Thus, appropriate planning and record-keeping is required to qualify such expenses for reimbursement.

These decisions by the PRRB will not permit providers to recover all costs attributable to patient telephone systems, but may permit hospitals to increase the share of telephone costs attributable to reimbursable patient care activities.

Of course, a hospital may have to appeal to the PRRB to secure these increases if the government opposes the PRRB's new allocations.

(As this newsletter goes to press, we have learned that the Administrator of the Health Care Financing Administration has overturned at least one of the PRRB's decisions involving a PBX system (Edgewater Hospital v. Blue Cross Association). However, we have not been able to review the written decision in the case and, therefore, cannot assess the precedential effect of this reversal. We will report on this decision in a future edition of this newsletter.)

1

CORPORATE & TAX DEPARTMENT NOTES

Franchising on the rise again

At a time when interest rates and inflation have made bank financing costly and weakened invested capital, there is a resurgence of interest in franchising. Why? Because it represents an alternative financing method for a company considering how to raise funds for expansion.

Always around in one form or another, the franchising concept reached a peak of popularity in the late 60's and early 70's. Even though it ebbed later in the 70's, it remained an important aspect of the economy. Now it is again expanding significantly.

While there are some drawbacks, franchising offers many companies an economical way to expand.

For a company that wishes to expand but does not want to dilute its equity or use costly bank financing, a soundly-managed franchise program offers the ability to add outlets without capital outlay, while creating an expanded income stream through franchise fees, royalties, and increased sales. The impact of common image and name identification through franchising is legendary. (The prime example is McDonald's.) Other potential benefits include the cost savings of mass purchasing and the use of pooled advertising funds to make an impact often greater than the sum of its parts.

Legally, franchising has some pitfalls that can be readily avoided with sound counseling and advance planning. A variety of state laws (including California's) regulate the offer and sale of franchises, and the Federal Trade Commission in 1979 adopted a Franchising Disclosure Rule that is similar in concept to most state laws. Coordination among the states and with the FTC in the franchising area began over a decade ago, and has continued to be reasonably effective. As a result, there are uniform standards, making compliance easier.

In general, the state laws consider a franchise to exist when a fee is charged for the right to use a name or logo while following a prescribed plan of business. The fee can be direct or indirect, and the courts and state regulators have been liberal in finding the indirect payment of a fee. The FTC definition is even less specific and more encompassing than most state laws.

Under either approach, where a franchise does exist, full disclosure to potential franchisees is required at the time of an offer and before a franchise agreement can be validly completed. This is accomplished in California by registering with the Commissioner of Corporations and preparing a formal disclosure document. The same basic document with certain cover pages will normally suffice in other states and with the FTC.

The preparation of registration and disclosure materials, the development of the franchise concept, and implementation of the franchise program must all be done with extreme care.

If the franchise agreement is prepared improperly, it can cause many otherwise avoidable problems. They range from antitrust violations to running afoul of state laws or standards, failure to properly deal with royalty payments, and failure to properly protect proprietary rights of the franchisor.

Apart from the legal work, the heart of every franchisor's success—or failure— lies in its marketing plan, its franchise operations manual and its training and field programs. They are quite different from those utilized by nonfranchised businesses because, in addition to knowledge of the business being franchised, they require unique knowledge of franchising. You know your business, but it is unlikely that you know franchising. Therefore, either hire a skilled and knowledgeable franchise director and staff (costly) or utilize a consultant (perhaps not as costly) and eventually train or develop your own knowledgeable staff.

There are a number of skilled and knowledgeable franchise consultants. But there are also some "consultants" who have been charging very big fees upfront for services that are, at best, unsatisfactory. Make sure you are dealing with a knowledgeable, legitimate and reputable consultant.

Many who should consider franchising never think about it. Many who try it, do it either prematurely, ill-advisedly, or improperly. But for those who use care, franchising may yield advantages they did not even expect.

Reagan Administration tax and stock policies to help business

Proposed tax and securities policies of the Reagan Administration should provide substantial benefits to business, said Joel Bernstein of Memel, Jacobs, Pierno & Gersh's Corporate Department, in an address to the American Electronics Association's recent Chief Executive Luncheon.

He reported how Administration proposals in the Economic Recovery Tax Bill of 1981 would affect companies in the electronics industry and other businesses by providing a faster method of writing off capital expenditures. The Accelerated Cost Recovery System, he explained, allows faster write-off periods for machinery and equipment used in business and for owner-occupied structures used for manufacturing and distribution. The accelerated depreciation schedules constitute a more liberal recovery allowance than presently allowed.

Bernstein also talked about recent and possible upcoming changes in federal securities laws, providing expanded exemptions from federal registration of securities offerings. The Small Business Investment Act of 1980 exempts from registration securities offerings to accredited investors if there is no public solicitation and the total amount sold is $5 million or less.

The Securities and Exchange Commission is also considering raising the sales ceilings on unregistered public offerings, limited offers, and sales of small offerings by closely-held businesses.

Recent and expected changes in securities regulations will assist many businesses in avoiding the time, trouble, and expense of federal registration of securities offerings.

2

An important tax reminder—exercise qualified stock options before May 21, 1981

Employees who received *qualified* stock options in their companies should exercise those options *prior to May 21, 1981*, assuming, of course, that the fair market value of the underlying stock is, or is expected to be, higher than the exercise price of the option.

Exercising qualified stock options on or after that date will cause them to be treated as nonqualified, so that the employee's tax liability is incurred at the time of exercise and is greater.

The value of a qualified stock option exercised prior to May 21 is not taxed at the time of option exercise. If the stock is held for three or more years before it is sold, the profit from that sale (calculated as the excess, if any, of fair market value at sale over the price paid at option exercise) is *taxed at time of sale as capital gain.*

In contrast, exercising a qualified stock option on or after May 21 causes it to be considered for tax purposes the same as a nonqualified stock option. Thus, profit at time of exercise (calculated as excess, if any, of fair market value at date of exercise over the option exercise price) is *taxed at time of exercise as ordinary income.*

Clearly, the tax advantages of qualified stock options over nonqualified, call for an employee to exercise his qualified stock option before the deadline.

A word of warning is necessary to employees who are also officers, directors, or principal shareholders of corporations registered under the Securities Exchange Act of 1934. They should check to see if they have sold any of their employer's stock within six months prior to exercise of stock options. Such exercise could violate the "short swing profit" rule of the Securities Exchange Act. This rule was set up to prevent insiders from using inside information to profit in stock transactions of their own company. It provides that if an insider buys stock and then sells it within six months or vice versa, any profit is assumed to be the result of inside information and is turned over to the corporation. Therefore, selling an employer's stock and within six months exercising an option could violate this rule.

With that exception, others should make sure to exercise their qualified stock options *before* the deadline, May 21, 1981.

REAL ESTATE DEPARTMENT NOTES

Timesharing regulations benefit consumers and developers

Proposed California regulations of timeshare real estate projects should benefit consumers and responsible developers alike.

This was the message David G. Ellsworth, partner in charge of the Real Estate Department of Memel, Jacobs, Pierno & Gersh, told the National Resort Timesharing Conference/81 at the Peachtree Plaza Hotel in Atlanta, Georgia, co-sponsored by the American Land Development Association (ALDA) and the publisher of *Resort Timesharing TODAY.* He explained, for example, that California now considers timeshare projects (comprising 12 or more timeshares) as subdivision offerings requiring public reports or disclosure documents, protecting the consumers in buying timeshares. The proposed regulations, he pointed out, follow in many respects the ALDA model timeshare ownership act, which he helped draft, and should be welcomed by the many respectable, responsible timeshare developers, whose business is hurt by the few unscrupulous or defaulting developers.

Timesharing, simply put, is the purchase by an individual of a fixed or floating time interval—the same recurring week each year or any time for seven days each year reserved on an advanced reservation basis—in a hotel, motel, apartment building, condominium or home. It enables those who cannot afford or do not want a year-round vacation home to own the right to that home for only the time each year they wish to use it.

With the passage in 1980 of California Senate Bill 1736, the DRE has express and specific jurisdiction over the sale of all timeshare projects in the state, as of January 1, 1981. Previously, right-to-use timeshares or timeshare uses—those in which the buyer obtained only the right to use the facility for a certain number of years, but not a proprietary

interest in the real property—were generally not included under DRE jurisdiction. The DRE has always had jurisdiction over the offering and sale of timeshare real estate projects—those in which a proprietary estate in real property is conveyed to the timeshare purchaser.

Projects located out-of-state and in foreign countries come under the new legislation and proposed DRE regulations if the sales are conducted in California.

Ellsworth also presented a complete overview of the regulations proposed for adoption by the DRE and the various methods to legally structure timeshare programs.

Tax rules simplified for installment sales

Congress recently enacted the Installment Sales Revision Act of 1980, modifying or eliminating some of the basic technical requirements which hindered use of the installment sales method of reporting income.

The installment method of reporting income (Internal Revenue Code Section 453) allows income from the sale of real property to be reported in the year each installment payment is received, recognizing gain and the taxes due on such gain in future years. The amount of gain on each installment payment is directly proportional to the total amount of gain (gross profit) on the total amount of installment payments (total contract price).

Often, taxpayers had difficulty qualifying for this method of reporting income because of strict technical requirements. Failure to comply with such requirements meant recognition of *all* gain in the year of sale.

3

Now, Congress has made it easier to qualify for installment reporting, by making the following requirement changes:

- **No maximum downpayment.** The previous requirement limiting downpayment to 30 percent or less of the sales price is entirely eliminated.
- **One payment rule.** In the past, a seller was forced to recognize at least a token downpayment in the year of sale. This is no longer the case. All payments can be deferred to a later year.
- **No election required.** Before, taxpayers had to elect the installment method. Now, if payment is received in a year later than year of sale, installment reporting is automatically applied.
- **Contingent sales price.** Previously, the sales price had to be fixed. Now, installment reporting is available when the sales price of real property is subject to a contingency (for example, when sales price is calculated as a multiple of gross income earned). Income is reported pro rata as each installment is received, using the maximum selling price specified in the sales contract for all computations. If the maximum selling price is not achieved, the taxpayer's income is recomputed.
- **Third-party guarantee.** Third-party guarantees used as security for installment payments are no longer considered as payments received on the installment obligation. To qualify, the guarantees must not be marketable or otherwise transferable before default by the purchaser.
- **Receipt of like-kind property.** The value of like-kind property received by the taxpayer as part of the sale is no longer included when calculating total sales price and the gain on each installment payment.

LITIGATION DEPARTMENT NOTES

Rights and obligations changed in subpoenaing records

Two recent additions to the California Code of Civil Procedure significantly affect the rights and obligations of businesses and persons from whom documents are subpoenaed.

Code of Civil Procedure, Section 1987.4 provides that the custodian of records is now entitled to obtain "reasonable costs" from the party issuing a Subpoena Duces Tecum for locating and producing records. The custodian of records is entitled to such reasonable costs, upon demand, *prior to* delivering the subpoenaed records.

"Reasonable costs" means "actual copying costs plus any additional reasonable clerical costs incurred in locating and making the records available. Such additional clerical costs shall be based on a computation of the time spent locating and making the records available multiplied by the employee's hourly wage."

The right is limited to a business "which is neither a party nor the place where any cause of action is alleged to have arisen." Although unclear, presumably this means that a business on whose premises an accident occurred would not be entitled to its reasonable costs for producing the records.

In a separate development, Code of Civil Procedure, Section 1985.3, which becomes operative on July 1, 1981, is intended to protect the privacy of a person whose personal records are subpoenaed from a physician, hospital, bank, savings and loan, credit union, trust company, insurance company, attorney, or accountant.

The statute requires that the party subpoenaing the personal records must, at least 15 days prior to the date called for the production of those records, serve the Subpoena Duces Tecum on the person whose records are being sought. At the same time, the subpoenaing party must serve the party holding the records a certificate attesting that the subpoena has been served on the person whose records are being sought.

The statute allows the person whose records are sought to bring a Motion to Quash or Modify the Subpoena. In that case, the agent holding the records is not required to produce the records, except upon order of the court or agreement of the affected parties.

Evidence disclosure required in administrative hearings

In an appeal brought before the Commodity Futures Trading Commission by Memel, Jacobs, Pierno & Gersh, the federal Commission decided that a defendant in an administrative proceeding is constitutionally entitled to force disclosure by the government of any evidence favorable to the defense.

By unanimous decision, the four-member Commission reversed a trial judge's order and held that its prosecutorial division must disclose any information it has which is helpful to a defendant in a license suspension proceeding. The decision may also encompass proceedings in which a fine alone may be imposed for misconduct by the licensee.

The disclosure of information by parties to litigation which aids the case of the opposing party, commonly known as "discovery," is required in most state and federal court civil cases and to a limited extent in all criminal cases. But it was not previously required in most administrative adjudications.

The Commission determined that "as a matter of due process" the government must supply the defendant evidence of which it is aware that helps disprove guilt or affects the degree of punishment appropriate. All doubts as to the necessity of disclosure must be resolved in favor of the defendant.

Other material which must be provided, according to the Commission, includes transcripts of testimony, signed statements, and substantially verbatim reports of interviews from the investigation or concerning witnesses to be called at the hearing.

While decisions of the Commodity Futures Trading Commission are not binding upon other federal or state admin-istrative agencies or courts, its decisions are persuasive authority for other tribunals and are often relied upon.

If the decision does serve as precedent in other adminis-trative areas, an accused will benefit from the investigatory resources of the government in that any favorable evidence discovered by the government will have to be disclosed.

TORTS DEPARTMENT NOTES

Do you have enough automobile insurance?

There once was a time in California when an automobile driver was adequately protected by insurance covering him for $100,000 per person for injuries/$300,000 in total for personal injuries/$25,000 for property damage. Of course, those were also the days when you could buy a car for $3,000, borrow money at 7 percent interest, and mail a letter for 8 cents.

Today anything less than $1 million of liability insurance coverage is inadequate. Unfortunately, insurance com-panies do not voluntarily offer excess coverage. You must specifically ask for it and insist on receiving it. You should secure a basic policy of $100,000 per person, $300,000 ag-gregate, and $25,000 property damage. However, an excess policy (with a $100,000/$300,000/$25,000 deductible) should be purchased covering the next $1 million of liability claims, both for personal injuries and property damage. This type of excess policy is relatively inexpensive, especially when you consider the possible catastrophic economic impact if you or any member of your family is involved in an accident.

Though the law requires that a motorist be covered for only $15,000/$30,000 in personal injury insurance, that is obviously inadequate. Even coverage for $100,000/$300,000/ $25,000 is penny wise and dollar foolish. Personal injury verdicts can easily exceed that coverage, leaving you to pay the difference. With the high cost of cars on the road and other property which could be involved, such damages could easily add up to more than the applicable coverage of $25,000. Totally destroy one Mercedes-Benz and you are over your limit. The difference comes out of your pocket—unless you have additional insurance.

Excess insurance is a smart investment, even if your income and assets are modest. From a social responsibility standpoint, if through your fault you cause serious injury to another person, shouldn't you at least be in a position to lessen the economic consequences of the injuries on that person's life? Also, from a financial standpoint, many people today have assets which would be jeopardized by accident settlements in excess of their insurance coverage. A home-owner is a perfect example, since the sharp rise in real estate values has resulted in equities that exceed the homestead protection provided by law.

Businessmen must also take into account their exposure due to the driving activities of their employees, agents or partners. Though the "going and coming rule" (traveling to and from work) excludes such travel from the scope of em-ployment, there are numerous exceptions to the rule and those exceptions grow each year. You should obtain a gen-eral comprehensive personal liability policy covering your-self individually and a comprehensive business liability policy covering your commercial enterprises.

LABOR DEPARTMENT NOTES

No Medicare money for hospitals' anti-union expenses

The Health Care Financing Administration (HCFA) recently reaffirmed its policy to deny reimbursement to hospitals for any costs incurred in persuading employees to reject unionization. Costs for influencing employees whether or not to organize, to form a union, or to join an existing union are not related to patient care and, therefore, not allowable Medicare costs.

Providers had objected that the policy violated manage-ment's right and responsibility to keep their employees informed. HCFA replied that it did not intend to interfere with such communication, but that the costs were nonreimburs-able.

Also, HCFA found no merit in the argument that union activity, by possibly causing discord in a hospital, could adversely affect patient care.

Rejected as well was the objection that unions cause higher wages and thus raise health care costs for patients.

To charges that it was pro-union, HCFA responded that its policy was neither pro- nor anti-union, but merely based on the union issue bearing no relationship to health care.

HCFA does allow reimbursement for expenses of collec-tive bargaining and related activities including contract negotiations and contract enforcement. Also, cost of con-sultants and attorneys retained to familiarize supervisors and employees with labor law are generally allowable Medi-care costs.

5

Office of Civil Rights limited in employment discrimination cases

The Department of Health and Human Services' Office of Civil Rights was restricted by a federal court of appeals to investigating employment discrimination only in programs funded primarily to provide employment.

When Cabrini Medical Center, a hospital receiving Medicare and Medicaid funds from the federal government, discharged a laundry employee, the employee claimed he was discriminated against because of a mental disability.

The Office of Civil Rights (OCR) contended it was authorized to investigate the complaint pursuant to Sections 504 and 505 of the Rehabilitation Act of 1973. The District Court granted OCR's petition to investigate, asserting that Section 504 was designed to eliminate discrimination under any program or activity receiving federal assistance without regard to the purpose for which the funds were received.

Reversing the District Court, the U.S. Court of Appeals concluded that OCR was not authorized to investigate. It cited Title VI of the 1976 Civil Rights Act which restricts OCR jurisdiction to investigate employment discrimination in those programs funded primarily to provide employment. The court determined that the hospital's receipt of Medicare and Medicaid funds did not constitute receipt of financial assistance for providing employment. Also rejected was OCR's argument that it be permitted to investigate whether or not the primary objective of the federal assistance was to provide employment.

OCR continues to aggressively investigate complaints of discrimination by terminated employees. The position of OCR appears to be that it will not follow *Cabrini* until there is a Supreme Court determination of its jurisdiction.

If *Cabrini* is upheld, OCR—while still having authority over facility and admission discrimination—will be restricted in investigating claims of employment discrimination. Also, upholding of this case will help prevent agency overlap, a problem commonly faced by personnel departments when several bites of the same discrimination apple are taken by the EEOC, state agencies and OCR. This was the case in *Cabrini*, for example, where the complaint had already been investigated by other agencies prior to OCR.

Employee in discrimination cases entitled to see own file

When the Just Horn Company, a division of Associated Drygoods Corporation, refused to turn over to the Equal Employment Opportunity Commission personnel records of employees charging the company with discrimination, because it did not want those employees to see their files, the Supreme Court ruled that each employee has the right to see the information in his own file.

During a two-year period, seven Horn employees filed employment discrimination charges with the EEOC, six alleging sex discrimination and one alleging racial discrimination. The EEOC began its investigation by requesting Horn to provide the employment records of the complainants, and statistics, documents, and other information relating to Horn's general personnel practices. Horn refused unless the EEOC agreed not to disclose these materials to the charging parties. The Commission refused to give this assurance, explaining its practice of making limited disclosure to a charging party of information in other files when he needs the information in connection with a potential lawsuit. When Horn continued to refuse to give any information without an assurance of secrecy, the EEOC subpoenaed the materials. Horn sued to stop the subpoena from being enforced.

The District Court decided that the EEOC's disclosure of confidential information to charging parties violated EEOC's scheme of negotiations on settlement set forth in Title VII of the Civil Rights Act of 1964. The Court enforced the subpoena only on the condition that the EEOC treat charging parties as members of the "public," to whom it legally cannot disclose any information in its files. The Fourth Circuit Court of Appeals affirmed the District Court's judgment.

But the Supreme Court overturned the lower courts, deciding that Congress did not include charging parties within the "public." The Court concluded that the employee charging discrimination was entitled to see the information in his own file. The Court also found that the EEOC may not disclose information to him from other EEOC files.

As a result of this case, if an employer has more than one ongoing EEOC investigation, he should keep separate files for each case. This will prevent the employee from going over all an employer's EEOC cases to see if there is a pattern of conduct or a similar case. Statistics and other information about the employer's general practice, in full or summary form, should be included in each charging party's file.

Legal Update from Memel, Jacobs, Pierno & Gersh is published for our friends and clients, to provide information on important legal trends. Articles are not exhaustive legal studies and are generalized in nature; applicability to any particular situation depends on the facts of that situation.

For more information on a particular article, contact the partner in charge of the appropriate department at (213) 556-2000:

Michael D. Saphier, Health Department
Anthony R. Pierno and David L. Gersh, Corporate & Tax Department
Arthur R. Chenen, Litigation Department
Stanley K. Jacobs, Torts Department
David G. Ellsworth, Real Estate Department
Edward B. Robin, Labor Department

INSIDE M J P & G

MJP&G is growing to fully serve client needs ... by Sherwin L. Memel

To provide the highest quality and most responsive service to its clients, Memel, Jacobs, Pierno & Gersh is continually growing.

When it was formed on May 29, 1975, the firm consisted of five partners and one associate. Since then, through a program of planned growth, it has expanded to 60 lawyers—20 partners and 40 associates. At the end of this summer, 13 additional attorneys, graduates recruited from the major law schools, will enter the firm upon completion of their bar exams. Also several experienced attorneys, with special expertise required by the firm's clients, will soon be joining the staff. By the end of this year, the firm will have over 75 lawyers to serve clients' needs.

In addition, our professional staff includes 10 highly trained, specialized paralegals and 2 law librarians who not only maintain an extensive library collection, but also handle specialized research.

Supporting all these professionals is an administrative staff led by a director of administration and two legal administrators. 125 others work as legal assistants, secretaries, accounting/data processing personnel, receptionists, word processing personnel, and in other capacities.

Working in offices in Century City, Sacramento, and Newport Beach—and soon in Washington, D.C.—the firm is structured into six departments: the **Health Department,** 7

administered by Michael D. Saphier, represents hospitals and other health care organizations (in 35 states) in bond financing, corporate organization, medical staff matters, reimbursement, certificate of need and other administrative hearings, and general health business legal affairs; the **Corporate Department,** chaired by Anthony R. Pierno and David L. Gersh, handles securities and commodities matters, mergers and acquisitions, franchising, tax matters, trademarks, savings and loan, banking and general corporate business matters; the **Real Estate Department,** headed by David G. Ellsworth, deals with commercial, industrial and residential development of all kinds, resort development as well as resort timesharing projects, both domestic and international, planning, zoning, sales, landlord-tenant law, real estate loans and Coastal Commission matters; the **Torts Department,** chaired by Stanley K. Jacobs, handles a wide variety of civil suits for wrongful acts and wrongful death, damages, and personal injuries; the **Litigation Department,** led by Arthur R. Chenen, handles all types of civil and business litigation including securities law, health law, real estate matters, breach of contract, administrative law, unfair competition, and defamation; and the **Labor Department,** headed by Edward B. Robin, deals with management-labor matters, employment discrimination, contract administration, and personnel practices.

In all matters, there is a constant combining of expertise from the appropriate departments to fully assist a client.

And that is the reason behind the firm's growth — to maintain the highest quality of expert legal services and greatest responsiveness in serving all of a client's legal needs.

from the law offices of:
MEMEL, JACOBS, PIERNO & GERSH
Twenty-Fifth Floor
1801 Century Park East
Los Angeles, California 90067

to:

ADDRESS CORRECTION REQUESTED
RETURN POSTAGE GUARANTEED

Sample Law Firm Brochure

Nutter, McClennen & Fish

Counselors at Law

Federal Reserve Plaza
600 Atlantic Avenue
Boston, Massachusetts 02210
(617) 973-9700

Federal Bar Building West
1819 H Street N.W.
Washington, D.C. 20006
(202) 296-3500

TABLE OF CONTENTS

INTRODUCTION TO THE FIRM

Nutter, McClennen & Fish has been engaged in the general practice of law since 1879 when the firm was founded by Samuel D. Warren and Louis D. Brandeis. The firm name was changed to Brandeis, Dunbar & Nutter in 1897 when Warren left to take over the management of his family's paper manufacturing business. When Brandeis was appointed to the Supreme Court of the United States in 1916, the name of the firm was changed again to Dunbar, Nutter & McClennen and in 1929, upon the retirement of Dunbar, it became known as Nutter, McClennen & Fish. Since that time, the firm has grown substantially from twenty-six lawyers in 1937 to thirty-six lawyers in 1960. Now it has over eighty lawyers and maintains a branch office in Washington, D.C. as well as the main office in Boston.

Lawyers in the firm are grouped in the following six departments, each constituting a distinct area of concentration. **Business**, including corporate finance, banking, acquisitions and mergers, securities regulation, corporate reorganization, commercial leases and other work of a business and commercial nature; **Litigation**, including antitrust, products liability, securities, business, commercial, bankruptcy, eminent domain, tax abatement and general trial and administrative agency work; **Probate**, including estate planning, wills and trusts and estate and trust administration; **Labor**, including collective bargaining — both public and private sector — and equal opportunity matters; **Real Estate**, including land use and environmental regulatory matters, conveyancing and real estate financing transactions; and **Tax and International**, including not only the broad range of federal, state and local tax problems, but also the tax, licensing and related aspects of various kinds of international transactions. In each of these areas there are members of the firm who are respected as leaders of their profession by their peers. The individual areas of concentration are supplemented by continuous cooperation and interaction among lawyers in all areas of our practice, a necessary ingredient in the firm's continuing effort to provide high quality, integrated legal services. Trained paralegal assistants are available to each department and work under the supervision of the lawyers.

1

There is no single profile of the firm's clients which include businesses, charitable and educational organizations, governmental agencies, trusts and estates, and individuals. They range from multi-national corporations to local businesses, from large real estate developers to purchasers of first homes, from wealthy individuals to persons of modest circumstances. Some of the industries in which the firm's clients are involved include banking, lending, venture capital, insurance, retailing, import-export, wholesale distribution, high-technology research and manufacturing, general manufacturing, real estate development, broadcasting, film and print media, automobile and heavy equipment manufacturing, pharmaceutical, printing and publishing and health care. The firm's clients also include a major university and an important cultural institution. This diverse client base is one of the firm's great strengths.

The firm's broad range of clients is matched by the diversity of the people who serve these clients. Today, lawyers at Nutter, McClennen & Fish are graduates of nearly twenty different law schools, were born in more than twenty different states and countries, have a working capacity in French, German, Italian, Portuguese and Spanish and represent several ethnic, religious, racial, economic and social backgrounds. Today, eleven women practice law at Nutter, McClennen & Fish. Among the firm's lawyers are former Assistant U.S. Attorneys, former Assistant Attorneys General (including a former First Assistant Attorney General) of the Commonwealth of Massachusetts, a former counsel to the Massachusetts Department of Public Utilities and numerous law clerks from both federal and state appellate and trial courts, including the Supreme Court of the United States. The common bond of all who practice at Nutter, McClennen & Fish has been and continues to be a commitment to excellence.

Over the years, the firm has had a strong commitment to public service. Leading the way was Louis D. Brandeis, one of our founding partners. Before appointment to the United States Supreme Court he had been instrumental in establishing savings-bank life insurance in Massachusetts and had earned a national reputation as "the people's attorney" in defending the constitutionality of wages and hours laws and other socially progressive legislation. Later partners have accepted appointment and served with distinction as judges on Massachusetts courts, including Arthur E. Whittemore, an Associate Judge of the Massachusetts Supreme Judicial Court. Others have held or now hold a variety of positions in local government, including those of town moderator, school committee member and zoning board of appeals member, and in national and local religious and charitable organizations.

Service to the legal profession has taken many forms. From our membership have come a president of the American Bar Association, three presidents of the Boston Bar Association, a president of the Massachusetts Association of Women

Lawyers, a president of Greater Boston Legal Services and chairmen of the Sections of Real Property, Probate and Trust Law and Corporation, Banking and Business Law of the American Bar Association. Several lawyers are active on various committees of the American, Massachusetts, Boston, District of Columbia and Interamerican Bar Associations and the American Society of International Law, as well as the boards of their law schools, the Massachusetts Law Review and the Journal of International Law and Economics. Other lawyers are active in the field of legal education, serving as lecturers at the Law Schools of Harvard University, Boston University and Boston College and at various bar-sponsored programs. Several members of the firm have published in their fields of expertise in recognized legal periodicals.

Besides holding membership in national, state and local bar associations and their sections for various specialties, members of the firm belong to the American College of Trial Lawyers, the American College of Probate Counsel and the American College of Real Estate Law.

The Washington office was opened in 1979, by coincidence the 100th anniversary of our founding. Oriented toward business, investment, international law and working with the federal agencies having jurisdiction in those areas, this office affords the firm and its clients an important new capability in handling many matters which require direct dealings with the federal government.

Members of the firm are admitted to practice in the state courts of Massachusetts, Maryland, Virginia, Maine, New Hampshire and New York, in the District of Columbia courts, in the United States District Courts for all of the above states, except Maine, in the United States Courts of Appeals for the First, Second, Fifth and District of Columbia Circuits, in the United States Supreme Court, in the United States Tax Court and the United States Court of Claims and before the more important federal and state administrative agencies having jurisdiction in the above-mentioned states and the District of Columbia.

The various types of matters handled by the respective departments are set forth on the following pages. Where a matter requires the expertise of more than one department, as commonly occurs, a team approach is used, combining the skills of the several departments as needed.

In sum, Nutter, McClennen & Fish has the capacity to bring a wide range of experience to bear on almost any legal issue and, after more than 100 years of law practice, continues to strive for professional excellence of the highest order, original and creative representation of its clients' interests and public service befitting the responsibilities of its members as leaders of the bar.

3

BUSINESS DEPARTMENT

Organization of Entities

- Advice on choice of business form — corporation, partnership, joint venture, business trust
- Organization of entity —
  Including drafting of all papers and carrying out all filings
- Qualification to do business in other states —
  Including advice and filing of papers
- Stock transfer restriction and buy-out agreements

Financing of Business Entities

- Equity capital —
  Public and private offerings
  Stock option plans
  Venture capital transactions (including venture capital investment partnerships)
- Institutional loans —
  Unsecured
  Secured by inventory, accounts receivable or other non-realty security
  Secured by real property (with Real Estate Department)
- Bond financings
- Sale and leaseback transactions —
  Personal property
  Real property (with Real Estate Department)

Real Estate Development, Leasing and Financing

- Leasing —
  Including preparation and negotiation of leases for all types of property, such as shopping centers and office, industrial and warehouse buildings
- Real estate development —
  Assisting real estate developers with site analysis
  Acquisition of land control, leasing, construction and permanent financings (with Real Estate and Tax Departments, as appropriate)
- Representations of banks, insurance companies and other institutional lenders (with Real Estate Department, as appropriate)
- Real estate syndications and private offerings
  Organization of joint ventures, limited partnerships, general partnerships (with Real Estate and Tax Departments)
  Preparation and analysis of private placement memoranda and public offerings

Other Business Agreements

- Acquisitions and dispositions —
  Buyer or seller
  Stock
  Assets
  Mergers
  Liquidations
  Recapitalizations
  Other reorganizations

4

- Franchise, distribution, dealer agreements —
  Including compliance with all federal and state disclosure and other laws and regulations
- Purchase order, invoice, acknowledgment forms, and advice under the Uniform Commercial Code generally
- Employment and sales representative agreements
- Proprietary information agreements
- Deferred compensation agreements (with Tax Department)
- Construction contracts (with Real Estate Department)
- Equipment leasing —
  Including leasing of computer hardware and software (or sales of equipment with license of software)

Other Areas of Expertise and Experience

- Corporate reorganization, bankruptcy, creditors' and debtors' rights (with Litigation Department)
- Bank regulation and operation, including mergers and all aspects of regulatory approvals
- Proxy contests and takeover strategies and defense
- Conduct of shareholder meetings
- Copyright law
- Trademark law
- Licensing —
  Including licensing of patents, trademarks, trade secrets, and copyrights
- Federal and state securities law —
  Including broker-dealer matters and all aspects of the Securities Act of 1933, the Securities Exchange Act of 1934, the Investment Company Act of 1940 and the Investment Advisers Act of 1940

LITIGATION DEPARTMENT

Complex Business Litigation
   Trial handling and pre-litigation counseling in areas such as:
- Antitrust — Sherman and Clayton Acts
- Price discrimination — Robinson-Patman Act
- Federal Trade Commission proceedings
- Securities — Private actions under Securities Act of 1933 and Securities
   Exchange Act of 1934 and administrative proceedings before the Securities
   and Exchange Commission
- Enforcement of license agreements for major film producers and distributors
- Trade secrets litigation
- Multi-district litigation
- Stockholder suits
- Class actions

General Business Litigation
- Franchising
- Licensing
- Employment contracts
- Computer industry
- Consumer Protection Act
- Commercial disputes arising under Uniform Commercial Code

Media-Related Litigation
- Defamation actions for libel and slander defending all aspects of press — news-
   papers, radio and television
- Invasion of privacy actions defending press
- Prosecution of actions, particularly on behalf of press, relating to federal and
   state Freedom of Information Acts
- Advice and litigation involving First Amendment guarantees

Products Liability Litigation
   Trial handling of matters involving primarily the defense of manufacturers in
   personal injury actions and commercial disputes involving product integrity

Regulated Industries Rate Setting
- Utilities
- Insurance

Aviation-Related Litigation

Outdoor Advertising Litigation
- First Amendment litigation
- State and local administrative agency litigation

6

Discrimination Litigation
- Administrative agency enforcement
- Title VII and constitutional litigation
- Federal contract compliance reviews

Domestic Relations
All aspects of contested matters pertaining to separation and divorce, property settlement agreements, contested divorce and custody trials and modification and contempt petitions

Probate Litigation
- Will contests
- Complaints for instructions
- Accounts of fiduciaries

Construction Litigation
Representation of owners, architects, engineers, contractors and subcontractors in arbitration proceedings and court trials

Real Property-Related Proceedings
- Urban renewal litigation
- Eminent domain/land takings
- Zoning and environmental matters
- Broker's commission suits
- Lease controversies
- Local property tax abatement

Local Administrative Agency Proceedings
- State discrimination commissions and the Equal Employment Opportunities Commission
- Industrial Accident Board
- Appellate Tax Board
- Industrial and professional regulatory boards
- Alcoholic Beverage Control Commission
- Zoning boards of appeals
- Planning boards

Miscellaneous
Torts, including such areas as negligence and malpractice

PROBATE DEPARTMENT

Estate Planning
- Lifetime or testamentary dispositions or retentions of property —
  Wills and testamentary trusts
  Revocable trusts
  Irrevocable trusts
  Instruments of transfer of personal property
  Special instruments including "standby" and "basket" trusts, legal life estates,
  "blind" real estate trusts
- Estate tax problems —
  Minimizing or avoiding federal and state estate taxes by use of lifetime
  transfers, marital deductions, trusts, orphan's deduction
  Special use valuations
  Deferral of estate taxes in certain estates
  Use of irrevocable trusts to minimize estate taxes
- Gift tax problems, including present interest problems —
  2503(c) trusts for minors
  Transfer to custodians under Uniform Gifts to Minors Act
  Trusts with "Crummey-type" powers
  Interest free loans
  Gift splitting
- Use of trusts to minimize income taxes —
  Short-term or Clifford Trusts
  Other irrevocable trusts
- Generation-skipping transfer tax —
  Grandfather provisions for certain trusts
  Grandchild exclusions
- Joint property problems —
  Estate and gift tax problems
  Qualified joint tenancy
  Severance
  Creditors' rights
- Lifetime or testamentary dispositions of business interests —
  303 redemptions (with Tax Department)
  Buy-sell agreements (with Business and Tax Departments)
  Disposition of employee benefits, including stock options, deferred compen-
  sation, pension and profit-sharing plan benefits and group insurance
- Questions relating to life insurance —
  Irrevocable lifetime transfers of life insurance, outright or in trust
  Protecting proceeds against claims by creditors or surviving spouse
- Charitable dispositions —
  Unitrusts and annuity trusts
  Gift annuities
  Charitable lead trusts
  Conditional gifts
  Conservation easements

8

• Special problems —
  Domicile and change of domicile
  Anatomical gifts
  Ante-nuptial and post-nuptial agreements
  Protecting assets against claims by surviving spouse or creditors

Administration of Estates and Trusts

• Estate administration —
  Probate proceedings involving both testate and intestate estates
  Will contests
  Post-death income tax planning including election of tax years and timing of
  distributions
  Estate tax returns
  Fiduciary income tax returns
  Licenses to sell or mortgage real estate
  Insolvent estates
  Claims by surviving spouse for statutory share
  Creditors' rights
  Probate accounting
  Estates of absentees

• Trust administration —
  Income tax returns and questions
  Generation-skipping tax problems
  Trust accounting
  Terminations and distributions

Probate Practice Other Than Estate or Trust Administration

• Matters in Probate and/or Superior courts —
  Conservators and guardians
  Adoptions
  Cy pres and complaints for equitable deviation
  Fee disputes
  Complaints for instructions or declaratory relief
  Partition
  Complaints under Management of Institutional Funds Act
  Actions for removal of fiduciaries

9

LABOR DEPARTMENT

All clients

Advice regarding compliance with the following federal and state laws, and representation before agencies and in court:

- National Labor Relations Act —
  Including all aspects of NLRB practice as described in more detail below
- Title VII of the Civil Rights Act of 1964 —
  Review of legality of personnel policies and practices
  Training of supervisors
  Representation before Equal Employment Opportunity Commission and various state agencies
- Fair Labor Standards Act —
  Minimum wage and overtime requirements
  Equal Pay Act
  Age Discrimination Act
  Representation before the Wage and Hour Division
- Executive Order 11246 —
  Advice regarding preparation, implementation and revision of affirmative action plans
  Representation during related compliance reviews by the Office of Federal Contract Compliance Programs
- Rehabilitation Act
- Viet Nam Era Veteran Readjustment Act
- Workers Compensation statutes
- Unemployment Compensation statutes
- Immigration and Naturalization statutes
  Including processing of visas and working permits
- Occupational Safety and Health Act —
  Including representation during investigations and administrative enforcement proceedings
- Railway Labor Act
- All related state statutes

Unionized Clients

In addition to the services provided to all clients, the following services are also provided:

- All aspects of collective bargaining negotiations
- Grievance and arbitration representation
- All other matters involving the relationship between the client and the union

Public Sector Clients

Representation of a number of public sector clients, including school committees, providing services which are basically the same as those provided to all other clients.

Non-Unionized Clients

In addition to the above-listed services, the following services are also provided:

- Advice on the maintenance of non-union status
  Review of personnel policies and practices
  Review of wage, salary and benefit plans
  Training of supervisors in proper employee relations
  Communication and human resources development in a union-free environment
- Representation during all National Labor Relations Board proceedings, including representation cases and unfair labor practice cases, from the investigation through any labor board and federal court hearings

REAL ESTATE DEPARTMENT

Real Estate Financing
- Negotiation of construction, interim and permanent mortgage loan commitments and documents
- Industrial revenue bonds
- Housing subsidy programs
- Loan participations
- Mortgage insurance

Condominiums and Cooperatives
- Creation of new condominums and cooperatives, including phased condominiums and planned unit developments
- Condominium conversion —
  Representation of owner/converter
  Representation of tenant groups and unit owner associations
- Purchase and sale of existing condominium and cooperative units
- Commercial and medical condominiums

Leasing
- Negotiation and drafting of residential leases
- Negotiation and drafting of commercial leases —
  Shopping centers
  Office space
  Warehouse
  Industrial

Mortgage Foreclosure Law, Practice and Loan Work-outs

Consumer Protection Laws
- Federal and state truth-in-lending laws
- Interstate Land Sales Act
- Massachusetts Consumer Protection Act
- Home warranties under the Magnuson-Moss Act

Historic Preservation
- Drafting legislation for historic districts
- Drafting restrictive covenants for historic districts
- Incentives for developing historic structures (with Tax Department)

Title Matters
- Examination and certification of title
- Massachusetts Land Court proceedings, including title registration, etc.
- Approved attorneys for all major title insurance companies

Representation of Seller, Buyer and Lender in the Purchase and Sale of Residential, Commercial and Industrial Property
- Broker's agreements
- Purchase and sale agreements
- Title insurance and title certification
- Financing documents —
  Promissory notes
  Mortgages
  Collateral documents
- Oversight of closing process

Land Control Documents and Land Assembly
- Industrial park covenants and restrictions
- Homeowners associations
- Options, right of first refusal
- Easements and cross easements
- Licenses
- Property management agreements
- Conservation restrictions and easements

Land Use and Environmental Controls — The Regulatory Process
- Zoning
- Subdivision
- State Building Code; handicapped regulations; OSHA
- Federal and state enviornmental laws and regulations —
  Wetlands
  Environmental impact statement
  Air pollution
  Water pollution
  Environmental code — Title V
  Hazardous waste
  Oil spills
- Urban renewal and related programs such as CARD designations and UDAG program
- Representation before all relevant federal, state, regional and local agencies

Construction Contracts and Architects' Contracts
- Construction manager agreements
- Bidding procedures
- Design-build contracts

TAX AND INTERNATIONAL DEPARTMENT

Tax Aspects of Corporate Transactions

- Incorporations —
  Including structuring interests of promoters and investors; incorporation of partnerships and proprietorships; debt v. equity questions
- Acquisitions —
  Tax-free
  Taxable (including taxable mergers)
  Hybrid and other "exotic" forms
  Loss carryovers
- Divisive Reorganization (spin offs and split ups)
- Recapitalization and other rearrangements of capital structure
- Liquidations —
  Complete
  Partial
  Subsidiary
- Stockholder distributions and redemptions
- Stockholder buy-back and cross-purchase agreements —
  Including uses of life insurance
- Bankruptcy and insolvency

Tax Aspects of Other Business Transactions

- Installment and other deferred payment sales —
  Including sales to related purchasers
- Sale, licensing and other transfers of intangible property
- Sales and exchanges —
  Like kind
  Involuntary conversion
  Wash sales
  Private annuities
  Investment annuities
- Industrial bond financing
- Real estate development
- REITS
- Regulated investment companies

Tax Aspects of Partnerships

- Formation —
  Including structuring interests of promoters and investors
- Tax shelters —
  Including real estate, equipment leasing, commodities, futures, cattle, oil and gas, Research and Development
- Terminations and dispositions

14

Executive Compensation

Employee Matters
- Qualified plans of all types —
    Including structuring, qualifying, administering and terminating
- Non-qualified plans —
    Restricted property
    Phantom stock
    Performance shares, etc.
- Withholding taxes —
    Including 100% penalty problems
- Reasonable compensation issues

Tax Aspects of Divorce and Separation
- Alimony, support, maintenance
- Capital transfers

Special Tax Problems
- Consolidated returns
- Net operating losses
- Unreasonable accumulations
- Investment credit
- Depreciation
- Personal holding companies
- Collapsible corporations
- Subchapter S
- Accounting methods and periods
- Fraud
- Minimum, alternative minimum and maximum taxes

Estate Planning and Taxation, Including Valuation and Administration Problems

Gift Tax

Income Taxation of Trusts, Estates and Beneficiaries, Including Uses of Trusts to Minimize Taxes

Exempt Organizations
- Organization
- Classification
- Qualification
- Private foundations
- Unrelated business income
- Dissolution

Charitable giving, including charitable remainder trusts, charitable annuities, bargain sales, conservation easements

International Transactions
- Doing business abroad —
  Licensing
  Franchising
  Branch operations
  Joint ventures
  Subsidiaries
  Repatriation
  Tax havens
  DISCs
  U.S. taxation of employees abroad
  Allocations of income and expense
- Foreign business and investment in the United States —
  Including structuring to avoid or minimize U.S. tax

State Taxation
- Multi-state taxation of business
- Massachusetts corporate excise tax
- Qualification for Massachusetts securities corporation classification
- Installment sales
- Sales and use taxes
- Massachusetts income tax
- Massachusetts estate tax
- Tax domicile questions
- Massachusetts business trusts
- Employment taxes and withholding

OTHER AREAS OF CONCENTRATION

General legal matters relating to Private colleges and universities

Hospital and nursing home certificates of need

Government-financed procurement contracts for health care service agencies

General legal matters relating to the delivery of health care services and to institutional care facilities

WASHINGTON OFFICE

Partnership
- Organization of general and limited partnerships and advice concerning applicability of federal and state securities laws
- Preparation of investment brochures for the sale of interests in limited partnerships
- Prosecution of litigation arising out of partnership interests

Trade Associations and Non-Profit Institutions
- Formation and qualification of tax-exempt trade associations and non-profit institutions
- Advice concerning maintenance of above status in antitrust matters

Taxation
Tax considerations incident to personal and business transactions

Regulatory Agencies
- United States International Trade Commission
- Federal Communications Commission
- Interstate Commerce Commission
- Civil Aeronautics Board
- Federal Aviation Administration
- Department of Labor
- Department of Agriculture
- Federal Maritime Commission
- Department of Interior
- Federal Energy Regulatory Commission
- Securities and Exchange Commission
- Commodity Futures Trading Commission
- Internal Revenue Service
- Office of Foreign Assets Control, Department of Treasury

Wills and Trusts

Estate Planning

Environmental Law

Intellectual Property

Legislation
- Drafting proposed legislation
- Monitoring pending bills
- Preparing testimony before congressional legislative committees

Litigation

All aspects of business litigation and proceedings before Federal departments and agencies, with particular emphasis on securities, partnerships, management disputes and energy and environmental related matters

International

* Overseas investments
* International financing and insurance
* Financing through international economic organizations —
  Inter-American Development Bank and International Finance Corporation
  Export-Import Bank
  Organization of Private Investment Corporation
  Agency for International Development
* Tax havens

International Trade Laws of the U.S. and the GATT and Other Treaties

Advice to foreign individuals and companies with respect to American federal and state laws and regulations affecting business investment and transactions in the U.S.

Energy

* Matters relating to companies engaged in solar systems engineering and manufacturing and in various aspects of international transactions involving oil and coal
* Exploration and development programs
* Pipeline regulations

Corporate

* Formation, qualification, maintenance and reorganization of corporations
* Mergers and acquisitions
* Tax considerations applicable to organizations, buyout and other agreements among promoters
* Franchise agreements and other contracts
* Organization of investment companies and registration under the Investment Company Act of 1940

Securities

* Registration under the Securities Act of 1933
* Preparation of investment brochures for private placement of securities
* Advice concerning state and federal regulations affecting the issuance and transfer of securities
* Common stock, limited partnership interests and other investment contracts
* Preparation of proxy statements and stock exchange listings
* Prosecution of litigation in the defense of issuers of securities and on behalf of persons defrauded in connection with the purchase of securities
* Broker-dealer registration and relations with NASD
* Investment Advisers Act registration

18

APPENDIX D
Sample Law Firm Portfolio

Benesch, Friedlander, Coplan & Aronoff

Attorneys at

1100 Citizens Building • 850 Euclid Avenue • Cleveland, Ohio 44114

Benesch, Friedlander, Coplan & Aronoff was founded in 1938 by attorneys Alfred A. Benesch and Jerome M. Friedlander. Mr. Benesch, a prominent civic leader in Cleveland and in Ohio, practiced until shortly before his death in 1973. Mr. Friedlander, in semi-retirement, is still active in the firm as counsel.

From an office of only five lawyers in general practice, Benesch, Friedlander has become one of Cleveland's leading law firms, comprising more than 50 lawyers, most of whom specialize in one or more of such diverse areas as corporate and securities law, commercial and bankruptcy law, real estate development and financing, personal, corporation, trust and estate taxation, labor law and litigation. The firm represents a broad range of clientele and carries its practice into various parts of this country and abroad.

This profile is intended to provide a guide to the range of services, background of attorneys, and overall philosophy of Benesch, Friedlander, Coplan & Aronoff.

At Benesch, Friedlander, we believe the practice of law requires expert advice, vigorous advocacy and thoughtful counseling. Because we know our clients expect the highest quality advice and the most efficient legal service, our services are available, if required, around the clock, seven days a week, to achieve those ends.

One of the premises of our philosophy is a commitment to the "make-it-happen" approach to practice—that is, to make sure clients' matters are brought swiftly to a successful conclusion with all necessary legal protection and required imagination and creativity. We have a reputation in the business community for getting the job done.

While we prefer to handle our clients' matters so as to avoid litigation or other adversarial proceedings, we employ all our resources promptly and effectively to act on our clients' behalf when such actions do occur.

To assure the most efficient service for our clients, we make use of all available personnel and equipment. We are among the leaders in Cleveland in our use of paralegal assistants to complement each of our major areas of practice. We use many high-technology machines in our work and, accordingly, stay abreast of the latest developments such as word and data processing, telecopying, interoffice communication and computer-aided research. Our word processing department operates seven days a week.

Continuing legal education is another premise of our philosophy. We regularly send our attorneys—partners and associates alike—as well as our paralegals, to legal seminars and meetings throughout the country. A significant reading list for our various specialists helps them stay informed of new legislation, the latest developments from the courts and regulatory agencies, and the thinking of legal scholars.

Entering lawyers attend in-house orientation sessions and practica to learn our methods, smooth the transition from student to practitioner, and learn the practical mechanics of a sophisticated law practice. Under the supervision of a partner, new lawyers receive assignments in several areas of specialization so as to acquaint them with much of the spectrum of the firm's practice.

ASSOCIATES

Benesch, Friedlander assures and maintains its continuity of quality and dedication by regularly recruiting the best recent law school graduates. When they join the firm, associates are placed in an unassigned "pool", where, under the direction of a partner, they work in various areas as required. Personal and thorough supervision and training are afforded each associate so as to provide the best possible service to the client.

When assigned a matter in a particular department, the associate will stay with that matter until it has been completed. For the most part, associates come into each situation early and have immediate contact with clients, attorneys for the other side, and other professionals involved in the transaction. For example, in a litigation case an associate is usually present at the initial interview and remains active until the matter concludes, even though that may take several years, and whether or not the associate goes into the Litigation Department. The firm seeks to place associates in positions of responsibility on a "fast track" basis.

After an orientation period of 18 months to two years, an associate usually develops an affinity for a particular area of the law and becomes a part of one of the firm's departments. Associates who become expert in more than one area will participate in two or more departments.

Associates are encouraged to develop clients for the firm, and will receive all assistance and guidance to handle these clients' matters effectively.

Associates participate fully in transactions in which they are involved. They are expected to use their imagination and ingenuity to obtain the best results for the client. This may require discussions, sometimes spirited, with partners, and sometimes with clients or their other professional advisors. We find such interplay is essential to effective representation of our clients.

SUMMER ASSOCIATES

Each summer the firm employs law students who are integrated into the work of the firm to permit the firm to observe them at work, frequently under the stress of pressing matters. Closely reviewed and monitored, these summer associates are expected to function as lawyers. They and their work are evaluated at least three times during the summer and prior to their return to law school, and they will work with as many of the attorneys in the firm as possible. We believe our summer associates have a rewarding experience with the firm.

Many of our current lawyers started as Benesch, Friedlander summer associates during their law school careers.

SCOPE OF PRACTICE

Because our clients do business and maintain offices in cities outside Cleveland and indeed, outside the country, our attorneys travel whenever the need arises. The firm also maintains a strong presence in Greater Cleveland, and many of our clients have worked with Benesch, Friedlander for more than 40 years. Benesch, Friedlander represents a wide range of clients, from multi-national corporations to "mom and pop" corner stores and all manner of other businesses and individuals, in their legal and financial affairs. We have helped a number of clients progress from small beginnings into large enterprises. We understand the growing business. We have found it most efficient to divide our practice into six major departments: Commercial and Bankruptcy; Corporate and Securities; Labor; Litigation and Antitrust; Real Estate; Tax, Probate and Estate Planning.

Each department is chaired by a partner who is responsible for all matters in that department, including work flow and client service. Many of our lawyers are experts in more than one area and will participate in two or more of our departments. Most of the firm's practice necessarily involves more than one area of legal specialization. For example, a client acquiring a business will require counseling by our lawyers skilled in corporate and securities law, taxes, and real estate law, all of whom work together to consummate the transaction.

THE ATTORNEY-CLIENT RELATIONSHIP

The departmentalization of law practice at Benesch, Friedlander adds depth and scope to the firm's ability to deal with complex legal problems of modern business and commerce. This permits the firm to develop strong relationships with its clients at all levels of the clients' needs.

As counselors we recognize the importance of personal rapport and continual involvement with each client. At the same time we realize when a particular matter requires special expertise, and we know who in the firm has the credentials to handle the matter properly at lowest cost to the client.

The originating attorney remains involved with the client and the specific file, but the ongoing activity may be assigned to the specialists best qualified to deal with its intricacies.

Index to Portfolio

---

1. The Firm Name
2. Commercial Law & Bankruptcy Department
3. Corporate & Securities Law Department
4. Labor Law Department
5. Litigation & Antitrust Department
6. Real Estate Law Department
7. Tax, Probate & Estate Planning Departments
8. Pool of Attorneys
9. Professional & Technical Support
10. Attorney Listings and Practical Matters.